Monographs in
Mediterranean Archaeology
7

Executive Editor
A. Bernard Knapp

Sheffield Academic Press

ENCOUNTERS AND TRANSFORMATIONS

The Archaeology of Iberia in Transition

edited by
Miriam S. Balmuth, Antonio Gilman and Lourdes Prados-Torreira

The conference was supported by
The Samuel H. Kress Foundation — Program for Cultural Cooperation Between
Spain's Ministry of Culture and United States Universities — Tufts University —
Comité Conjunto Hispano - Norteamericano — Individual Donors —
Leon Levy and Shelby White

Published by Sheffield Academic Press Ltd
Mansion House
19 Kingfield Road
Sheffield S11 9AS
England

Printed on acid-free paper in Great Britain
by Bookcraft Ltd
Midsomer Norton, Bath

British Library Cataloguing in Publication Data

A catalogue record for this book is available
from the British Library

ISBN 1-85075-593-0

Dedicated to Manuel Fernández-Miranda

Contents

List of Figures

List of Plates

List of Tables

List of Contributors

Miriam S. Balmuth

Department of Classics
Tufts University
Medford, MA 02155, USA

Teresa Chapa Brunet

Departamento de Prehistoria
Universidad Complutense de Madrid
Ciudad Universitaria, 28040 Madrid, Spain

Alicia Perea Caveda

Departamento de Prehistoria, Centro de Estudios Históricos
Consejo Superior de Investigaciones Científicas
Serrano 13, 28001 Madrid, Spain

Robert Chapman

Department of Archaeology
University of Reading
Reading RG6 2AA, England

José Clemente Martín De La Cruz

Departamento de Ciencias Humanas Experimentales
    y de Territorio
Universidad de Córdoba
Plaza del Cardenal Salazar 3, 14071 Córdoba, Spain

María Belén Deamos

Departamento de Prehistoria y Arqueología
Universidad de Sevilla
41071 Sevilla, Spain

Manuel Fernández-Miranda[†]

María Dolores Fernández-Posse

Instituto del Patrimonio Histórico Español
Ministerio de Cultura
El Greco 4, 28071 Madrid, Spain

Manuel Bendala Galán

Departamento de Prehistoria y Arqueología
Universidad Autónoma de Madrid
Cantoblanco, 28049 Madrid, Spain

Juan Manuel Vicent García

Departamento de Prehistoria, Centro de Estudios Históricos
Consejo Superior de Investigaciones Científicas
Serrano 13, 28001 Madrid, Spain

Antonio Gilman

Department of Anthropology
California State University, Northridge
18111 Nordhoff Street, Northridge, CA 91330-8244, USA

Almudena Hernando Gonzalo

Departamento de Prehistoria
Universidad Complutense de Madrid
Ciudad Universitaria, 28040 Madrid, Spain

Annie Grant

Department of Archaeology
University of Reading
Reading RG6 2AA, England

Katina T. Lillios

Department of Anthropology
Ripon College
Ripon, WI 54971, USA

Concepción Martín

Instituto del Patrimonio Histórico Español
Ministerio de Cultura
El Greco 4, 28071 Madrid, Spain

Marisa Ruíz-Gálvez Priego

Departamento de Prehistoria
Universidad Complutense de Madrid
Ciudad Universitaria, 28040 Madrid, Spain

Lourdes Prados-Torreira

Departamento de Prehistoria y Arqueología
Universidad Autónoma de Madrid
Cantoblanco, 28049 Madrid, Spain

Juan A. Santos Velasco

Departamento de Ciencias Humanas y Sociales Edificio Vives
Universidad de La Rioja
Luis de Ulloa s/n, 26004 Logroño, Spain

Acknowledgments

Tufts University acted as host to the conference, organized by Miriam Balmuth and Lourdes Prados. Antonio Gilman translated several of the articles (those by María Belén, Teresa Chapa, Manuel Fernández-Miranda, José Clemente Martín de la Cruz, Marisa Ruiz-Gálvez and Juan Vicent) and, with Balmuth and Prados, edited the contributions. Financial support came from the Samuel H. Kress Foundation, the Program for Cultural Cooperation Between Spain's Ministry of Culture and United States Universities, Tufts University, Leon Levy and Shelby White, and other individual donors. Julio Jacoiste, Consul General of Spain in Boston, was a gracious presence at the conference.

Preface

Miriam Balmuth, Antonio Gilman and Lourdes Prados-Torreira

Since 1979, colloquia have been held at Tufts University for the purpose of discussing the latest archaeological developments on the Tyrrhenian island of Sardinia. It is as the result of an encounter — between Lourdes Prados and Miriam Balmuth — that in 1991 we went westward, beyond the Tyrrhenian, and eastward as well, for possible Phoenician 'influence', and extended the chronology to an earlier date in the Neolithic than we have normally treated, to organize the colloquium that we referred to as 'The First International Conference in America on Iberian Archaeology' and called 'Encounters and Transformations: The Archaeology of Iberia in Transition'.

Our personal discussions began with Iberian and Sardinian bronze figurines; soon they extended far beyond the figurines to the differences in date and concept of derivation for objects from both places, a continent and an island, as well as for the dates and ideas of Phoenician influence that we began with. We ultimately came to the state of archaeology in both areas, and the extent to which the introduction of new approaches, and the very recent changes that could be perceived in both fieldwork and literature, were challenging old procedures with new methodologies and redefining the problems.

In recent years, of course, the term 'encounter' has come to be used as a neutral way of referring to the vast consequences of the journey of Columbus from Spain to the New World. 'Discovery' and 'conquest' imply the passivity and subjugation of the inhabitants of the Americas, while 'encounter' implies the equality of the parties at the meeting. Referring to the 'encounter' between two worlds also minimizes the political and economic aspects of the process because, as members of an 'encounter', Europeans are not dominators or exploiters, but rather participants in an exchange of ideas. Use of the term suggests, then, that this exchange is the most important outcome of Columbus's voyage: it privileges an idealist conception of history.

A theory of culture change that views encounters between societies as the catalyst for the transmission of new ideas will, of course, be very familiar to students of the pre- and protohistory of the Mediterranean generally and the Iberian peninsula in particular. From the foundation of the discipline in the last century until the last fifteen years, one explanatory paradigm dominated research (Martínez Navarrete 1989): changes in archaeological assemblage types (*cultures* in Childe's [1929:v–vi] sense) in Iberia reflected changes in cultural norms, in the capabilities and habits the makers of those assemblages had acquired as members of their society, and were to be explained as the direct or indirect effect of foreign settlers or visitors. Such an approach clearly was relevant and appropriate in the context of Iberian protohistory, and it was applied freely to explain all changes in earlier time periods. The great achievements of humanity — agriculture, metallurgy, and the other arts of civilization — would have spread from their original hearths until they reached the most remote and backward corners of the earth. The task of those who studied the prehistory of an area as evidently peripheral as the Iberian peninsula was to document the arrival and spread of these advances on the basis of the similarities of archaeological assemblages. Prehistorians would discuss the details of this scheme (should a particular trait be traced to one or another origin, foreign or indigenous? through what agencies and by what routes would the diffused traits have spread? and so on), with divisions existing between those who saw an Oriental origin for virtually all novelties and those who gave greater weight to indigenous traditions. But everyone agreed on what research strategy should be pursued: what was essential was to identify in the archaeological record the 'typical' stylistic elements (the norms) that would permit the derivation and periodization of the ideas embodied in that record.

This theoretical approach was, of course, the consensus view of European prehistory until the 1960s, but in Spain it continued to be dominant for nearly twenty more years. During the Franco regime professional opportunities for archaeologists were limited, and the ties of patronage were correspondingly strong: senior archaeologists were all normativists and were in a position to exclude dissidents. In the late 1970s, however, the vast increase in the number of university students and the transition to a democratic regime provided opportunities for change (Ruíz Zapatero 1993). Existing departments of archaeology and prehistory were greatly expanded and new ones were established. The devolution of administrative regulation and funding of archaeological projects to the newly established regional governments within Spain also provided increased archaeological employment. This expansion meant that juniors who were less faithful to the precepts of their mentors could also make their way. The transition to democracy set the institutional stage for a pervasive change in archaeological theory and practice.

The proceedings of a conference such as this one necessarily reflect the state of the art: they are intended to give voice to the diversity of viewpoints of the profession. The prehistoric contributions demonstrate the great changes that have been over the past fifteen years. By the 1970s certain claims about the prehistoric development of Iberia made by the normativist school were encountering considerable empirical difficulties in some areas. In particular, the view that the development of both megalithism in the later Neolithic and of metallurgy in the Copper and Bronze Ages had occurred under the stimulus of people or influences from the eastern Mediterranean had become incompatible with the increasing number of radiocarbon dates for those periods (Renfrew 1967). The trajectory of later Iberian prehistory needed to be reconsidered: it would have to be seen, not as the product of encounters between Iberian natives and oriental visitors, but as a process of local, independent transformations from simpler to more complex social formations. Prehistorians of the Iberian peninsula began to develop accounts of that region's prehistory and protohistory from a processual perspective. Here, Childean cultures are not seen as configurations of learned behaviors, but as systems of adaptation, and are to be explained functionally. The positive effect of this, in Iberian archaeology as elsewhere, has been to amplify vastly the range of ecological and social questions that must be asked, and to require the deployment of appropriate interdisciplinary techniques to obtain the answers. The prehistoric chapters in this volume make clear how solid the commitment to a processual approach has become: all the contributors adopt a functionalist approach in their choice of

material, and many are explicitly problem-oriented and theoretical.

The contributions to protohistory demonstrate, as one would expect, a far greater diversity of approaches. For prehistorians to give weight to a processual approach is relatively easy: after all, they deal with evidence in which the actions of individuals, with their historically particular motivations, are hardly identifiable. In this time range, however, encounters (in the sense discussed above) unquestionably took place: the influence of eastern Mediterranean societies is dramatic and requires documentation by the traditional archaeological methods of the normativist school. Literary and epigraphic sources provide information and the integration of these with the archaeological record would surely be desirable. Some contributors address these issues by sticking to their normativist guns: contributions such as Bendala's, for example, illustrate the deeply-rooted commitment of many Spanish archaeologists to the traditional, or normative approach. Others are clearly committed to the integration of archaeological and historical sources into a social history that will account for the transmission of ideas and styles according to processual methodology.

Spanish archaeology in the 1980s and 1990s is going through a transition from a normativist to a processualist prehistory that resembles the emergence of the New Archaeology in North America and Britain in the 1960s and 1970s. This delay affords Spanish archaeology the opportunity to learn from the mistakes of their Anglo-Saxon colleagues. In North America, in particular, the positive aspects of processualism have been bought at a very high price, namely the adoption of a Fordian view of *history as bunk*: the dominant current of opinion is committed to a cultural ecology that sees the previous trajectory of a cultural system as a source of random noise that obscures scientific explanation of the system's operation. A choice was made, in Flannery's (1967) terms, between culture history and culture process. The processually-oriented contributors to this volume, i.e. the majority of the participants, will have none of this dichotomy, and we believe it will be of interest to non-Iberianists to see how well the papers succeed in combining both functionalism and historicism. By applying approaches derived from Marxism or from the *Annales* school to current issues; they demonstrate brilliantly (in our opinion; which is hardly impartial) that an integration between history and process is entirely feasible. In any event, the reader of this volume will know that the archaeology of the Iberian peninsula provides grist to all theoretical mills. Coming at a time of transition in the definition and interpretation of cultural change, the conference papers presented here illustrate the ongoing transformation of Spanish archaeology.

Bibliography

Childe, V.G.

    1929   *The Danube in Prehistory*. Oxford: Clarendon Press.

Flannery, K.V.

    1967   Culture History vs. Culture Process: A Debate in American Archaeology. *Scientific American* 217: 119–22.

Martínez Navarrete, M.I.

    1989   *Una Revisión Crítica de la Prehistoria Española: la Edad del Bronce como Paradigma*. Madrid: Siglo XXI de España.

Renfrew, C.

    1967   Colonialism and megalithismus. *Antiquity* 41: 276–88.

Ruíz Zapatero, G.

    1993   The Organisation of Archaeology in Spain. In M.I. Martínez Navarrete (ed.), *Theory and Practice of Prehistory: Views from the Edges of Europe*, 45–73. Santander: Universidad de Cantabria.

1.   The Island Filter Model Revisited

Juan Manuel Vicent García

This paper will discuss certain issues concerning the diffusion and the adoption of domesticated species in the Iberian peninsula. An examination of certain ideas about the historical interpretation of this process will serve as a point of departure for a critical alternative to the theories most widely accepted by Spanish archaeologists.

At present, the dominant theoretical position with respect to the process of neolithic developments in the Iberian peninsula is substantially diffusionist. According to an orthodox formulation of this approach, the Iberian Neolithic developed as the result of the introduction of a 'cultural current', which installed itself at the beginning of the fifth millennium BC on the eastern coasts of the peninsula, in particular in the País Valenciano (Valencia). This initial 'focus' initiated a process of 'acculturation' of the local Epipalaeolithic 'substrate', a process which would eventually reproduce itself across the whole peninsula. This interpretation has guided research over recent decades and has attained a high degree of elaboration and empirical support. In fact, the Neolithic archaeological sequence in the Spanish Levant constitutes the reference point for discussions of the periodization and radiocarbon dating of the Neolithic in the rest of the peninsula.

Whether or not it is feasible in archaeological terms, this point of view is, in my opinion, highly unsatisfactory in its implications for the understanding of the historical, social, and cultural processes that derived from the introduction of domesticates to Iberia. The way in which the archaeological evidence is presented, the categories by which that evidence is organized, indeed the very idea of a 'cultural current' forces the diffusionists to link the process of neolithic development to a 'demic' hypothesis; i.e. one related to a movement of people.

In this article I shall present in some detail the archaeological underpinnings of the most elaborate and coherent expression of the diffusionist point of view, namely the 'dual' theory proposed by the most influential group of Levantine neolithic specialists. I do not propose to criticize the archaeological foundation of this theory, but rather to argue against it as an interpretation of historical processes, and to show how other points of view that can account for the same evidence without recurring to 'demic' explanations. In particular, I will argue against two of the basic assumptions of the diffusionist interpretation:
1) the substantial unity of the 'neolithic package' (cereals + animal domesticates + pottery); and
2) the disjunctive character of the technological and typological relationship between the Epipalaeolithic/Mesolithic and the Neolithic.

I will discuss the first assumption in relation to the concrete mechanisms by which domesticates were introduced to Iberia, and the second in relation to the problem of how a real economy of production was established.

The ideas I will propose are not in themselves original. The central goal of this contribution is, rather to relate the development of the Neolithic more within the sphere of social relations than of techno-economic determinants. In the final analysis, all I seek to do is to apply *Ockham's Razor* to some of more dogmatic extremes of diffusionism, such as cultural influences or prehistoric colonizations, and thus to reestablish the social logic of this process within a historical perspective.

The diffusionist paradigm

Recent investigations of the origin of the Neolithic in the Iberian peninsula have been based on a general consensus that accepts the theses of Bernabò Brea (1946–56) concerning the unity of the so-called western Mediterranean Impressed Ware horizon, its chronological position as the earliest neolithic facies in each region, and its external origin, namely the eastern Mediterranean. Within this consensus there is some theoretical variation. Levantine prehistorians defend a 'dual' approach that attributes the introduction of the Neolithic to a cultural group (possibly consisting of settlers), while most Catalans subscribe to a more eclectic 'acculturationism' that limits the mechanism of neolithic development to the assimilation of external 'cultural influences' by native populations (cf. Bosch and Tarrús 1991: 63). The general agreement about the significance of the 'Cardial horizon' has occasionally been challenged by autochthonist alternatives, usually linked to evidence from areas that are peripheral to the Levantine 'nuclear zone'. As we shall see, the development of research over the past twenty years has been guided by the debate between these positions. At no time, however, has the Cardial horizon' consensus lost its position as the dominant paradigm.

Concensus was initially gained at the expense of the old Africanist tradition of the years before the Civil War (e.g., Bosch Gimpera 1932), which derived the Iberian Neolithic from the Capsian of North Africa. The 'collapse of the African myth' — the phrase is Martínez Santa Olalla's (1946: 22) — was supported by archaeological research in the 1940s and 1950s (San Valero 1946, 1947, 1950; Jordá and Alcácer 1949; Pericot 1945; Tarradell 1960; etc.). The principal arguments involved the priority of Cardial pottery, its Mediterranean parallels, as well as the lack of viability of the existence of an independent African centre.

The final triumph of these claims was a direct consequence of the impact of the stratigraphy of Arene Candide and its subsequent use as an independent external reference point for Cardial wares in Spain (San Valero 1947), but it was also the product of a general movement among Spanish prehistorians of the post-Civil War period towards Orientalist positions. This change was really directed against the latent evolutionism of the Occidentalism of Bosch and his followers, who at that time were politically suspect (Martínez Santa Olalla 1946: 19–20). This anti-evolutionism was transmitted directly to later research, which postulated the oriental origin of the Spanish Neolithic as undisputed.

At the same time, excavations at important sites such as Cova de l'Or (Fletcher 1962, 1963), Cova de la Sarsa (San Valero 1950), and Cueva de la Carigüela (Pellicer 1964) permitted the definition of the scope and characteristics of the Cardial horizon, which was assimilated, for better and for worse, to the 'Early' section of the Early/Middle/Late tripartition that was adopted at this time as the general organizational framework for the Neolithic of the Iberian peninsula.

The Orientalist approach received its definitive backing with the study and dating of the cereals from the Cardial levels of Cova de l'Or (Hopf 1966; Schubart and Pascual 1966). These results confirmed the oriental origins and the early

chronology (beginning of the fifth millennium) of the Cardial complex, as well as its techno-economic significance, as the cultural context for the introduction of domesticates to the peninsula.

As a result of these developments, from the mid-1960s the groundwork was set for a rare phenomenon in Spanish prehistory; a coherent research program with well-defined archaeological objectives. In terms of the principal, testable implications of the diffusionist thesis, these objectives may be summed up as follows:

1) demonstration of the essential unity of the Cardial horizon in the western Mediterranean and of the place of the Spanish Cardial complex within that whole;
2) demonstration that this horizon was the first to have pottery and a 'production economy', and that it was independent from local cultural traditions; and
3) demonstration of the secondary, derived character of the Neolithic of the rest of the Iberian peninsula.

The 'dual' theory

This approach directed the research in the 1970s and 1980s of a group of prehistorians (notably Martí Oliver, Bernabeu, and Fortea) committed to carrying out the program I have just described. As a result of the continued, coherent, and conscientious efforts of these and others, the Spanish Levant has become the general point of reference for the whole process of neolithic development of the peninsula. Likewise, the 'dual' theory has become the underlying assumption in all discussions of the issue and its regional sequences. This gives it a decisive importance, one that goes beyond its original regional context.

The 'dual' hypothesis postulates the existence in the Spanish Levant of two groups, one the 'pure' Neolithic, the other the local Epipalaeolithic 'substrate'. This view was put forward by Jordá and Alcácer (1949), and received its definitive form after Fortea's (1971, 1973) systematization of the Mediterranean Epipalaeolithic and the renewed excavations at Cova de l'Or by Martí Oliver (1977; Martí Oliver *et al.* 1980). The pure group, identified at sites like Or, Sarsa, and Cendres, is characterized by what the proponents of the approach consider to be a fully developed neolithic set of traits, both economic (there is evidence of domesticates) and cultural (there is pottery). These features of this group appear fully formed and without possible local predecessors: the domesticates are fully differentiated (and so presumably have a foreign origin), and this is confirmed by the parallels which the Cardial pottery has in other groups of the Mediterranean Impressed Ware horizon. In accordance with the underlying diffusionist theses, the 'pure' Neolithic demonstrated at the sites described above, would constitute a nucleus, both for the region and for the peninsula as a whole. In contrast, the substrate would be constituted by the indigenous inhabitants, who received the acculturating influence of the pure Neolithic while maintaining their local Epipalaeolithic tradition. These influences are manifested by the independent occurrence of isolated neolithic traits in contexts that otherwise would be classified within the 'geometric' Epipalaeolithic of Fortea (1973). In effect, the dual theory simply transfers to historical reality the taxonomic dichotomy between the Cova de l'Or and Cocina III–IV assemblage types (Bernabeu and Martí 1992: 215).

The arguments of the proponents of this theory stress the incompatibility of the characteristic elements of the two groups (Bernabeu 1989: 10; Bernabeu and Martí 1992: 214). The contrasts are seen in economic patterns (presence/absence of domesticated species, ratio of domesticated to wild animals, killing patterns, settlement locations, etc.), the material culture (the lithic and bone industries, ornaments, etc.), and in recent publications (Martí and Hernández 1988) even rock art (linear-geometric vs. macro-schematic representations). Confirmation of discontinuity in all aspects of the archaeological record is a critical feature of the model in that it is evidence of an external Cardial origin.

No less crucial an implication of the underlying diffusionist thesis is the substantial unity of the foreign neolithic 'package' that includes Cardial pottery and domesticated plants and animals (Fortea and Martí 1985). Validation of the thesis requires that anomalies like the presence of animals in aceramic contexts or of pottery in Epipalaeolithic contexts without domesticates be explained away. These facts cease to be anomalous, and indeed reinforce the theory as proof of the neolithic influence on the substrate, if one can demonstrate that:
1) no access to domesticates is possible except through their Cardial introducers; and
2) there is no ceramic horizon earlier than the Cardial one.

The first proposition refers to the possibility of either a local process of domestication or of an independent transmission of domesticates prior to Cardial Ware. Both issues have been raised repeatedly.

Early domestication has been discussed in relation to the Epipalaeolithic contexts with domesticated sheep/goat at Cova Fosca (Castellón), whose excavators have argued for the existence of a local process of domestication during the seventh millennium BC (Olaria de Gusi *et al.* 1982; Olaria and Gusi 1983; Olaria 1988a, 1988b; Estévez 1988). Similar problems have arisen in Andalusia: domesticated animals have been identified in epipalaeolithic levels at Cueva de Nerja (Boessneck and Driesch 1980; Pellicer 1983; Muñoz 1984). In both cases proponents of the dual hypothesis have attacked the anomaly with arguments that allude to problems of the radiocarbon dates with regard to their stratigraphic and techno-typological contexts (as this would be defined by the sequence in the Spanish Levant, of course), to the doubtful integrity of the contexts themselves and to problems with the identification of the faunal remains (extensive discussions along these lines are presented by Fortea and Martí 1985; Bernabeu 1989; Bernabeu and Martí 1992; Zilhão 1993, etc.). The basic arguments, however, are still the absence of domesticable wild species on the Iberian peninsula, on the one hand, and the lack of nearby areas from which domesticates could have been introduced in pre-Cardial times, on the other. This last argument has been raised against parallel claims of local or pre-Cardial domestication in southern France (Geddes 1980).

As far as the question of pre- or non-Cardial ceramic horizons are concerned, the discussion has also centreed on the acceptance or rejection of radiocarbon dates, based on whether or not they fit with the Levantine sequence. Frequently, the dates under discussion are the same ones that are rejected in discussions of early domesticates. As the reader will recall, the rejection of early domesticates is generally based on comparative typological considerations, so that the matter of the ceramic sequence is of critical importance. Be that as it may, the interdependence of the two issues frequently leads to circular arguments in which the assumptions about domestication and comparative typology support one another.

The priority of the Levantine Cardial centre was initially discussed in relation to a possible pre-Cardial phase of undecorated pottery radiocarbon dated to 6000±150 bc at Verdelpino (Cuenca) (Moure and Fernández-Miranda, 1977; cf. detailed discussions in Fortea and Martí 1985:

174ff. and Bernabeu 1989: 128). The initial proponents of this pre-Cardial horizon did not respond to the numerous criticisms they received, and the Verdelpino evidence has for the moment been shelved. Implicitly, the early date at Verdelpino is argued to be the result of mixing in the deposits. At present, then, the typological-comparative debate centres on the independence of the Levantine centre from the oldest contexts with pottery in Andalusia. Here Cardial pottery does not dominate the ceramic assemblages (as in the earliest phase of the Levantine sequence), but is present in association with other decorative techniques, such as non-Cardial impressions, incisions, relief decoration, and 'almagra' (red, burnished) surfaces. Generally, these contexts had been considered representative of an Andalusian Middle Neolithic referred to as the 'Cultura de las Cuevas' (Navarrete 1976), an attribution based on the stratigraphy at Cueva de la Carigüela (Granada) (Pellicer 1964) and the dates from Cueva de los Murciélagos (Córdoba) (Vicent and Muñoz 1973). The publication in the 1980s of a series of very early radiocarbon dates (in the sixth and seventh millennia bc) for some of these contexts (Nerja, Dehesilla, Cueva Chica de Santiago) brought into question the idea that the Levantine Cardial centre should be considered the nuclear zone for the Iberian Neolithic (e.g., Olaria 1986; Acosta 1986). Other less extreme dates from other regions (Chaves in Aragón, Barranco de los Grajos in Murcia, Can Ballester and Cova Fosca in Castellón) reinforced the crisis of the model of absolute priority for the Levantine Cardial complex.

The reaction of the proponents of the dual theory has consisted of a refinement of the Levantine ceramic sequence, based on a comparative analysis of the series from Or and Cendres (Bernabeu 1989). This revision substitutes the earlier tripartite periodization with a sequence of two phases (Neolithic I and II), which are interpreted explicitly as successive 'cultures' (Bernabeu 1989: 10; Bernabeu and Martí 1992: 213). The first of these cultures encompasses the old Early and Middle Neolithic into a single cultural tradition that is part of the Mediterranean Impressed Ware complex. The ceramics at Or and Cendres would permit the subdivision of this thousand-year long tradition into three horizons (A, B, C), which in turn could be subdivided into phases (A1, A2, B1, B2). The criterion for this ceramic periodization is the continuous decrease in the proportion of Cardial motifs in relation to other forms of decoration over the course of the two stratigraphic sequences. Accordingly, the Neolithic IA would be properly denominated the 'Cardial ware horizon,' while the Neolithic IB would be termed the 'Impressed-Incised ware horizon' (Bernabeu 1989: 113). Only phase IA1 could be considered to have an absolute predominance of Cardial ware, and thus to represent the first moment of the process of neolithic development.

This existence of this phase, only identified at Or and Cendres, fulfills the need to maintain the chronological priority of the Levantine centre against the pretensions of autonomy (or, more modestly, synchrony) for the contexts that are not strictly Cardial and have absolute dates that are 'too' early. In effect, these contexts have their clearest parallels in horizon IB of the Levantine sequence. In accordance with the logic of a cultural interpretation of the ceramic sequence, the parallels are interpreted in terms of 'genetic' relations and therefore of contemporaneity (e.g., Bernabeu 1989: 118). Thus, the model postulating the Levantine as a nucleus for the transition to agriculture receives archaeological support.

By taking typological similarities as indicators of strict synchrony this view is in open disagreement with the available absolute chronology. The arguments must, therefore, be directed to establishing the inferiority of absolute chronologies with respect to the coherence of the relative sequence and, what is even more, to the fundamental diffusionist thesis. As Bernabeu (1989: 128) puts it:

> The model assumed ... to explain the origins of the Neolithic leads us to a first selection in accepting radiocarbon dates that refer to the initial chronology of this process: if the initial Neolithic horizon corresponds ... to impressed wares, then its chronology must be put into relation with what is proposed for those same wares in the diffusionary centre or centres.

These problems do not completely disappear, however, if one accepts the arguments of the proponents of the dual theory and throws out all the dates from the sixth millennium and earlier (Nerja, Dehesilla, Cueva Chica de Santiago, Fosca, Barranco de los Grajos: see the detailed discussion in Bernabeu 1989), since some 'acceptable' dates (e.g., Cueva de los Murciélagos, Chaves) suggest the possibility that the two early horizons of the Levantine sequence are contemporaneous.

As we have just seen, the dual theory depends upon a complex interpretation of the archaeological record, an interpretation whose critical points are, firstly, the discontinuity between a pure Neolithic and an Epipalaeolithic that is becoming Neolithic and, secondly, the unity of the Cardial neolithic package, together with supplementary arguments about the inability of the substrate to obtain independent access to the components of that package. The purely archaeological aspects of this interpretation are not indisputable, as we have seen, but they are sufficiently supported by the evidence to constitute a solid framework for organizing the archaeological record. It must be said, however, that this solidity is relative to the extreme fragility of the arguments put forward by opponents of dualism. Zilhão (1993: 38–46) has analyzed in detail the most important cases brought forward against the dualists (Cueva Dehesilla, Cova Fosca, and Cueva de Nerja) and has shown that they are all affected by serious problems of archaeological credibility. This, of course, does not subtract validity from the dualists' own evidence, but needs to be taken into account when evaluating that evidence.

I now wish to consider the historical implications of this theory, that is to say, what it argues about the actual way in which the process of neolithic development unfolded, given that the empirical basis on which it stands has been accepted as valid. The defenders of the dual hypothesis are usually ambiguous on this point. One has the impression that, rather than resolve the issue, they try to avoid it, suspending their judgment. Thus, in Martí Oliver's (1983) comprehensive and popular account of the Levantine Neolithic, its extra-peninsular origin is practically not discussed, beyond a mere affirmation of its oriental provenance.

The most salient feature of the dual theory is, however, its complete dependence on arguments for demic diffusion as the basis for the process of cultural diffusion. In effect, the interpretation of the record is based on the assumption that the pure Neolithic of the Or facies is something more than a taxonomic abstraction. The way in which the proponents of this model write about the pure Neolithic suggests, indeed demands, that it should have a real ethnic basis, since reference is always made to the 'bearers' of that culture. Ultimately, in the words of Bernabeu (1989: 138), 'the only model capable of explaining the origin of our Neolithic without entering into logical contradictions when it is applied to the facts of the archaeological record is a diffusion that involves the displacement of human groups.'

In the formative phase of the diffusionist paradigm the search for oriental parallels of Cardial ceramics went hand in hand with discussions about the navigability of the Mediterranean and the possible routes of diffusion (San Valero 1946). These preoccupations have never been abandoned, and the majority of authors feel the obligation to pay tribute to the 'unquestionable role which navigation played in this process' (Bernabeu 1989: 123). All the same, the weight of the facts has imposed a certain realism when the concrete mechanisms of diffusion are interpreted:

The acceptance of a diffusionist model cannot imply a negation of the role the substrate may have played in any given case. The diffusion of neolithic culture along the coasts of the western Mediterranean cannot be interpreted from the perspective of concepts such as an invasion — in the classic and dramatic sense which is usually attributed to this term — or a classic colonization. There are models more appropriate to the socio-economic structure of these prehistoric societies that would better explain the phenomenon. In this sense, a model of population expansion seems a more acceptable alternative (Bernabeu 1989: 121).

In effect, the 'wave of advance model' of Ammerman and Cavalli-Sforza (1973) constitutes the theoretical horizon of the dual approach in that it links the transmission of domesticates with a demic model that is compatible both with the chronological pattern documented in Central Europe and the Mediterranean as a whole, and with the absence of clear evidence for a colonization in the classic sense mentioned above. This permits one to maintain the idea of a cultural 'current' without abandoning the underlying principle, derived from Kossinna, of the unity between race and culture:

> We propose that the appearance of the first Neolithic groups, the bearers of the earliest Cardial ceramics, is to be related to a process of population expansion from the eastern Mediterranean just as Ammerman and Cavalli-Sforza have proposed (Bernabeu and Martí 1992: 214).

In short, the demic hypothesis of Ammerman and Cavalli-Sforza serves to redeem the coherence of the dual model, a model compromised by the apparent theoretical insufficiency of its ingenuous normativism. Under these circumstances the dual interpretation of the process of neolithic development would appear to be rendered immune from all possible refutation. On the one hand, it is impossible to explain the early presence of domesticates in Iberia without resorting to diffusionist arguments. On the other hand, there is no longer any need to explain the absence of data relating to both the exact origin of the bearers of these domesticates, and the means by which they arrived from abroad.

The 'Island Filter' model

A general reconsideration of the problem of the westward diffusion of domesticates would seem to be required in order to overcome the theoretical impasse just described. In my opinion, the elements for such a reconsideration were first put forward by Lewthwaite (1986b) in what he termed the 'island filter model.' His formulation is empirically weak, but it embodies as many valuable elements as other suggestions he has made. Thus, Lewthwaite (1982) was the first to point out that 'complex hunter-gatherers' constituted possible ethnographic analogues for the subsistence strategies that seemed to be revealed by a dispassionate analysis of the oldest neolithic groups of the western Mediterranean. He was also the first to suggest the essentially social role played by the elements of the neolithic package in those contexts (Lewthwaite, 1981, 1986a, 1986b, 1987). The ideas I present in the rest of this work are simply intended to derive general principles from proposals, that have unfortunately, made an insufficient impact on Spanish research.

The island filter model (Lewthwaite, 1986b) seeks to account for the palpable differences that are observed in the transition to food production in the eastern and western basins of the Mediterranean. In the east, mesolithic foraging economies seem to be replaced very early (about 6000 bc) and rather abruptly by village farming economies, after a relatively brief episode of intensification, the most distinctive feature of which is deep water fishing. In the west however, the appearance of village farming economies is delayed at least until the fourth millennium, after a long period (at least two millennia) in which pastoral exploitation of domestic animals is integrated into subsistence strategies and ways of life that continue the patterns of the preceding period with just a few modifications.

From a Western perspective, these contrasts suggest at least two questions concerning (1) the prolonged stability of mixed strategies of hunting-gathering and animal-keeping and (2) the delay in the adoption of the village farming pattern. These really involve two aspects of the same general question: Why does the so-called 'Early Neolithic' of the western Mediterranean (which corresponds in culture-historical terms to the 'Cardial horizon') seem so un-neolithic when judged by the standard of eastern Mediterranean patterns? Or more generally still, why did access to the techniques of food production not lead the inhabitants of the western Mediterranean to adopt a village way of life?

The island filter model claims that explanation of the palpable difference between the sequences of neolithic development in the eastern and western Mediterranean basin is based on the selective role played by the islands of the western Mediterranean in the process of the transmission of neolithic traits. The specific conditions which the populations of these islands would have faced would explain why they adopted certain features, such as domesticated sheep and goats, and remained indifferent to others, such as village dwellings.

The underlying principle in all of this is that, under normal conditions, the traits that are assimilated are those that would guarantee the preservation of previous ways of life, not those that would bring about their transformation. Raising small mammals would permit the maintenance of a way of life based on the exploitation of local wild equivalents after these had become extinct due to excessive human pressure in another chronological context (this is the case for *Myotragus balearicus*). Naturally, these wild *equivalents* would have no reason to be the genetic *antecedents* of any domesticated species.

Logically, as a consequence of the operation of this principle, the recipients of the 'Neolithic' further to the west would only have access to those features which had been of interest to their intermediaries, so that the Early Neolithic of Iberia would resemble its post-Palaeolithic predecessors more than would the societies in which agriculture originated.

This hypothesis has become indefensible for empirical reasons: there is no evidence for the priority of the islands in the process of neolithic development in the western Mediterranean basin. It contains, however, a series of assumptions which make it an important milestone in the development of research on the issue, assumptions whose logic outlive their refutation on empirical grounds. I believe two of these assumptions are of particular importance: (1) the importance attributed to the contrasts between the sequences of eastern and western neolithic development, contrasts considered to be at the root of the problem; and (2) the emphasis on the concrete mechanisms by which the complex of domestication spread.

The island filter model places the difference between the eastern and western Mediterranean at the centre of the problem, underlining the characteristic contrast between discontinuity and continuity in the two areas. Naturally, this involves an interpretation of the evidence to which defenders of the dual theory would not subscribe. For them, sites like Cova de l'Or represent a 'pure Neolithic', for which a fully developed economy of food production is assumed. Now, as they themselves recognize (Martí Oliver 1983), the absence of the village type settlements which would be expected in this case is paradoxical. The dual theory usually resolves this problem with *ad hoc* hypotheses or by proposing that judgment on the matter be put off; ('village settlements are unknown, but they may be found in the future'). The intensification of research in some regions and the recent introduction of systematic, intensive surveys has permitted the identification of a growing number of such settlements, although few have been excavated as yet. These discoveries have been hailed by dualists as a confirmation of one of their theory's critical predictions, which, until the 1980s, had been seen as an embarrassing paradox.

For its part, the island filter model emphasizes this contradiction, but gives it a diffusionist interpretation: village settlements were an element 'filtered' by the selective self interest of the intermediary transmitters of the neolithic complex.

It is impossible to accept this argument, because the system of village farming cannot be considered a cultural feature that can be transmitted in itself. It is not, for example, an isolated technology. On the contrary, it is a complex phenomenon that affects all aspects (economic, ideological, political) of the social whole, as well as the particular form in which that whole is articulated.

We can accept, however, that the contrast between the process of neolithic development in the eastern and western Mediterranean must be the point of departure for any discussion of the issue. The crucial question is the one that was formulated above: why did access to the techniques of food production *not* lead the inhabitants of the western Mediterranean to adopt a village way of life?

Naturally, this approach questions, not only the basic model of diffusion, but also the interpretation of the significance and historical role of the introduction of domestication to the western area. We accept as given that domesticated plants and animals came from the east, but we refuse to accept that fully developed neolithic economies were present in the west until well into the fourth millennium at the earliest, in spite of the presence of those same plants and animals. Accordingly, we must accept that important aspects of the neolithic process, (such as the economic, social, and even ideological characteristics of village settlements) are not immediately tied with the diffusion of domesticates, since their appearance seems to be deferred for almost two millennia.

The island filter model is right in attributing this anomaly to the concrete mechanisms by which diffusion took place. Its principal weakness, however, is its emphasis on the route of diffusion as a central factor of explanation. Although it substitutes the demic vehicle of diffusion with the more logical process of relations between neighbours, it still accepts the traditional idea of the diffusionary 'current' as a single, directional vector of cultural transmission.

The capillary diffusion model

I believe the logic of the capillary diffusion model approach can account for the westward diffusion of domesticates and other cultural features without the need to resort to suppositions about the movement of human populations. To develop the model we must consider what is known about social relations among hunter-gatherers as well the evidence about the conditions of human occupation in the western Mediterranean during the early Holocene.

Everything appears to indicate that the social organization of the post-palaeolithic populations of the Mediterranean did not surpass the complexity attributed to the ideal type of 'band' society. At any rate, social relations would have been segmentary, and in known segmentary societies different kinds of relations of reciprocity between groups play an important role. These relations form wide ranging networks through which goods and social gifts flow, as a vehicle of kinship obligations, political alliances, social competition, and even conflict. In a certain sense, the capacity of these social relations to serve as the base for flows of material elements may be considered as a form of 'conductivity.'

It seems reasonable to suppose that domesticated plants and animals — and with them their genetic properties — circulated through these networks of reciprocity, be it as products, as means of production or even as status objects. That is to say, we may speak of a certain conductivity of the post-palaeolithic social world with respect to domesticates. Naturally, the nature of this phenomenon would have to be determined in each particular case. What seems certain, however, is that the segmentary social dynamic favored — or at least did not impede — the expansive pressure of domesticated genotypes. To paraphrase a well-known neo-Darwinian formulation, we might say that certain plant and animal species used post-palaeolithic social networks very efficiently to maximize their adaptive success and dispersal.

Under the segmentary conditions we attribute to the post-palaeolithic populations of the Mediterranean, the conductive properties of the complex of intergroup relations must have been isotropic, equal at all points in the network. As we shall see later, the homogeneity of the conductivity would probably only be distorted by ethnic/cultural boundaries and by specific geographic limitations. The absence of pronounced differences of potential in demography, economy, and socio-political scale between the various parts of the network would exclude the possibility of long-distance, directional movement of goods and information. Thus, it seems appropriate to propose a capillary model for the process of transmission, in lieu of the traditional axial or arterial model.

This model implies a large-scale pattern similar to the 'wave of advance' of Ammerman and Cavalli-Sforza, and it accounts for the same geographical and chronological pattern of westward diffusion of domesticated species, but is based on assumptions other than the principle of demic diffusion. In effect, the capillary model presumes a relatively static situation in the distribution of human populations. This does not exclude the possibility of movement of human populations, but eliminates a dependency on demic explanations for arguments about the process of transmission.

We must also bear in mind the probable existence of exogamic practices among post-palaeolithic societies, and thus for the likely circulation of 'reproducers' along the same networks 'used' by domesticated species. It is even possible that the circulation of both were linked by specific exogamic institutions, such as dowry or brideprice. In any case, it seems possible to explain phenomena of genetic spread through relatively static populations, so that we can reject the wave of advance model, even if we accept the existence of the genetic evidence Ammerman and Cavalli-Sforza adduce in its support. If a static model of transmission is reasonable for human genetic features, it should be reasonable also for technological or cultural elements, which can be transmitted independently of human movement.

The processes of capillary transmission suggest possible explanations of some specific facts that characterize how domesticated species spread within the Iberian peninsula, making discontinuous and uneven progress from the coast toward the interior. To understand this pattern we must now consider the factors of differential spread of relative anisotropy, mentioned above. We may suppose that the circulation between groups of objects diffused socially would be affected by the particular configuration of relations between societies. Effectively, the web of segmentary social relations would exhibit discontinuities due to differences in ethnic/cultural identity, linguistic communities, transitory political circumstances, and so on. Furthermore, the influence the landscape itself had on social and productive processes would impose severe modifications on the model of isotropy. This, in fact, is the logic of the filter effect.

At the same time, the dynamics of different anisotropic factors are not synchronous, but develop over different Braudelian *durées*. Thus, the existence of a political conflict between neighbouring communities may interrupt or impede the transmission of goods between them, but such phenomena represent conjunctures that would barely affect the distribution of goods over *archaeological* time scales. Ethnic or cultural discontinuities would exert a much more lasting influence, filtering flows of material goods associated with the interchange of social information (since the possibility of such interchange is affected by cultural diversity) over long periods of time. Finally, discontinuities in the landscape, to the extent that they determine the conditions of infrastructural production permanently, would generate fractures and lines of force in the systems of interregional transfer of information, according to well-known principles of complementarity, incompatibility, and so on.

The combined effect of these factors is what leads to the archaeological impression that the advance of domesticates into the Iberian peninsula was discontinuous, a pattern easily interpreted in terms of demic colonizations and agricultural frontiers. The origins of the Neolithic in the various natural regions (or in the different cultural facies that represent these regions in the archaeological record) *appear* to occur all at once. In reality, the domesticates (or Cardial pottery, as the case may be) first occupy the system of intergroup exchange, saturating it to its outer limits relatively rapidly. These limits would themselves be a restriction on further transfers to areas beyond the system, at least as long as the material flows in question remained associated with specific social institutions.

The pattern of diffusion of Cardial pottery is a good example of this kind of phenomenon, one that may perhaps apply to the earliest domesticates as well. There is a certain consensus, based on solid analytical evidence, about the non-functional character of Early Neolithic decorated pottery. It is a highly elaborated ware, made from very fine clays, and is fragile and difficult to fire. This is true both of Levantine and of Andalusian assemblages (Martí *et al.* 1987; Navarrete *et al.* 1991). At the same time, the recent discovery that motifs on Cardial pottery are also found in rock art (Martí and Hernández 1988) supports the view that these ceramics somehow propped up the identity of social groups, although at a level which is difficult to specify. I do not mean to suggest that decorated pottery was an authentic ethnic marker, but rather that its patterns of distribution were related to aspects of intergroup relations that were not directly functional.

This hypothesis was first put forward in general terms by Lewthwaite (1981), and interesting case studies have been made for Languedoc (Barnett 1990) and southern Italy (Malone 1985). According to these studies, regional analysis of the distribution of Early Neolithic decorated pottery shows that some decorative types have a local distribution, while others are uniform across broad areas. Malone (1985: 122–24) considers these to be reflections of the formation of local alliances and Barnett (1990: 864) suggests they demonstrate intergroup prestige networks.

Thus, what seems to characterize the earliest ceramic phases of the prehistory of Iberia is not so much the spread of a particular type of pottery as the spread of the social need to possess and exchange decorated pottery. This need would be manifested differently in different regions, thus producing the impression that different cultural areas existed. On this account, the spread of pottery would be related to aspects of the internal social dynamics of Epipalaeolithic groups, possibly as a symptom of the gradual dissolution of the previous social order.

The stylistic fragmentation which follows the Cardial episode seems to coincide with the conversion of pottery production towards directly functional uses, with a partial loss of its sociotechnic character as a vehicle for, and sign of, social relations.

Some of this argument might perhaps also be applied to domesticates, as Lewthwaite (1987) suggests, on condition that the role they played in the internal social dynamic of post-palaeolithic groups be clarified.

Discussion

By accepting intergroup reciprocity as the vector for the transmission of neolithic traits, we assume that the transmission was social in nature, rather than specifically economic or generally techno-adaptive. Accordingly, we should attempt to formulate a hypothesis concerning the way in which the first domesticated plants and animals were integrated into the new social and productive contexts in which they were accepted. This is what the dual theory tries to do when it proposes that the first appearance of domesticated cereals and sheep/goats were part of a fully developed economy of food production (Bernabeu and Martí 1992). The general argument against this interpretation has already been mentioned: its central point is the absence of village farming in the western Mediterranean until a very late phase of the Neolithic. The human populations of that area appear to integrate the potential elements of a production economy into their previous way of life, adjusting them to the productive strategies of foragers by using them as complementary resources which reduce the risk of subsistence production (Lewthwaite 1986b). This would relate the process to the practice of social storage, a factor which appears to be as critical to the process of transition to food production as it is to the process of the emergence of social complexity (Testart 1982; Halstead and O'Shea 1982; Ingold, 1983). At the same time it would bring to the fore the social potential of Mediterranean domesticates as accumulators of use value.

Indeed, social storage strategies are easily related to risk reduction, but, as Testart (1982) has demonstrated, its practice requires profound transformations in the social structure of hunter-gatherers, since it requires a severe restriction of the norms of generalized reciprocity that constitute one of the central principles of band organization. At the same time, the control of risk by such accumulation has clear implications for the development of inequalities and differentiated forms of political power.

This line of analysis should lead us to ask about the nature of the social and political dynamics among the post-palaeolithic inhabitants of the western Mediterranean. If indeed the role of the earliest domesticates is to be interpreted in relation to the concept of social storage, we must suppose that they were received into a context in which the decomposition of the social structure characteristic of hunter-gatherers was already under way: the conditions for accumulation which the domesticates would provide must already have been in existence to some extent. Otherwise, the features in question would have been filtered out. This is in fact what occurs with respect to some of them, when we consider the extreme scarcity (and spatial restriction) of cereals in comparison with sheep/goat during the first phases of the process.

Unfortunately, we do not as yet have an adequate empirical basis for the discussion either of social relations during the Early Neolithic of the Iberian peninsula or of the links between the earliest use of domesticates and social storage strategies. Notwithstanding, the same contextual arguments that have been used by proponents of the dual theory as evidence for the productive maturity of Cardial neolithic societies can be interpreted so as to support a hypothesis that postulates a social use for domesticates, such as the argument outlined above. The cereals at Cova de l'Or have been presented as the product of a mature production technology on the basis of their advanced degree of processing and their concentration in a storage deposit (Bernabeu and Martí 1992). At the same time, it has been suggested that the abundance of young individuals among the sheep/goat at the site represent a selective cull pattern characteristic of surplus-oriented livestock keeping (Pérez Ripoll in Martí *et al.* 1980: 203; see also Martí *et al.* 1987; Bernabeu and Martí 1992, etc.) There is little doubt that the finds at Or reflect a technically sophisticated use of domesticates, but this in no way implies their predominance within the totality of production. As Barandiarán and Cava (1992: 194) have correctly indicated:

> The high percentage of plant and animal domesticates present in the Or deposit guarantees that the people there were intensively

engaged in the exploitation of agricultural and pastoral resources, but this does not necessarily mean that those people did not practice the hunting and gathering of wild resources with equal intensity in other places.

This issue is directly related to the possibility that early neolithic groups may have practiced various spatial and temporal diversifications of production like those that are documented among the epipalaeolithic populations of southern France and the Spanish Levant (Davidson 1976). Thus, the classic Levantine sites may be showing us only a part of the subsistence system, thanks to their functional specialization in activities related to the exploitation of domesticates.

This leads me to a final reflection on the nature of the facts available for the Early Neolithic. In reality, the entire characterization of the socio-economic aspects of the pure Cardial phase is based on evidence from very few sites, which may in some way be a product of very special circumstances. Thus, for example, Cova de l'Or has produced remains of a grain storage facility, but not a single trace of grain processing (in fact, the site is located on a steep slope in mountainous terrain, a place highly unsuitable for grain cultivation.) Likewise, with respect to cull patterns, the predominance of young animals could be the result, not of general economic patterns, but of the seasonal use of the site. Clark's (1985: 257–258) suggestion that differences in age at death may be due to the import or export of animals from a site should also be considered. These interpretations could be consistent with one another and with a third piece of evidence: the outstanding quality of the Cardial ware from the site. These three considerations may lead to the suggestion that the site was not so much the permanent seat of a residential group as a place linked to important activities within economic and social cycles the complete variability of which eludes us. We may suppose, in effect, that the concentration in the cave of grain silos, of the remains of the intensive consumption of young sheep/goats, and of exceptional decorated pottery is a reasonable indication of the existence in that place of an authentic accumulation of use values, in the sense discussed earlier. If this conjecture is accurate, Cova de l'Or would have been a locality functionally specialized not in the exploitation of domesticates, but in social storage. This would require us to give a different interpretation to the differences between the classic Levantine Cardial facies and the presumed substrate. These would, in reality, be the product of the same people observed at distinct moments in the deployment of their subsistence and social activities.

Of course, all these ideas are yet to be tested archaeologically. For such testing to take place, however, it is essential that researchers set aside certain clichés that have hitherto been beyond discussion. This article seeks to invite this large scale and much-needed revision, without which little progress in our knowledge of the Neolithic in the Iberian peninsula will be possible.

Bibliography

Acosta, P.

1986   El Neolítico en Andalucía Occidental: Estado Actual. In *Homenaje a Luis Siret (1934–1984)*, 136–50. Sevilla: Consejería de Cultura, Junta de Andalucia.

Ammermann, A.J., and L.L. Cavalli-Sforza

1984   *The Neolithic Transition and the Genetics of Populations in Europe*. Princeton: Princeton University Press.

Barandiarán, I., and A. Cava

1992   Carácteres Industriales del Epipaleolítico y el Neolítico en Aragón: Su Referencia a los Yacimientos Levantinos. In P. Utrilla (ed.), *Aragón/Litoral Mediterráneo: Intercambios Culturales durante la Prehistoria*, 181–96. Zaragoza: Institución Fernando el Católico.

Barnett, W.K.

1990   Small-scale Transport of Early Neolithic Pottery in the West Mediterranean. *Antiquity* 64: 859–63.

Bernabeu, J.

1989   *La Tradición Cultural de las Cerámicas Impresas en la Zona Oriental de la Península Ibérica*. Servicio de Investigación Prehistórica, Serie de Trabajos Varios 86. Valencia: Servicio de Investigación Prehistórica.

Bernabeu, J., and B. Martí

1992   El País Valenciano de la Aparición del Neolítico al Horizonte Campaniforme. In P. Utrilla (ed.), *Aragón/Litoral Mediterráneo: Intercambios Culturales durante la Prehistoria*, 213–34. Zaragoza: Institución Fernando el Católico.

Bernabó Brea, L.

1946–56 *Gli Scavi nella Caverna delle Arene Candide*. Bordighera: Instituto di Studi Liguri.

Boessneck, J., and A. von den Driesch

1980   Tierknockenfunde aus vier südspanischen Höhlen. *Studien über frühe Tierknockenfunde aus der Iberischen Halbinsel* 7: 14–19.

Bosch, A., and J. Tarrús

1991   Canvi Cultural i Hàbitat en el Procés de Neolitització de Catalunya. *Travaux de Préhistoire Catalane* 7: 61–70.

Bosch Gimpera, P.

1932   *Etnología de la Península Ibérica*. Barcelona: Editorial Alpha.

Clark, G.

1985   Beyond Subsistence Reconstruction: The Potential of Faunal Remains in the Study of Social and Economic Complexity. In C. Malone and S. Stoddart (eds), *Papers in Italian archaeology IV*, 2: 252–71. British Archaeological ReportsInternational Series 244. Oxford: British Archaeological Reports.

Davidson, I.

1976   Les Mallaetes and Mondúver: The Economy of a Human Group in Prehistoric Spain. In G. de G. Sieveking, I.H. Longworth, and K.E. Wilson (eds), *Problems in Economic and Social Archaeology*, 484–99. London: Duckworth.

Estévez, J.

1988   Estudio de los Restos Faunísticos. In C. Olaria (ed.), *Cova Fosca: Un Asentamiento Meso-Neolítico de Cazadores y Pastores en la Serranía del Alto Maestrazgo*, 281–337. Castellón de la Plana: Diputación de Castellón.

Fletcher, D.

1962   Toneles Cerámicos Neolíticos. *VII. Congreso Nacional de Prehistoria, Barcelona 1960*, 148–51.

1963   Nuevos Datos Sobre las Relaciones entre las Costas Españolas y el Mediterráneo Oriental. In *A Pedro Bosch Gimpera en el Septuagésimo Aniversario de su Nacimiento*, 167–72. México, DF.

Fortea, J.

1971   *La Cueva de la Cocina*. Servicio de Investigación Prehistórica, Serie de Trabajos Varios 40. Valencia: Servicio de Investigación Prehistórica.

1973   *Los Complejos Microlaminares y Geométricos del Epipaleolítico Mediterráneo Español*. Memorias del Seminario de Prehistoria y Arqueología 4. Salamanca: Seminario de Prehistoria y Arqueología.

Fortea, J., and B. Martí

1985   Consideraciones Sobre los Inicios del Neolítico en el Mediterráneo Español. *Zephyrus* 37–38: 176–99.

Geddes, D.

1980   *De la Chasse au Troupeau en Méditerranée Occidentale*. Archives d'Écologie Préhistorique 5. Toulouse: École des Hautes Études en Sciences Sociales.

Halstead, P., and J. O'Shea

1982   A friend in need is a friend indeed: social stor-

age and the origins of social ranking. In C.
Renfrew and S. Shennan (eds), *Ranking,
Resource and Exchange: Aspects of the
Archaeology of Early European Society*, 92–99.
Cambridge: Cambridge University Press.

Hopf, M.

1966   *Triticum monococcum* L. y *Triticum dicoccum*
Schübl en el Neolítico Antiguo Español. *Archivo
de Prehistoria Levantina* 11: 53–73.

Ingold, T.

1983   The Significance of Storage in Hunting
Societies. *Man* 18: 553–71.

Jordá, F., and J. Alcácer

1949   *La Covacha de Llatas (Andilla)*. Servicio de
Investigación Prehistórica, Serie de Trabajos
Varios 11. Valencia: Servicio de Investigación
Prehistórica.

Lewthwaite, J.

1981   Ambiguous First Impressions: A Survey of
Recent Work on the Early Neolithic of the West
Mediterranean. *Journal of Mediterranean
Anthropology and Archaeology* 1: 292–307.

1982   Cardial Disorder: Ethnographic and
Archaeological Comparisions for Problems in
the Early Prehistory of the West Mediterranean.
In R. Montjardin (ed.), *Le Néolithique Ancien
Méditerranéen: Actes du Colloque International
de Préhistoire, Montpellier 1981*, 311–18. Sète:
Fédération Archéologique de l'Hérault.

1986a   From Menton to Mondego in Three Steps:
Applications of the Availability Model to the
Transition to Food Production in Occitania,
Mediterranean Spain and Southern Portugal.
Arqueologia 13: 95–119.

1986b   The Transition to Food Production: A
Mediterranean Perspective. In M. Zvelebil (ed.),
*Hunters in Transition: Mesolithic Societies of
Temperate Eurasia and their Transition to
Farming*, 53–66. Cambridge: Cambridge
University Press.

1987   Essai pour faire sortir de sa coquille le facteur
social dans le cadre du Néolitique ancien
méditerranéen. In J. Guilaine, J. Courtin, J.L.
Roudil and J.L. Vernet (eds), *Premières
Communautés Paysannes en Méditerranée
Occidentale*, 737–43. Paris: C.N.R.S.

Malone, C.

1985   Pots, Prestige and Ritual in Neolithic Southern
Italy. In: C. Malone and S. Stoddart, (eds),
Papers in Italian Archaeology IV, 2: 118–51.
British Archaeological ReportsInternational
Series 244. Oxford: British Archaeological
Reports.

Martí Oliver, B.

1977   *Cova de L'Or (Beniarrés, Alicante), I* Servicio
de Investigación Prehistórica, Serie de Trabajos
Varios 51. Valencia: Servicio de Investigación
Prehistórica.

1983   *El Nacimiento de la Agricultura en el Pais*

Valenciano: Del Neolítico a la Edad del Bronce.
Valencia: Universidad de Valencia.

Martí Oliver, B., V. Pascual Pérez, M.D. Gallart Martí, P.
López García, M. Pérez Ripoll, J.D. Acuña Hernández and
F. Robles Cuenca

1980   *Cova de L'Or (Beniarrés, Alicante)*, vol. 2.
Servicio de Investigación Prehistórica, Serie de
Trabajos Varios 65. Valencia: Servicio de
Investigación Prehistórica.

Martí, B., J. Fortea Pérez, J. Bernabeu Aubán, M. Pérez
Ripoll, J.D. Acuña Hernández, F. Robles Cuenca and M.D.
Gallart Martí

1987   El Neolítico Antiguo en la Zona Oriental de la
Península Ibérica. In J. Guilaine, J. Courtin, J.L.
Roudil and J.L. Vernet (eds), *Premières
Communautés Paysannes en Méditerranée
Occidentale*, 607–198. Paris: C.N.R.S.

Martí, B., and M.S. Hernández

1988   *El Neolitic Valenciá: Art Rupestre i Cultura
Material.* Valencia: Servicio de Investigación
Prehistórica.

Martínez Santa Olalla, J.

1946   *Esquema Paletnológico de la Península Ibérica*,
2nd edition. Madrid: Seminario de Historia
Primitiva del Hombre.

Moure, A., and M. Fernández-Miranda

1977   El Abrigo de Verdelpino (Cuenca): Noticias de
los Trabajos de 1976. *Trabajos de Prehistoria*
34: 31–68.

Muñoz, A.M.

1984   La Neolitización en España: Problemas y Líneas
de Investigación. In J. Fortea (ed.), *Scripta
Praehistorica Francisco Jordá oblata*, 349–369.
Salamanca: Universidad de Salamanca.

Navarrete, M.S.

1976   *La Cultura de las Cuevas con Cerámica
Decorada en Andalucía Oriental.* Granada:
Universidad de Granada.

Navarrete, M.S., J. Capel, J. Linares, F. Huertas and E.
Reyes

1991   *Cerámicas Neolíticas de la Provincia de
Granada: Materias Primas y Técnicas de
Manufacturación.* Granada: Universidad de
Granada.

Olaria, C.

1986   La Problemática del Neolítico Andaluz y sus
Conexiones con el Litoral Mediterráneo
Peninsular. In *Homenaje a Luis Siret
(1934–1984)*, 130–35. Sevilla: Consejería de
Cultura, Junta de Andalucia.

1988a   *Cova Fosca: Un Asentamiento Meso-Neolítico
de Cazadores y Pastores en la Serranía del Alto
Maestrazgo.* Castellón de la Plana: Diputación
de Castellón.

1988b   El Neolítico en las Comarcas Castellonenses. In
P. López (ed.), *El Neolítico en España*, 101–30.
Madrid: Editorial Cátedra.

Olaria de Gusi, C., J. Estévez Escalera, and E. Yll

1982   Domesticación y Paleoambiente en la Cova Fosca (Castellón). In R. Montjardin (ed.), *Le Néolithique Ancien Méditerranéen: Actes du Colloque International de Préhistoire, Montpellier 1981*, 107–20. Sète: Fédération Archéologique de l'Hérault.

Olaria, C., and F. Gusi

1983   Cova Fosca: Cazadores y Pastores en el Maestrazgo. *Revista de Arqueología* 27: 18–36.

Pellicer, M.

1964   *El Neolítico y el Bronce de la Cueva de la Carigüela de Piñar (Granada)*. Trabajos de Prehistoria 15. Madrid: Seminario de Historia Primitiva del Hombre.

1983   Neolítico Meridional Hispano: la Cueva de Nerja (Málaga). In *Premières Communautés Paysannes en Méditerranée Occidentale: Résumé des Communications*, 171–72. Montpellier.

Pericot, L.

1945   La Cueva de la Cocina (Dos Aguas). *Archivo de Prehistoria Levantina* 2: 39–71.

San Valero, J.

1946   El Neolítico Español y sus Relaciones. *Cuadernos de Historia Primitiva* 1: 5–33.

1947   La Caverna de las Arenas Cándidas y el Neolítico de Europa Occidental. *Rivista di Studi Liguri* 13: 184–186.

1950   *La Cueva de la Sarsa (Bocairente, Valencia)*. Servicio de Investigación Prehistórica, Serie de Trabajos Varios 12. Valencia: Servicio de Investigación Prehistórica.

Schubart, H., and V. Pascual

1966   Datación por el C14 de los Estratos con Cerámica Cardial de la Cueva de L'Or. *Archivo de Prehistoria Levantina* 11: 45–51.

Tarradell, M.

1960   Problemas Neolíticos. In: J. Maluquer de Motes (ed.) *Primer Symposium de Prehistoria Peninsular (Pamplona, 1959)*, 45–67. Barcelona: Instituto de Arqueología.

Testart, A.

1982   The Significance of Food Storage among Hunter-gatherers: Residence Patterns, Population Densities and Social Inequalities. *Current Anthropology* 23: 523–537.

Vicent, A.M., and A.M. Muñoz

1973   *Segunda Campaña de Excavaciones en la Cueva de los Murciélagos, Zuheros (Córdoba), 1969*. Excavaciones Arqueológicas en España 77. Madrid: Ministerio de Educación y Ciencia.

Zilhão, J.

1993   The Spread of Agro-pastoral Economies across Mediterranean Europe: A View from the Far West. *Journal of Mediterranean Archaeology* 6: 5–63.

2. Types of Fortification in Sites in Southern Italy and Spain During the Neolithic and Copper Ages

José Clemente Martín De La Cruz

The function of the large trenches commonly found in copper age sites in the Iberian peninsula (and in other areas and times as well) has been the object of particularly extensive discussion. These trenches are the focus of this paper, but given the complexity of this phenomenon, we will limit ourselves here to presenting our views about the function of these features in two regions, Spain and Italy (Figure 2.1), leaving other areas to future studies.

Spain

The excavations at Valencina de la Concepción (Sevilla) (Fernández and Oliva 1980, 1985, 1986; Ruíz Mata 1983) and Papa Uvas (Aljaraque, Huelva) (Martín de la Cruz 1985, 1986a, 1986b, 1989), beginning in the 1970s, brought to light a variety of subsurface features. These include large ditches of various sizes with more or less open U-shaped or V-shaped cross-sections. Associated with these trenches are circular features, known as 'wells', with a diameter of about 1 m that can reach a depth of up to 10 m Another series of features, known as 'silos'[1], can be divided into two groups by their sizes, the first

about 0.80 m by 1.60 m by 0.80 m in depth, the second about 0.65 m by 2.60 m by 0.95 m in depth. In some cases these silos have been interpreted as the remains of a hut the superstructure of which has disappeared (Martín de la Cruz 1989). Further work at copper age sites in Andalusia (La Minilla: Ruíz Lara 1991; Los Pozos: Hornos *et al.* 1987), Extremadura (El Lobo: Molina Lemos 1980; Pijotilla) and adjacent parts of Portugal (Santa Vitoria) has revealed similar features.[2] Surface finds suggest the existence of further instances, but we will not take them into account in this preliminary report.

Studies of the contents of these features, and more particularly the trenches, show that they belong culturally and chronologically to a moment subsequent to an advanced phase of the neolithic process. They belong to a neolithic community that has undergone population growth thanks to technological improvements that permitted them to optimize their exploitation of the ecosystem. The manufacture of some products and the use of animals for traction facilitated work, transport, and relations of exchange, while slowly transforming the traditional egalitarian ties between individuals into relations of a clearly stratified character.

The transition from one form of organization to another may have begun in the Neolithic, but it is completed during the Copper Age. An argument that a community is Copper Age must depend on the recognition of a distinctive strategy of exploitation and manipulation of the bases of production, as well as on technological and social complexity: it cannot depend on traces of mining and metallurgy, since in early times these are only found occasionally and do not determine the level of development. The discovery of mining and metallurgy would not be the starting point of the change; rather, it would form part of a complex process in which demographic growth, the exploitation of, and control over, access to new lands and resources, technological improvements, and the slow consolidation of social inequalities would be related to one another so

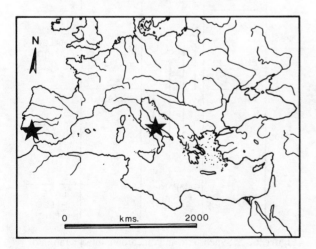

Figure 2.1 Location of areas in the Italian and Iberian peninsulas compared in this study.

dynamically that it would be difficult to specify which was the prime mover that generated such effects. Probably the impact of all of these factors, acting differentially according to the diverse potential of local ecosystems, produced the diversity presented by the different cultural manifestations of the Copper Age.

Detailed studies of the period of transition and of slow transformation from one phase to the other, from the Late Neolithic to the supposedly *ex novo* communities of the Millares-Orce type (Arribas *et al.* 1983; Schüle and Pellicer 1966; Schüle 1980) with fortifications and fully developed agriculture, did not exist until the 1970s. This led scholars to resort to a diffusionist explanatory theory in order to account for this cultural reality. Criticism of this theoretical reasoning in the 1970s and 1980s was based on field studies carried out with an elaborate and precise methodology. This involved theoretically guided fieldwork, data collection, and analytical procedures, as well as an integrated understanding of the problem under study. This has permitted a definitive appraisal of the transformative capacities of local communities.

In southeast Spain, the transition from the Neolithic to the Copper Age is little understood. The work carried out by the Siret brothers at sites which might be characteristic of the later neolithic Almerían Culture did not succeed in defining that entity (Siret and Siret 1887), which remains rather poorly defined to this day. In our opinion, however, the problem has resided not only in the lack of reliable archaeological records, but also in the orientalist predilections of those who studied the problem from the time of its formulation until the 1980s (see Martínez Navarrete 1989 for a review of Spanish prehistoriography).

The socio-economic transformations that must have occurred in the southeast with the development of the Almerían Culture are perceptible, but are not sufficiently demonstrated in the archaeological record to permit us to establish a cause-and-effect relationship with the Los Millares Culture. In contrast, however, we believe that this transition, the change from neolithic to copper age communities, can be documented in the southwest by correlating the stratigraphies at Papa Uvas, Cerro de los Vientos, and Valencina de la Concepción (Figures 2.2 and 2.3).

As in any transitory phase, one is better able to recognize its cultural manifestations negatively than positively. We know with greater precision what is *not* similar about the Almerían culture to what went before and to what followed. The

transition always ends up evading our understanding, but undoubtedly those are the times at which cultural, technological, social, and material changes are most marked. By contrast, we identify the end of the process by its continuity, by the precipitation of those elements (not always the most logical or reasonable ones) which resolved or retarded the conflict, and consequently by the elimination of those other traits which were archaic or non-functional (or which, on the contrary, were up-to-date and useful, but were abandoned for some reason which the human group would have had at the time).

All that has been said only contextualizes the difficulty of attributing function to the features we are discussing.

Papa Uvas is a flatland settlement located on the coastline about 34 m above sea level. Palaeoenvironmental reconstructions (Belén *et al.* 1977; Figueroa and Clemente 1979; Figueroa *et al.* 1987) indicate that the mouths of the rivers Tinto and Odiel formed a bay that was affected by the tidal movements of salt and fresh water and by fluvial and marine sedimentation. This, together with the redeposition of sediments caused by a rise in sea level in the last phases of the Flandrian transgression, silted up the old bay until the sea came to be, as it is now, 8 km away from the site.

The site is located on land formed during the Tertiary, and consists of compact and fairly impermeable marls with limestone and gypsum outcrops. Its occupation began towards the end

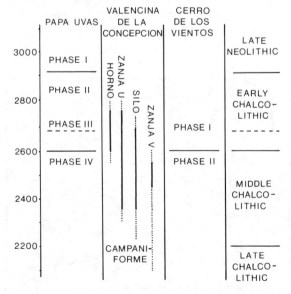

Figure 2.2   Synchronic and diachronic interpretation of the phases and structures in the archaeological sites analyzed.

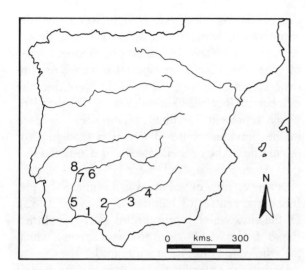

Figure 2.3   The Iberian peninsula with the location of sites mentioned in the text: 1. Papa Uvas; 2. Valencina de la Concepción; 3. Minilla; 4. Pozos; 5. Cerro de los Vientos; 6. Pijotilla; 7. Lobo; 8. Santa Vitoria.

of the fourth millennium. The economy was based on agriculture and animal husbandry, with a predominance of gathering activity and little hunting (although the inhabitants did not pass up the chance to consume the large marine mammals occasionally speared in the shallow waters of the bay that was silting up) (Martín de la Cruz 1986a: 294).

This first community dug a group of ditches that were approximately circular but probably not fully closed, with a maximum diameter that we estimate to be about 15 m Elsewhere, there is another set of ditches, sometimes superimposed on one another. These have a meandering layout (Figure 2.5) which we have excavated over a length of about 60 m (and we know from our geophysical survey that they extend some 30 m further). All of these ditches have U- or V-shaped sections with rounded bottoms; they are between 1 and 1.5 m wide at the surface and between 0.9 and 1.3 m deep (Figure 2.6).

We do not know for what purpose these ditches were dug because we always find them filled with remains linked to the life of the village, that is to say, belonging to a period when these features were no longer in use. The chronology which we can estimate from the fill (about 3200/3100 to 2900 BC) must always be a *terminus ante quem* for the occupation.

Following the arguments outlined earlier and presented more extensively at the 1991 Round Table on the peninsular Copper Age held at

Sevilla (Martín de la Cruz in press), the continuity of the site at Papa Uvas is maintained into the Copper Age phase. In this period the site goes through two building episodes, which permit us to distinguish an *initial* and a *full* phase of the Copper Age. The two new ditches, one north, and one south of their neolithic predecessor, are of a larger size, reaching a maximum width of 6 m for the Early Copper Age and 6.5 m for the for the Full Copper Age. The depths are 2.4–2.6 m and 3 m respectively, and the more or less open cross-sections are clearly V-shaped (Figures 2.7 and 2.8). At Valencina de la Concepción V-shaped ditches reach depths of almost 7 m.

Analysis of the materials which filled these two sets of trenches, together with the radiocarbon chronology, indicates that there were no more than two generations between the people who dug these features and those that filled them up. We are able to demonstrate, therefore, that in each of the phases recognized for the Late Neolithic, Initial Copper Age, and Full Copper Age, took place a restructuring of the area that was occupied (Martín de la Cruz 1994: 174).

The chronology which we propose, on a preliminary basis, (and which we will no doubt revise somewhat in our final published work) is as follows:

Phase I   Final Neolithic: 3200/3100–2900 BC
Phase II   Early Copper Age A and B: 2900–2800 BC
Phase III   Early Copper Age C: 2800–2700 BC
Phase IV   Full Copper Age: 2700/2600–2500 BC

What could have induced this population to have made the ditches described above? On the occasion of the publication of Papa Uvas II (Martín de la Cruz 1986a), we discarded the possibilities that their primary functions were to serve as trash pits, water channels, traps or sheepfolds. This left a defensive function as the most parsimonious one, although we argued that in order to increase their effectiveness the trenches should have had an earthen embankment (which could have supported a palisade), made from the earth extracted when they were dug out (Martín de la Cruz 1986a: 211). Nevertheless, since we do not know the complete layout of each of these three enclosures, we cannot be sure that they were built to defend the occupants and to dissuade attackers. If this interpretation is correct, however, we must accept the fact that neolithic communities were not as egalitarian as previously thought.

Italy

Recently Tiné (1983) has published an interesting study of the region of Apulia in Italy, paying particular attention to the district of the Tavoliere (Foggia). He has made use of an aerial survey of the territory, and has conducted extensive excavations of the site of Passo di Corvo. As a result, Tiné has been able to articulate the neolithic sequence on the west coast of the Adriatic and to indicate the particular characteristics of the exploitation of the landscape during that period. The soils are particularly suited to agriculture, although there are some drainage problems. The neolithic groups of the Tavoliere also dug ditches around their sites. Studies of the size of these enclosures have permitted differentiation of the villages or settlements with respect to their overall dimensions. The sites can also be classified according to several types depending on the number and the shape of the trench enclosures that surrounded them (Tiné 1983: 24, fig. 8).

In his study Tiné assigns up to 180 localities to the Earliest Neolithic (not the earliest phase, exemplified at the sites of Prato Don Michele and Coppa Nevigata, but the phase represented by the settlements of Guadone and Lagnano da Piede, datable to the end of the seventh millennium BC). These have features dug in the ground that form one or two circular trenches, the types

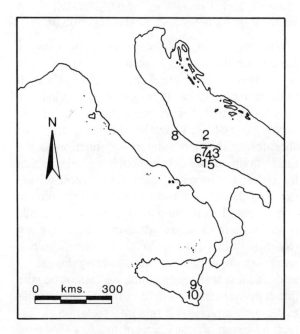

Figure 2.4   The Italian Peninsula with the location of the sites mentioned in the text: 1. Passo di Corvo; 2. Prato Don Michele; 3. Coppa Nevigata; 4. Guadone; 5. Laguna da Piede; 6. Amendola; 7. Monte Aquilone; 8. Ripoli; 9. Megara Hyblaea; 10. Stentinello.

designated A1 and A2, which would be the simplest and which cover an area of less than 2 hectares. There are also other, less frequent types of sites with a larger number of trenches or with oval layouts. During the Middle Neolithic the number of localities diminishes to 58, many of which represent continuations of sites occupied in the previous phase. There is a tendency for population to be concentrated: it is estimated that the Amendola district near Passo di Corvo covering an area of 90km^2 was dominated by just four large centres of habitation (Tiné 1983: 32). Of the sites which represent this Early Neolithic, Passo di Corvo has been the axis around which the whole study has been structured.

During the Later Neolithic, dated to the end of the fourth millennium, the number of localities diminished to 28, some of which continue occupations of the previous phase, although others are secondary occupations of Early Neolithic localities that had been abandoned in the middle period. It appears that it is during this phase, the Later Neolithic, that the abandonment of the Tavoliere (which had begun in the previous phase) takes place.

The occupations from the end of the seventh to the fourth millennium provide evidence for predominantly agricultural communities who dug ditches around their villages. Although one cannot establish a clear evolutionary sequence in the complexity of the layouts, it appears that the simplest layouts belong to the Early Neolithic and the most complex to the Middle Neolithic, when villages protected by two to five enclosures are common. Since stratigraphic superpositions are infrequent, the studies that have established these phases have been based on stylistic analyses that have confirmed and refined the proposals formulated by Tiné (1973).

The ditches must have had multiple functions. These may include the drainage of areas that were either occupied or intended for agricultural use. It must be specified that their use was not necessarily related to defence, but may be the result of a cultural trait: "...è un costume non ignoto nei paesi della costa mediorientale da dove gli agricoltore colonizzatori del Tavoliere provenivano" (Tiné 1983: 32). The ditches could even have been built before the foundation of the village and may also have been independent of a real necessity.

If the function was drainage, this would have been dictated by the characteristics of the ground and by the need to use it for agriculture, so that the smallest, C-shaped ditches[3] could be considered the reduction to a domestic scale of the

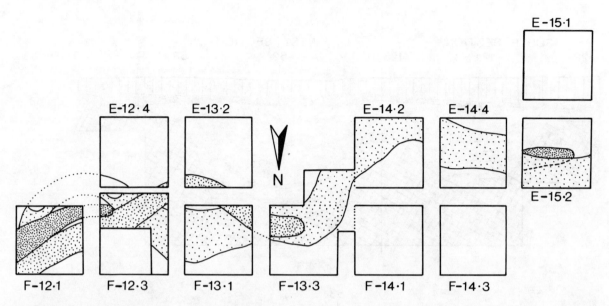

Figure 2.5 Plan of Late Neolithic ditches at Papa Uvas.

various exterior enclosures of the village at the community level. It is likely that one of the most important functions would have been to dry out the soil, not to conduct water, which would be allowed to filter into the ditches, there to be stored and/or to evaporate.

All the same, we cannot reject the idea that the ditches served to protect or separate groups from each other, even though there is no reason for us to suppose that a warlike situation existed. The ditches could be a general response to the ned to protect property and be evidence for the latent hostility between culturally similar groups (Manfredini 1972). Bearing in mind that all localities did not have the same problem of drainage, it is possible to interpret some of the ditches at Passo di Corvo (6 m wide and about 4 m deep) (Figure 2.9) and Monte Aquilone (2.3 m wide with vertical walls 3 m deep), as well as the great trenches at Ripoli (Cremonesi 1965, Grifoni Cremonesi 1989) (7.2–7.5 m wide and 4.5–4.8 m deep) as having a defensive function, and this is even more clearly demonstrated at the settlement of Megara Hyblaea (Orsi 1921), which had a ditch 2.5 m wide and 3 m deep, above which a wall was built up to 2 m thick with rock taken from the trench. A similar situation has been documented at the settlement of Stentinello (Orsi 1890; Tiné 1961). Thus, it is likely that the drainage function (where required) of early period ditches was gradually transformed into a defensive one (without losing other possible functions).

In all cases the fill in these features does not appear to be the result of deliberate action. In the lower levels, artefactual remains are found infre-

quently because this deposition corresponds to the phase when the feature was in active use. The middle layers indicate that the ditch was partly filled by natural causes: stones only appear in the ditch as a result of the destruction of sections of wall around the ditch and are not clearly stratified; the presence of rocks, pottery, and so on can be attributed to rains, particularly if these were intense (Tiné 1983: 19). At Monte Aquilone the upper layers were formed when the ditch was used as a rubbish dump (Manfredini 1972).

The effort required to create these features would have required the group to have a certain degree of hierarchy and a notable sense of community among its components. It also is indicative of another important function; the delimitation and differentiation of one territory with respect to others. The ditches would be the external emblem of the power exercised by the settlement or by some of its families, or perhaps they would delimit the areas which were occupied by the various clans or families that lived together in the same settlement.

Discussion

Taking geographical and chronological differences into account, and without any intention of establishing a concrete historical linkage, we have the impression that the settlements in Andalusia, Extremadura, and the Alentejo represent a pattern of occupation and territorial exploitation similar to that which has been described for the Tavoliere.

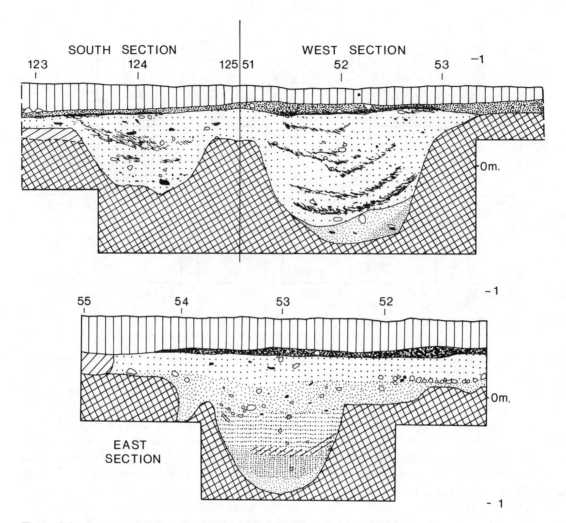

Figure 2.6   Sections of the Late Neolithic structure at Papa Uvas.

All that we have said about settlements in Apulia and Sicily is valid for their counterparts in the Iberian peninsula, except that, in the case of Papa Uvas (the best known site up to now), the settlement does not seem to have been planned *ex novo* with three ditches (also, we do not know whether the ditches completely surrounded the settlement area.) From the differing sizes of the features and from their contents, it appears that the settlement grew little by little, so that the ditches of the Early and Full Copper Age would be the result of the demographic, technological, economic and social development of a community that had its origins in the late Neolithic.

Given the geomorphological characteristics of the surroundings, one of the purposes of the ditches could have been drainage, but we believe that, just as in the Italian settlements, the feature later had defensive functions.

The settlement areas in which these trenches are best documented are those of Papa Uvas and Valencina de la Concepción. These sites are 80 km apart and are at different elevations, but they are similar in terms of their immediate surroundings. They dominate what would have been wide estuaries that were gradually silting up, a sort of amphibious landscape through which the various channels of the rivers Tinto-Odiel and Guadalquivir would flow into the Atlantic Ocean.

Both sites are located on Tertiary terrain, have the same geological formation, and both have agriculture as their preferred mode of subsistence. Under these circumstances, the existing ditches could have served to drain the surroundings. However, as we shall see shortly in the case of Cerro de los Vientos (Piñón Varela 1987), chronologically and culturally similar groups in areas with a different ecosystem and abundant stone built clearly defensive constructions. This shows that from the beginning the ditches had the defense of the settlement as one of their functions.

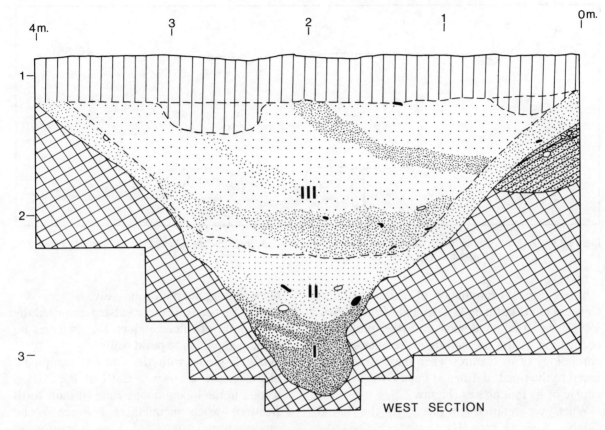

Figure 2.7   Sections of the Early Copper Age structure at Papa Uvas.

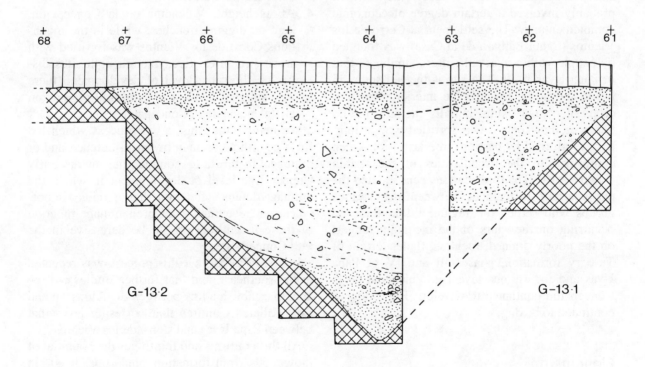

Figure 2.8   Section of the Full Copper Age structure at Papa Uvas.

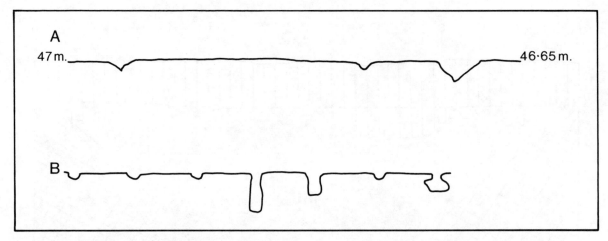

Figure 2.9   A: North–south section showing the relative positions of the three ditches at Papa Uvas. B: Section of part of the site of Passo di Corvo.

In our critical examination of Valencina de la Concepción (Martín de la Cruz and Miranda Ariz 1988), we tried to demonstrate the prolonged occupation of the site and the differences in the chronology of its features when these were compared to the trends defined at Papa Uvas over the course of its four phases (Figure 2.2).

When we referred to phase II, the Initial Copper Age, at Papa Uvas, we explained the features of its new cultural development: the exploitation of new lands and resources and the control over these were linked to a demographic and perhaps technological development which probably involved a certain degree of economic complementarity. The settlement at Cerro de los Vientos (Santa Bárbara de la Casa) was founded by people with a material culture similar to that of Papa Uvas II–III. The site is located some 55 km to the north, towards the interior, near outcrops of copper oxide. Initially the site had no defences, but soon it was fortified with a rampart, reinforced by bastions, the layout of which conformed to the irregularities of the terrain (Figure 2.10). The fortifications consolidated the existence of differences between the various groups who settled the region. While this was occurring on the spurs of the mountain ranges; on the poorly drained, rockless, flatter terrain of Tertiary formation, phases III and IV of Papa Uvas and the various layers at Valencina de la Concepción continued to develop. There ditches continued to be dug.

Conclusion

All of this indicates that:

1. The initial function of the ditches was possibly drainage, but not exclusively.

2. Defensive needs, if these existed, required the excavation of ditches, since the area has no stone with which to build walls.

3. When a group with the cultural equipment characteristic of phases II–III at Papa Uvas settled in the mountainous zone (it built fortifications when inequalities between social groups were manifested after a period in which groups became acquainted with the local habitat). In this case, because the area which was occupied had plenty of stones, the defences were built with them.

4. At its height, Valencina de la Concepción, kept on digging trenches, while in the mountains Cerro de los Vientos was fortified with stone structures. Even though both sites displayed the same level of development, there was a higher level of agricutltural production at Valencina de la Concepción.

We believe that this is the process which led from neolithic communities with defence and/or drainage features, to communities at an Early Copper Age level of development in which the drainage/defense function has similar importance, and eventually the predominant function of these localities came to be defensive in the Full Copper Age.

It is very likely that this process was repeated in the southeast, and that further studies will be able to establish a link between the Almerían and Los Millares Cultures that corresponds to that between Papa Uvas and Cerro de los Vientos.

All this confirms and reinforces the potential of indigenous transformation and our need to understand local cultural developments. The similarities which exist between the features at Italian and Iberian settlements reflect similar responses to the problems of drainage and of

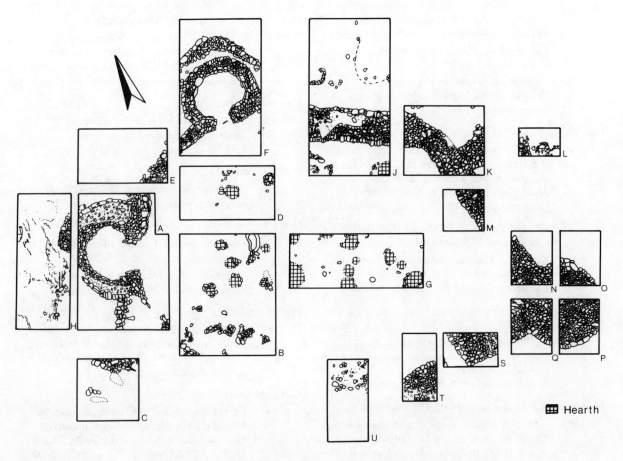

Figure 2.10 Plan of the fortified settlement of Cerro de los Vientos (after Piñón 1987:318).

inter-community relations. They occur far apart in spac and time and may be the product of environmental conditions. They may, then, have arisen as a result of cultural convergence. It is also possible, however, that in some way the similarity was produced by contact with the central Mediterranean, a contact hidden in the Cardial horizon of the Early Neolithic (or the more diverse Middle Neolithic), a horizon which is usually documented in caves and only rarely at open air sites.

Studies of the distribution of this type of fortification in Italy, France, Spain, and Portugal, and of their associated material culture and chronologies, will bring us closer to an understanding of this phenomenon.

Notes

1. The term 'silo' covers a variety of features of different shapes, contents, and time periods. Sometimes the term 'fondo de cabaña' [hut floor] is used. Neither one designation nor the other has any clear functional definition.

2. We thank Dr. Victor Hurtado and Ms. Ana Mosa Carvalho Dias for information on their work in progress at Pijotilla and Santa Vitoria (Campo Maior), respectively.

3. The C-shaped structures bear a great similarity to those which are currently being excavated at the site of Santa Vitoria by Ms. Ana Mosa Carvalho Dias.

Bibliography

Arribas, A., F. Molina, L. Sáez, F. de la Torre, P. Aguayo, A. Bravo and A. Suárez

    1983   Excavaciones en Los Millares (Santa Fe de Mondújar, Almería). *Cuadernos de Prehistoria de la Universidad de Granada* 8: 123–47.

Belén, M., M. Fernández-Miranda and J.P. Garrido

    1977   Los Orígenes de Huelva. *Huelva Arqueológica* 3: 13–375

Cremonesi, G.

    1965   Il villaggio di Ripoli all Luce dei Recenti Scavi. *Rivista de Scienze Preistoriche* 20: 85–155.

Fernández, F., and D. Oliva

    1980   Los ídolos Calcolíticos del Cerro de la Cabeza (Valencina de la Concepción, Sevilla). *Madrider Mitteilungen* 21: 20–44.

1985   Excavaciones en el Yacimiento Calcolítico de
        Valencina de la Concepción (Sevilla): El Corte
        C (La Perrera). *Noticiario Arqueológico
        Hispánico* 25: 8–125.

1986   Valencina de la Concepción (Sevilla):
        Excavaciones de Urgencia. *Revista de
        Arqueología* 58: 19–33.

Figueroa, M.E., and L. Clemente

1979   Dinámica Geomorfológica del Estuario de los
        ríos Tinto y Odiel (Huelva). In R. Juliá, M.A.
        Marqués, A. Mir, D. Serrat and F. Gallart (eds.),
        *Actas, IV Reunión del Grupo de Trabajo del
        Cuaternario, Bañolas*, 79–95. Gerona: AEQUA.

Figueroa, M.E., J.M. Fernández Palacios, E. Castellanos, L.
Clemente and P. Silgestrom

1987   Estuarios y Marismas del Litoral de Huelva (SO
        de España). In *Actas, VII Reunión sobre el
        Cuaternario, Santander*, 211–14. Santander:
        AEQUA.

Grifoni Cremonesi, R.

1989   Le Strutture del Villaggio di Ripoli. In
        *Interpretazione Funzionale dei "Fondi di
        Capanna" di Età Preistorica*, 63–66. Milan:
        Istituto Italiano per l'Archeologia Sperimentale.

Hornos Mata, F., F. Nocete Calvo and C. Pérez Darea

1987   Actuación Arqueológica de Emergencia en el
        Yacimiento de los Pozos de la Higuera de
        Arjona (Jaén). In *Anuario Arqueológico de
        Andalucía, 1986*, 3: 198–202. Sevilla:
        Consejería de Cultura, Junta de Andalucía.

Manfredini, A.

1972   Il Villaggio Trincerato di Monte Aquilone nel
        Quadro del Neolitico dell'Italia Meridionale.
        Origini 6: 29–154.

Martín de la Cruz, J.C.

1985   *Papa Uvas I: Campañas 1976–1979 (Aljaraque,
        Huelva)*. Excavaciones Arqueológicas en España
        136. Madrid: Ministerio de Cultura.

1986a   *Papa Uvas II (Aljaraque, Huelva)*.
        Excavaciones Arqueológicas en España 149.
        Madrid: Ministerio de Cultura.

1986b   Aproximación a la Secuencia de Hábitat en Papa
        Uvas (Aljaraque, Huelva). In *Homenaje a Luis
        Siret, 1934–1984*, 227–42. Sevilla: Consejería
        de Cultura, Junta de Andalucía.

1989   L'insediamento Neolitico e Calcolitico di Papa
        Uvas. In E Giannitrapini, L. Simone and S. Tiné
        (eds.), *Interpretazione Funzionale dei "Fondi di
        Capanna" di Età Preistorica*, 82–86. Milan:
        Istituto Italiano per l'Archeologia Sperimentale.

1994   *El Tránsito del Neolítico al Calcolítico en el
        Litoral del Suroeste Peninsular*. Excavaciones
        Arqueológicas en España 169. Madrid:
        Ministerio de Cultura.

in press Diacronía cultural. *Actas, mesa redonda sobre el
        Calcolítico peninsular*.

Martín de la Cruz, J.C., and J. Miranda Ariz

1988   El Poblado Calcolítico de Valencina de la
        Concepción (Sevilla): Una Revisión Crítica.
        *Cuadernos de Prehistoria y Arqueología de la
        Universidad Autónoma de Madrid* 15: 37–67.

Martínez Navarrete, M.I.

19989   *Una Revisión Crítica de la Prehistoria
        Española: La Edad del Bronce como
        Paradigma*. Madrid: Siglo XXI de España.

Molina Lemos, L.

1980   El poblado del Bronce I de El Lobo (Badajoz).
        Noticiario Arqueológico Hispánico 9: 91–127.

Orsi, P.

1890   Stazione neolitica di Stentinello. *Bullettino di
        Paletnologia Italiana* 16: 177–209.

1921   *Megara Hyblaea*. Monumenti Antichi 27.
        Rome: Accademia Nazionale dei Lincei.

Piñón Varela, F.

1987   Los Vientos de la Zarcita (Santa Bárbara de
        Casa). In *Anuario Arqueológico de Andalucía,
        1986*, 2: 317–24. Sevilla: Consejería de Cultura,
        Junta de Andalucía.

Ruíz Lara, D.

1991   Excavación Arqueológica de Urgencia en La
        Minilla (La Rambla, Córdoba): Campaña de
        1989. In *Anuario Arqueológico de Andalucía,
        1989*, 3: 157–63. Sevilla: Consejería de Cultura,
        Junta de Andalucía.

Ruíz Mata, D.

1983   El Yacimiento de la Edad del Bronce de
        Valencina de la Concepción en el Marco
        Cultural del Bajo Guadalquivir. In *Actas, I
        Congreso de Historia Andaluza: Prehistoria y
        Arqueología*, 183–208. Córdoba: Monte de
        Piedad y Caja de Ahorros de Córdoba.

Schüle, W.

1980   *Orce und Galera*. Mainz am Rhein: Philipp von
        Zabern.

Schüle, W., and M. Pellicer

1966   *El Cerro de la Virgen (Orce, Granada)*.
        Excavaciones Arqueológicas en España 46.
        Madrid: Ministerio de Educación Nacional.

Siret, L., and H. Siret

1887   *Les Premiers Ages du Metal dans le Sudest de
        l'Espagne*. Antwerp.

Tiné, S.

1961   Notizie Preliminari sui Recenti Scavi nel
        Villaggio di Stentinello. *Archivo Storico di
        Siracusa* 7: 113–17.

1973   I villaggi Neolitici nel Tavoliere di Foggia
        (Puglia): La Successione degli stili Ceramici. In
        Atti, VIII Congresso, U.I.S.P.P., 386–92.

1983   *Passo di Corvo e la Civiltà Neolitica del
        Tavoliere*. Genoa: Sagep.

3. Groundstone Tools, Competition, and Fission: The Transition from the Copper to the Bronze Age in the Portuguese Lowlands

Katina T. Lillios

Introduction

The Copper and Early Bronze Age of the Portuguese lowlands have traditionally been viewed in sharply contrasting terms. The Copper Age, the period between 3000 and 2000 BC, has been seen as a period of marked social complexity, and the Early Bronze Age, between 2000 and 1500 BC, as a period of social collapse or devolution. This characterization has been applied since the Copper and Bronze Ages were first recognized in Iberia during the late 19th century. The Swedish writer Åberg noted in 1921 that "the finds in the tombs and settlements (of Portugal) show that there is a very clear delineation between the period of the Palmella tombs (the Copper Age) and the period of the cists (Early Bronze Age). The latter period is a retrogression of civilization" (Åberg 1921: 112). Almost fifty years later, Savory stated that "during the rest of the second millennium, the peninsula, as a whole, appears to have become progressively more isolated from the principal centers of development of barbarian Europe, and stagnated" (Savory 1968: 198). Most recently, Gilman noted that "the absence of a distinctive Bronze Age along the Tagus River in the second millennium BC is the final manifestation of an involution which had started in the Final Copper Age" (Gilman 1987: 28).

While the conceptual frameworks used to describe the shifts between the Copper and Bronze Ages of Portugal have changed, archaeologists have generally operated under the shared premise that any society with metallurgy, long-distance exchange, monumental construction, craft specialization, and intensive agriculture, such as that of Portugal in the Copper Age, would be on the developmental path toward state formation, and if this did not occur, something 'went wrong'. Often rather simplistic models (e.g., invasions, climate change, environmental degradation) are offered to explain this 'unexpected turn of events'. I argue that such a premise is problematic, considering that incipient complexity led more often to social fragmentation or fission than to pristine state formation. I argue that too little attention has been devoted to fragmentation and fission and that more sophisticated models be developed to account for these alternate trajectories of social evolution.

In this paper, I develop one such model to account for the changes in the archaeological record between the Copper and Bronze Ages in the lowlands of west-central Portugal. Specifically, I demonstrate that more continuity exists between these periods than has been acknowledged, and that those discontinuities that are apparent reflect a decline in the consumption of prestige good as well as a decrease in the use of social markers such as defensive walls and decorated ceramics. I will suggest that these changes reflect a phase of fission, and that the exchange of groundstone tools may have played an important role in generating this transformation.

The archaeological background

The transition from the Copper to the Bronze Age of the Portuguese lowlands was a period of marked changes in settlement pattern, burial practices, and material culture. Many copper age settlements, some of which had been occupied throughout the third millennium BC, were abandoned at the end of the millennium. These sites were commonly walled and situated on hilltops overlooking river valleys. Particularly in the Lisbon and Setúbal areas, copper age settlements are densely distributed in the landscape. Because many of these settlements appear to have been occupied for long periods of time, it is likely that they were contemporaneous. The evidence for subsistence indicates that copper age societies relied principally on agricultural produce (wheat, barley, flax, fava beans), animal domesticates (sheep, goat, cattle), wild game (deer, pig), and fish (Sangmeister and Schubart 1981; Paço 1954).

The few Early Bronze Age settlements which are known , such as Agroal (Lillios 1991), were unwalled and seem not to have been continuously occupied. Furthermore, their distribution over the landscape is more dispersed than copper age settlements. However, like copper age sites, Early Bronze Age settlements, including Agroal, were situated on hilltops. The only evidence for the subsistence economy of Early Bronze Age lowland sites comes from Agroal. A narrower range of fauna than is normal for copper age settlements was recovered at Agroal, and included mainly older cattle, and sheep and goat. Fishing and agriculture was also practiced, as is demonstrated by a copper fishhook, sickle blades with silica gloss, groundstone adzes, and grinding stones.

The typical burials of the Copper Age were collective inhumations in caves, rock-cut tombs, and megaliths, often associated with abundant prestige goods, such as beakers, copper daggers, schist plaques, ostrich eggshells, and dozens of unused groundstone tools (Spindler 1981; Paço 1954; Leisner *et al.* 1961, 1969). Harrison makes the important point that some of these burials are perhaps better described as 'repeated single burials', that is, although many individuals are buried in one tomb, they were deposited at different times, the earlier burials pushed aside for more recent ones (Harrison 1977: 25–26). Such emphasis on collective unity at death was replaced in the Early Bronze Age by a focus on the individual; typical of this period are individual inhumations in cists, pits, and caves with, at most, a few ceramic vessels and a copper dagger.

There is, nonetheless, an important continuity between third and second millennium artefact assemblages. This is in the form of metallurgy. Despite the fact that the early second millennium BC in Portugal is known as the Early Bronze Age, true copper-tin alloying did not take place until the end of the second millennium BC, or the Late Bronze Age. Metal objects during both the Copper and Early Bronze Ages were made of a 'natural alloy' of copper and arsenic, which is found in Portuguese ores. Furthermore, the forms and functions of metal objects are similar through the Copper and Early Bronze Ages. Finally, the fact that copper ores are found throughout the lowlands in quantities and forms that could have been exploited by prehistoric communities, although they do not often appear on modern metallurgical maps, suggests that metallurgy can neither be considered an important marker of social change nor a factor in the transformations which occurred between the third and second millennia.

Previous explanations for these changes have focused on the climatic shifts associated with migrations (Savory 1968), which are not supported by palaeoenvironmental evidence, and on systems of control over natural resources such as water (Chapman 1982, 1990) and land (Gilman 1981, 1987).

Chapman (1982, 1990) compares the transition in Portugal from the Copper to the Bronze Age to that of southeast Spain. He argues that water was a critical resource in Spain during the Copper Age and thus, technological developments, such as irrigation, and social changes, namely the evolution of a managerial class, evolved to control it. For Portugal, however, Chapman has argued that water was not a critical resource, and thus no managerial elites were needed in order to control access to it. Despite the fact that precipitation levels in Portugal are indeed higher and less variable than for southeast Spain (400–800mm mean annual rainfall) (Ribeiro 1987: 180–181), they are, nevertheless, still low enough to produce a Mediterranean landscape.

Gilman (1981, 1987) adopted a Marxist approach to later Portuguese prehistory and focused on the conflicting goals of elites and 'peasant cultivators' and the ritual means by which these discordances were masked (e.g., communal burials). He suggested that the absence of significant land management works, such as irrigation canals, in Portugal would have encouraged disenfranchised groups to abandon their settlements and fission. While I agree in principal with Gilman's model and while his and Chapman's arguments go some way toward pointing out the environmental factors that weakened social cohesion, they do not pay sufficient attention to the forces that drove the social network apart.

The archaeologial evidence for groundstone tools: a comparison with the ethnographic record

A number of factors point to the importance of groundstone tools in Portuguese prehistory, both as a sensitive indicator of social organization as well as a potentially powerful generator of social transformation.

Most groundstone tools from late prehistoric sites in Portugal are made of amphibolite (Figure 3.1). Amphibolite is a metamorphic mafic rock, which is dark-green to dark-grey in colour and typically consists mainly of phaneritic amphiboles and feldspars (usually hornblende and plagioclase) (Best 1982: 397). The nearest source of amphibolite is 200 km from the Lisbon and Setúbal peninsulas, at the border of the lowlands and the uplands of Portugal (Figure 3.2). Other sources are known in the mountains of northeast Portugal (Comissão Nacional de Ambiente 1982). Amphibolite tools from copper age sites are found in the form of axes, adzes, chisels, and hammerstones. Some appear to have served first as axes or adzes, then, as the edges wore down, were used as hammerstones. These tools would have been crucial for a number of activities, including agriculture, forest clearance, woodworking, limestone quarrying, and boat building.

Although there are basalt sources in the lowlands, they were rarely quarried for stone tools in Portuguese prehistory. The reason for this preference of amphibolite over basalt seems to be the

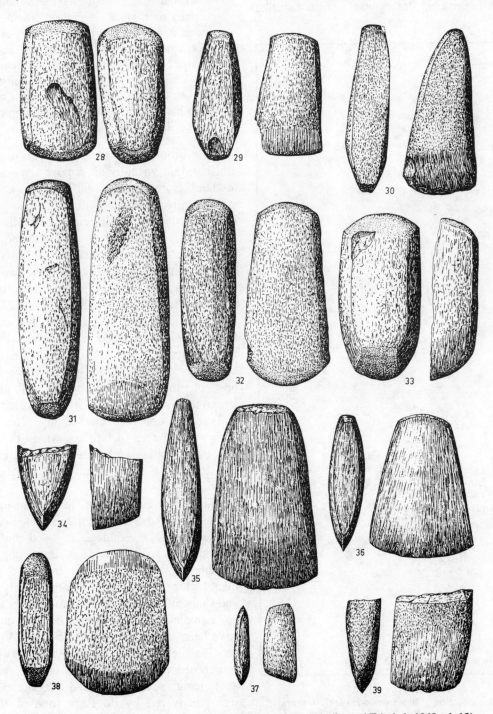

Figure 3.1 Ground stone tools from the copper age site of Penedo (from Spindler and Trindade 1969: pl. 12).

physical properties of the two stones. As a metamorphosed rock, amphibolite's fibrous structure renders it less likely to fracture during use as an axe or an adze (Howard Snyder: personal communication).

Because amphibolite tools were a necessary component of the economy of copper age agricultural communities and because amphibolite was not locally available in the lowlands, dependable exchange partners would have been critical to the survival of these communities, particularly those at a great distance from the source. In this way, the prehistoric Portuguese were not unlike

the Kulin (McBryde 1984), the Yir Yoront of Australia (Sharp 1952); the Tungei (Burton 1984); the Siane of New Guinea (Salisbury 1962), or the Maori of New Zealand (Best 1912; Firth 1929). These agricultural peoples live in areas devoid of hard stone, and only acquire the raw materials used for necessary groundstone tools through a well-established exchange networks. Sharp wrote:

> Yir Yoront men were dependent upon interpersonal relations for their stone axe heads, since the flat, geologically recent alluvial country over which they range, provides no stone from which axe heads can be made. The stone they used comes from known quarries 400 miles to the south. It reached the Yir Yoront through long lines of male trading partners... Almost every older adult man had one or more regular trading partners. (Sharp 1952: 74)

While groundstone tools made of amphibolite are found on virtually all copper age sites in the lowlands, some sites appear to have accumulated significantly greater quantities than others. The hilltop settlement of Leiceia is particularly noteworthy for its abundance of groundstone tools. The 1 hectare site is located 6.5 km from the margin of the Tagus river, and has evidence of occupation during the Early, Middle, and Late Copper Age (Cardoso 1989). Over 300 groundstone axes, adzes, chisels, and hammerstones from Leiceia are housed in the National Museum for Archaeology and Ethnology, in Lisbon. This high number may partially reflect the fact that one of the early excavators of the site, Vasconcelos, was particularly interested in axes and adzes, and collected many from private homes in the area of Leiceia, where they served magical purposes and were placed in chinks in the stone walls (José Arnaud: personal communication).

What is intriguing about the groundstone from Liceia in the Lisbon museum is that, in addition to the typical assemblage of used and broken groundstone tools found at most copper age settlements, some are tools in the process of manufacture. These 'blanks' are roughly the size and shape of an adze or axe, but none of the sides are completely polished nor do they appear to have been used as hammerstones. At Vila Nova de São Pedro, located mid-way between the source of amphibolite and the coastal sites, such as Leiceia, several hundred groundstone tools were recovered by do Paço, one of the early excavators of the site in the 1940s (Paço 1970

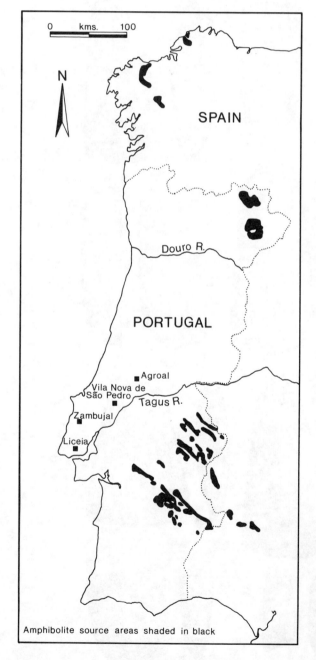

Figure 3.2   Location of sites mentioned in the text and of amphibolite sources in western Iberia.

[1942]: 282). Some of these are also unfinished blanks. If a simple down-the-line exchange was operating in the Copper Age, we would expect to see a decline in the abundance of groundstone tools the further away from the source one went. In fact, there is a concentration of settlements and groundstone tools furthest from the source, along the coast.

Could Leiceia and Vila Nova de São Pedro have functioned as manufacturing and redistribution areas for groundstone tools? It would certainly appear so. A similar argument has been put forth to explain the distribution of neolithic axes made of volcanic tuff found in England. While the source of the raw material is in northwest England, axes made of the tuff are principally found around the Humber estuary in eastern England (Phillips 1980: 153). Likewise, a concentration of obsidian artefacts from neolithic contexts were found in Pescale, northern Italy, whose source has been identified in Sardinia (Hallam *et al.* 1976).

How would such a bulky raw material be transported to the Portuguese sites? Given the weight of the stone, overland transport would have been tiresome, even for pack animals. Transport down the Tagus would have been most likely, particularly in light of Daveau's reconstruction of the extent of the Tagus at around 3000 BC. Her study indicates that the river had a more northerly course than it has now, and in fact, would have been only a few kilometers from Vila Nova de São Pedro, suggesting that water transport may have played a significant role in the functioning of the site (Gonçalves 1984, after Daveau). The importance of the Portuguese riverways as conduits for prehistoric exchange and interaction has also been recently discussed by Kunst (1991).

The fact that not all groups had equal access to the source of stone, and that central distribution and manufacturing places for groundstone tools may have existed in the Copper Age is not surprising, given patterns displayed in the ethnographic record. Best (1912: 24) clearly describes a comparable situation among the Maori, for which the source of stone was often in enemy territory (thus prohibiting equal access to all) or kept secret.

> In obtaining material for his stone implements, the Maori was often much hampered by the restriction of his social system — the division of people into tribes, independent of each other, and often at war, certainly always suspicious of each other. Hence he could not range at will over distant lands in search of desirable material for his implements. Thus it often occurred that stone, more especially greenstone or nephrite, was an article of barter between them. In other cases, a party of natives would make an expedition on to the lands of another tribe (with or without permission), in order to obtain some desirable kind of stone that was not found in their own territory... Natives state that when a good quality of stone was found...the situation of the deposit was kept secret as far as possible, so that other tribes, and even other divisions of the same tribe, should not become acquainted with it. (Best 1912: 24)

Among Portuguese copper age communities, groundstone tools were not only commodities critical to their survival, but appear to have also been highly valued prestige or ritual goods. In a number of burials, such as Cascais and São de Estoril, there are axes and adzes which show no evidence of having been used, as well as others which are so small and delicate that it is difficult to imagine their having been used. These are often found in association with beakers and artefacts of non-local origin, such as ivory. In other burials, such as São Martinho de Sintra and Cascais, there are hafted adzes carved in limestone. These would clearly have been quite useless in working wood or tilling soil, and may have been symbols of power used in rituals. Among the Maori, ritual adzes made of finely polished greenstone and mounted on elaborately carved handles had a purely ceremonial function, and "...were effectively brandished in the vigorous gesticulations so inseparable from Maori oratory in the days of yore" (Best 1912: 119).

In summary; larger, more roughly hewn tools are generally found on settlements, and the smaller, more finely polished and unused tools are found in burials. The different forms and qualities of groundstone tools at copper age sites in Portugal suggest that they may have circulated in different spheres of exchange. Exchange spheres are circuits of exchange for different sets of goods. The concept was first used by Hoyt in the 1920s (Hoyt 1924) and later developed by Bohannan (1955) for the Tiv.

There appear to have been two spheres of exchange for groundstone tools during the Portuguese Copper Age. In one of these, the larger, more roughly hewn groundstone tools may have circulated. One might hypothesize that these were acquired through reciprocal exchange, involving food or other subsistence-related items, between individuals of equal status. The second sphere may have included the smaller, finer, and unused tools, and circulated with metal items, fine ceramics, and other craft specialist goods. This sphere might have been operated through redistribution by leaders of communities and/or in important feasts and rituals associated with births, marriages, alliances, and deaths.

There is a good deal of ethnographic data for exchange spheres involving groundstone, some of which are suggestive of the Portuguese case. Among the Siane, of New Guinea, for example, three exchange spheres are responsible for the circulation of different groundstone items; these have been called the subsistence sphere, the valuables sphere, and the luxury sphere (Salisbury 1962). In the subsistence sphere, goods are circulated that "maintain the productive organiz- ation of society" and move between members of the same clan (Salisbury 1962: 105, 187). These include groundstone tools made from common stone, as well as food, birds, rats, aprons, and skirts.

Valuables, which are goods that are owned personaly by individuals, and include ornamental greenstone axes from the Mount Hagen area and pigs, are circulated in the second sphere. They are distributed at both public and ritualized events. While the exchange of valuables pre- serves relations between "corporate, inter-marry- ing groups" (Salisbury 1962: 104), they also function to maintain social distance (Salisbury 1962: 90–91). This sphere among the Siane is similar to that documented for the Yir Yoront, for which the exchange of groundstone took place during feasts, and thus was a public event (Sharp 1952: 75).

By contrast, the exchange of luxury goods for the Siane does not take place publicly (Salisbury 1962: 84). Included in this sphere are axe stones which come from the northeast, near the Korefa tribe, as well as tobacco, salt, and pandanus nuts. No individual is self-sufficient in luxury goods. Salisbury notes that "the system of distribution works, not by a strict accounting system but through self-interest, since individuals wish to keep their friends satisfied and so preserve their relationship" (Salisbury 1962: 90).

Firth describes the two principal exchange spheres among the Maori. The first occurs within social groups, and involves mainly subsistence goods (including common groundstone), and the second is between groups/communities, and cir- culates food not used in everyday subsistence, as well as shellfish, birds, and, most importantly, greenstone or nephrite adzes (Firth 1929: 202).

The two spheres of exchange proposed for the Portuguese Copper Age offer a mechanism for the changes which took place in the early second millennium BC. As stated above, the subsistence sphere is most often of a reciprocal nature. The valuables sphere, however, is more competitive. Very often individuals invited to another's feast will return the 'favour' by putting together an even more lavish display of food and goods. The Maori engage in this exercise of one-upmanship, as do the Kabre of Togo. Firth noted that for gifts made to a Maori chief, "...a return was expected, of equivalent or even greater value" (Firth 1929: 288). Among the Kabre:

> The return invitation...typically involves an increase in the quantity and quality of drink and food served. Thus, a small pot of beer is replaced by a medium-sized pot, and a chicken by a guinea hen...Each increment not only opens a new debt but also symbol- izes the growing nature of the relationship (Piot 1991: 12).

These public displays often involve such large quantities of goods that serious damage is done to the private economy of the leader, and divorce is not uncommon. A common lament among wives is that:

> He spent money on others, outside the fam- ily (that is, on his exchange partners), but not on me (Piot 1991: 15).

The archaeological correlates to such behavior would be agricultural intensification accompa- nied by environmental degradation, and, in fact, these are documented archaeologically. A marked decline in tree species, such as pine and oak, during the transition of the Copper and Bronze Ages has been documented by the Dutch palynologists Leewaarden and Janssen (1985). As the quality of the land declined, the ability of some groups to compete effectively in these exchange alliances would have been diminished to the point that some realignment in the social order would have been necessary for their survival. Settlements were abandoned and social groups dispersed in the landscape in what was probably a series of fission events, as demonstrated by generalized abandonment at the end of the Copper Age.

A collapse of the two exchange spheres opera- tive in the Copper Age appears to have taken place by the Early Bronze Age, leaving only the subsistence sphere in operation. Throughout the early second millennium BC, groundstone tools are still used, but they are only found in settlements. An overall decline in prestige good consumption seems to have taken place between the third and second millennium BC. Much more research on Early Bronze Age settlements and burials is needed, however, in order to be completely certain about these patterns.

Conclusions

In this paper I have explored the function (both utilitarian and ritual) of an artefact which has been neglected in the research of prehistoric Portugal and which may have played a critical role in the dramatic changes accompanying the transition from the Copper to Bronze Age. Much more attention has been paid to the isolated finds of North African ostrich eggshells and ivory on copper age sites than to groundstone tools which, as I have mentioned, are present on almost all copper age sites.

The ethnographic literature has been instructive in demonstrating that among many primitive agricultural communities living in forested landscapes, the groundstone axe and adze are powerful symbols (usually male) of authority, wealth, and prestige. Groundstone tools are often mythified or personified, their manufacture and use is associated with taboos, and they are so highly valued that their theft can be a cause for battle (Best 1912). I have used the ethnographic record not to prove the 'truthfulness' of my model, but as a means of lending strength to the possibility that the patterns suggested could have actually taken place. Secondly, the ethnographic record points to the complexity of exchange behaviour — a fact that can easily by underestimated by the archaeologist given the static nature of the evidence.

Most importantly, I have used the record as an heuristic device, that is, in order to discover avenues for future research. These include:

1) Where, precisely, are the sources of the amphibolite?
2) How is the production of the groundstone axes organized? Is the stone made into blanks at the source or is it transported in rough form? Are, there, in fact, central distribution areas for groundstone? Are they worked into finished products at these places or distributed to individuals who later work them? What was the technology involved in the extraction and manufacture of groundstone tools?
3) Are there settlements near the sources? Is there any evidence for working of groundstone at these sites?
4) How were groundstone tools used? What are the different contexts in which they are found? How does the function of the tool vary by context? What was the use life of a groundstone tool? Were groundstone tools collected as heirlooms by prehistoric communities?
5) What meaning did groundstone tools have for Portuguese communities in the Copper Age?

Future investigations into these issues will help to clarify our understanding of the functioning of late prehistoric Portuguese society as well as strengthen our evolutionary models for non-state societies.

Acknowledgments

I would like to thank Michael Dietler and William Barnett for their help in developing some of the issues presented in this paper.

Bibliography

Åberg, N.
    1921   *La civilisation Énéolithique dans la péninsule Ibérique.* Arbeten Utgifna med Understöd af Vilhelm Ekmans Universitetsfond 25. Uppsala: Akademiska Bokhandeln.

Best, E.
    1912   *The Stone Implements of the Maori.* New Zealand Dominion Museum, Bulletin 4. Wellington: New Zealand Dominion Museum.

Best, M.
    1982   *Igneous and Metamorphic Petrology.* New York: W.H. Freeman.

Bohannan, P.
    1955   Some Principles of Exchange and Investment among the Tiv. *American Anthropologist* 57: 60–69.

Burton, J.
    1984   Quarrying in a Tribal Society. *World Archaeology* 16(2): 234–37.

Cardoso, J.L.
    1989   *Leceia: Resultados das Escavações Realizadas 1983–1988.* Oeiras: Câmara Municipal de Oeiras.

Chapman, R.W.
    1982   Autonomy, Ranking, and Resources in Iberian Prehistory. In C. Renfrew and S. Shennan (eds),

Ranking, Resources, and Exchange: Aspects of the Archaeology of Early European Society, 46–51. Cambridge: Cambridge University Press.

1990   *Emerging Complexity: The Later Prehistory of South-East Spain, Iberia and the West Mediterranean.* Cambridge: Cambridge University Press.

Comissão Nacional do Ambiente

1982   *Carta Litológica.* Scale 1: 1,000,000. Lisbon.

Firth, R.

1929   *Primitive Economics of the New Zealand Maori.* London: George Routledge and Sons.

Gilman, A.

1981   The Development of Social Stratification in Bronze Age Europe. *Current Anthropology* 22: 1–23.

1987   Unequal Development in Copper Age Iberia. In E.M. Brumfiel & T.K. Earle (eds), *Specialization, Exchange, and Complex Societies*, 22–29. Cambridge: Cambridge University Press.

Gonçalves, V.

1984   Programa para o Estudo da Evolução das Sociedades Agro-pastorais, das Origens a Metalurgia Plena, dos Espaços Abertos aos Povoados Fortificados, no Centro do Portugal. *Clio/Arqueologia* 1: 207–11.

Hallam, B., S. Warren and C. Renfrew

1976   West Mediterranean Obsidian. *Proceedings of the Prehistoric Society* 42: 85–110.

Harrison, R.J.

1977   *The Bell Beaker Cultures of Spain and Portugal.* Cambridge, MA: Peabody Museum of Archaeology and Ethnology, Harvard University.

Hoyt, E.

1924   *Primitive Trade.* London: K. Paul, Trench, Trubner.

Kunst, M.

1991   Copper Manufacture at Central Places? Some Aspects of the Importance of Iberian Copper Age Fortifications. Paper presented at the Annual Meeting of the American Anthropological Association, Chicago.

Leewaarden, W. van, and C.R. Janssen

1985   A Preliminary Palynological Study of Peat Deposits near an Oppidum in the Lower Tagus Valley, Portugal. In *Actas, I Reunião do Quaternário ibérico, Lisboa, 1985*, 2: 225–36. Lisbon: Grupo de Trabalho Português para o Estudo do Quaternario.

Lillios, K.T.

1991   Competition to Fission: the Copper to Bronze Age Transition in the Lowlands of West Central Portugal (3000–1000 B.C.). Unpublished Ph.D. dissertation, Department of Anthropology, Yale University.

McBryde, I.

1984   Kulin Greenstone Quarries: The Social Contexts of Production and Distribution for the Mt. William Site. *World Archaeology* 16: 267–85.

Paço, A. do

1970   A Povoa Eneolítica de Vila Nova de S. Pedro. In *Trabalhos de Arqueologia de Afonso do Paço (1929–1968)*, 275–305. Lisbon: Associação dos Arqueólogos Portugueses.

Phillips, P

1980   *The Prehistory of Europe.* Bloomington: Indiana University Press.

Piot, Charles D.

1991   On Persons and Things: Some Reflections on African Spheres of Exchange. *Man* 26: 405–24.

Ribeiro, O.

1987   *Portugal: O Mediterrâneo e o Atlântico*, 5th edn. Lisbon: Augusto Sá da Costa

Salisbury, R.F.

1962   *From Stone to Steel: Economic Consequences of Technological Change in New Guinea.* London: Cambridge University Press.

Sangmeister, E., and H. Schubart

1981   *Zambujal: Die Grabungen 1964 bis 1973.* Madrider Beiträge, 5. Mainz am Rhein: Philipp von Zabern.

Savory, H.N.

1968   *Spain and Portugal: The Prehistory of the Iberian Peninsula.* London: Thames and Hudson.

Sharp, L.

1952   Steel axes for Stone Age Australians. In E.H. Spicer (ed.), *Human Problems in Technological Change*, 69–90. New York: John Wiley.

Spindler, K.

1981   *Cova da Moura.* Madrider Beiträge 7. Mainz am Rhein: Philipp von Zabern.

Spindler, K., and L. Trindade

1969   A Povoa Eneolítica do Penedo (Torres Vedras). In *Actas das I Jornadas Arqueológicas*, 57–192. Lisbon: Associação dos Arqueólogos Portugueses.

4. Preliminary Report on a Survey Program of the Bronze Age of Northern Albacete Province, Spain

Antonio Gilman, Manuel Fernández-Miranda, María Dolores Fernández-Posse and Concepción Martín

Until the development of the New Archaeology some thirty years ago, European prehistory was thought to have developed under oriental auspices. Europe was like the Third World to the Near East, the beneficiary (as the Third World is supposed to be) of the knowledge developed in the heartland. The New Archaeology replaced this account with a functionalist, adaptively-orientated one, which negated the categories describing progressive human social evolution from mesolithic bands, thorough neolithic tribes, to bronze age chiefdoms. Since the European prehistoric trajectory was a particular case that conformed to a general pattern, prehistorians sought to apply the same functionalist, adaptively-orientated models that were supposed to explain social evolution elsewhere. Thus, the development of social complexity in Europe would have been the result of the regulatory requirements of intensified systems of production and exchange (Renfrew 1973: 155–59). In place of the old diffusionist orientalism the functionalists proposed a sociological model, in which the emergent elites of later prehistoric Europe differed from the managers of Near Eastern temple economies only in terms of their smaller scale.

Some scepticism may be warranted with respect to the relevance of higher-order regulation models to European cases. It would be preferable, perhaps, to think in more 'Germanic' (and less 'Asiatic') terms, so to speak, to consider how stratification may arise under more anarchic circumstances. To explore such alternatives, we have recently conducted a survey of archaeological settlement patterns and land-use of the Bronze Age in the province of Albacete, Spain. This communication constitutes a preliminary account of the background, orientation, and progress of that work.

Bronze age settlements in the southern Meseta of the Iberian peninsula are among the best preserved in Europe. The large-scale and well-preserved character of the fortified settlements and the relative stability of the landscape in which they are situated allows, we believe, systematic documentation of how the centres of political control were located with respect to productive resources and to each other. The survey we report on here is intended to provide that documentation.

Background

Our survey program covers a climatically and geomorphologically stable region. The Mancha is a broad depression formed by the Alpine orogeny and filled with late Miocene, Pliocene, and early Pleistocene sediments. It is now a largely endorrheic plain with permanent or seasonal lagoons in its lower areas (López Bermúdez 1978). In Albacete the plain is bordered to the south and east by outliers of the Betic and Iberian mountain systems. Relief is generally low (with permeable parent rocks in hillier areas), so that erosion has probably not greatly changed the landforms since prehistoric times. The Mancha has a semi-arid continental Mediterranean climate, with rainfall of 350 to 450 mm per year falling mainly from October to May, and a high degree of variation in temperature between summer and winter. The natural vegetation, still present in some areas, consists mostly of oak and pine parkland, with thicker woodlands in hilly regions and gallery forest along major watercourses. Palaeoclimatological evidence is restricted to a few pollen diagrams (López García 1977, 1983a, 1983b), the interpretation of which is consistent with the view that changes in vegetation over the past 5000 years have been caused mainly by human action, and no recourse to climate change is necessary to account for them (see also López García 1978, 1986; Dupré Ollivier 1988). The uniform character of La Mancha facilitates the comparative interpretation of the ancient landscapes on which the region's prehistoric sites depended.

It is only in the past twenty years that the density of bronze age settlements in La Mancha has been recognized. Perhaps because of the inhospitable reputation of the Meseta's climate, prehistorians of the Iberian peninsula (e.g., Savory 1968) were inclined to accept at face value the relative scarcity of later prehistoric sites in the interior: sparse populations practicing a pastoralist economy in a harsh environment would not be expected to leave many archaeological traces. Local archaeologists had long known of massive piles of stone that they dated to the Bronze Age, and some of these piles had even been excavated. However, they had either been thought to be burial mounds (Sánchez Jiménez 1947, 1948) similar to bronze age barrows in central and northern Europe, or they had been interpreted as peripheral examples of the copper and bronze age cultures prevalent in southeast Spain (Martínez Santa-Olalla 1951). As recently as two decades ago, the Bronze Age of the southern Meseta was essentially unknown, despite what we now know to be a very rich archaeological record.

The first evidence of the presence of permanent, large, fortified bronze age settlements in La Mancha came with the excavations of two sites in Ciudad Real, El Azuer and Los Palacios by the University of Granada in 1974 (Molina and Nájera 1978). The mounds of stone rubble were revealed to be the remains of a central tower surrounded by two rings of walls. Now, twenty years later, about a dozen similar settlement sites have been excavated in La Mancha, clearly showing that the region has an exceptionally rich archaeological record from the Bronze Age. In the province of Ciudad Real the University of Granada team identified over twenty flatland settlements as well as many others on hilltops (Nájera Colino 1984:7). A survey of the municipality of Almansa, 500 km² (Albacete province) has identified 43 sites (Simón García 1987), and similar densities are reported for parts of the provinces of Cuenca (Díaz-Andreu García 1990) and Toledo (Ruíz Taboada 1993). Our knowledge of the Bronze Age in La Mancha comes from recent work, some still in progress, the data being published mostly in preliminary reports. All the same, the available information, makes clear that La Mancha has an exceptionally complete bronze age archaeological record.

The archaeological record

The bronze age archaeology of La Mancha is an archaeology of settlements. Recent research has concentrated on the resolution of the problems presented by deeply stratified sites with complex histories of defensive construction. This work (which we have summarized elsewhere [Martín *et al.* 1993]) shows the following:

1. The Bronze Age in La Mancha broadly resembles the Bronze Age 'culture' long known from eastern Andalusia and Murcia to the south (the Argaric) and the Spanish Levant to the east (the 'Bronce' Valenciano). All three areas are characterized by individualized burial rites, by permanent settlements of a strongly defensive nature, as demonstrated either by their construction or by their location, and by typological features such as riveted daggers and undecorated carinated pottery. The Bronze Age in La Mancha seems to be more like the 'Bronce Valenciano' than like the Argaric, but this similarity is based less on positive resemblances than on the rarity of some of the special items found in the richest Argaric grave contexts, such as chalices and halberds.

2. The Mancha Bronze Age occupies the same time span as the Argaric and the Bronce Valenciano. Radiocarbon dates from recently excavated settlements generally fall between 3750 and 3300 BP. Based on calibrated radiocarbon years the Bronze Age in La Mancha runs from about 2250 to about 1500 BC, a period that matches the time ranges of its analogues to the south and east. The stylistically nondescript character of the pottery and lithics and the scarcity and uniformity of the metal artefacts has prevented investigators from subdividing the Bronze Age of La Mancha into subperiods.

3. Two basic types of settlement characterize the Mancha bronze age: '*morras*' and '*motillas*', on the one hand, and '*castillejos*', on the other (cf. Martínez Navarrete 1988). The former sites (called '*morras*' in Albacete and '*motillas*' in Ciudad Real) are circular forts consisting of ringed walls (and in some cases a central tower) with habitation spaces in their interiors. These sites can be located either in low-lying river valley bottoms and marshes or on promontories and hill-tops. Some of these fortifications have adjacent settlement areas outside the defensive perimeter, but most seem to be isolated strong points. Some of these forts are quite large (El Azuer, for example, measures fifty metres in diameter and has internal walls that are still seven metres high), but many are small mounds of rubble two metres or less high and twenty or less in diameter. The castillejos are settlements located on hill-tops and terraced hill slopes. Some of the larger examples cover several thou-

sand square metres, are deeply stratified, and may have fortifications protecting the more accessible slopes, but many are quite small sites, occupying platforms of a few hundred square metres and with correspondingly shallower deposits. Excavations have concentrated on the larger sites of both groups, and the radiocarbon dates from them show that they were sites of long-term occupation that at least partly over-lapped in time.

4. Faunal analysis from El Azuer and Los Palacios sheds light on subsistence patterns in La Mancha during the Bronze Age. Cattle outnumber sheep/goat, and both show a relatively high proportion of adults, indicating that the animals were exploited both for traction and for milk, that is, for 'secondary products' (Harrison and Moreno López 1985). Both of these sites also yielded large quantities of grain (mostly emmer and bread wheat). Sickle blades and milling stones, found at all sites, testify to the importance of nonpastoralist pursuits (the sickle blades from El Acequión have heavy gloss).

The location of sites also suggests a relatively intensive agriculture. The density of settlements appears to be greater along watercourses and in swampy zones than in areas suitable only for dry farming. Hydraulic resources may have been exploited to provide permanent pasture and stable harvests. What we know appears to indicate that the subsistence base of the Bronze Age in La Mancha consisted of a Mediterranean agriculture with some degree of intensification.

5. The Bronze Age of La Mancha fits the pattern shown elsewhere in the Iberian peninsula of the development of intensive agriculture, which is generally associated with incipient class stratification. The few burials that are known from La Mancha, however, reveal little wealth differentiation, but the highly defensive orientation of the settlement sites implies differential wealth. The same is indicated by large stores of grain inside fortified settlements and the production of valuable materials at some sites (metal at Azuer, ivory [imported no doubt from North Africa: Harrison and Gilman 1977] at El Acequión).

Theory and problem

The overall archaeological record for the Copper and Bronze Ages of the Iberian peninsula clearly indicates the development of increasing social stratification (Chapman 1990). The many fortified settlements, changes in burial rituals with increasing differentiation in grave goods, the development of metallurgy, and long-distance trade in exotic materials all testify to this. Different processual explanations for this development have been offered over the last decade by a number of scholars. One school considers social stratification to arise from the leadership necessary to organize and maintain long-distance trade and intensive subsistence production, which in turn arose from population pressure (Ramos Millán 1981) or from the need to meet the uncertainties that a Mediterranean climate presents for food production (Chapman 1982, 1990). Another school considers inherited social status to arise from the consolidation of power by an elite; this power may result from the control of commodity exchange between communities with differential access to metallurgical resources and technology (Lull 1983) or from the diminished social fission — and hence greater opportunities for the collection of tribute — stemming from intensified systems of cultivation (Gilman 1976, 1987). The debate over these various scenarios, comprising the range of current thinking on the origins of social complexity, is ongoing. The preference of one scenario over another depends mainly on assessment of its feasability, given the paucity of concrete evidence about the causes that gave rise to social stratification. The goal of our research in Albacete has been to obtain evidence that would test these contrasting approaches.

These various explanations clearly posit rather different types of prehistoric settlement pattern. Proponents of managerial theories who propose that control over resources was a key to the emergence of social complexity in the Bronze Age suggest that archaeological evidence for settlement hierarchies can be used as indicators of stratified societies. Brumfiel (1976) and Steponaitis (1981) stress that such a hierarchy is marked by the non-correspondence between the size of a settlement and the agricultural productivity of its site catchment area. Given a constant catchment productivity, administrative settlements will be larger than those inhabited by direct producers because the former collect tribute from the latter, accumulate hangers-on, and so on. Renfrew and others who have favoured a managerial account of the origins of social stratification see a necessary correlation between settlement hierarchies and social inequalities (see, for example, Milisauskas 1978).

Similarly, commodity exchange between an organically integrated society of farmers and miners would result in mining settlements that would seem too large with for the agricultural resources in their vicinity, since the mineral-producing population would receive food from their agricultural trading partners. Proponents of this approach, such as Lull, have developed this idea in detail.

By contrast, that capital investments in subsistence production makes it possible for 'protectors' to exploit primary producers is a theory that need involve no disparity between the size of a settlement and the agricultural resources in its vicinity. Under such a system those who give tribute may live side-by-side with those who take tribute, and the population will be distributed in the landscape proportionally to the resources that can support it. It is a system similar to that of feudal Europe, and it may in fact be possible to trace the roots of the latter back to the manorial systems of feudal Europe (whose roots, one may argue, go back to the social organization of European barbarians).

Site hierarchies have been broadly accepted as a hallmark of the development of social complexity in later prehistoric Europe, but the nature of the archaeological record from Europe makes their existence hard to prove. The relevant chronological horizons are quite ancient, so that often one cannot be sure that the sites recorded in a survey constitute a representative sample of what once existed. Natural or cultural factors the impact of which is difficult to evaluate may have produced the differential loss of sites of varying characteristics. Furthermore, the size differences between settlements may be due, not to to differences in the number of their prehistoric occupants, but to the intensity or the time span of their occupation, factors a survey program may find it difficult to assess. These difficulties are compounded by the coarseness of periodizations based on radiocarbon: occupations with the same archaeological diagnostics may in fact have flourished at different times within a single period of some centuries. Finally, it may be hard to assess the agricultural productivity of the landscapes in which sites are situated at the remote time of their occupation (and without an at least comparatively reliable measure of this productivity the definition of some sites as being of a higher order than others is, as we have noted, impossible). These difficulties have made it easy both for some Europeanist prehistorians to doubt claims for the existence of hierarchies and for others to accept those claims as reasonable under the circumstances.

The Bronze Age of La Mancha constitutes an archaeological horizon of emergent social com-plexity in which the problems outlined above can be controlled to some degree. The settlements that constitute the record were built of stone and were often quite large, so that it seems likely that many of them have survived. 3500 years of sub-sequent agriculture and alluviation may have destroyed or obscured smaller sites, but the larger *morras* are too massive to make their removal worthwhile, and *castillejos* are on high ground which is rarely subjected to any subsequent use. Some of the larger sites may have been destroyed by massive building projects (like the *morra* at Balazote [790/111: cf. Appendix and Figure 4.1], destroyed by the construction of the Albacete-Jaén highway [Instituto Geológico y Minero de España 1931]), and others may be obscured by subsequent constructions (some of the Medieval castles may have bronze age components undetected beneath their foundations), but we feel confident that above a certain threshold virtually all the larger fortified sites will have survived and are susceptible to identification by a systematic survey program. The problem of untangling chronological palimpsests is a serious one in the Bronze Age of La Mancha, given the lack of reliable chronological diagnostics with which to subdivide its 750 year time span, but radiocarbon dates obtained in excavations conducted recently, all on larger sites, show that these were occupied for most of the period. Some sites were founded later, and others abandoned sooner, but we feel it is reasonable to suppose that the larger, more deeply stratified sites were all being occupied around 2000 to 1800 BC. Finally, the landscape of La Mancha appears, on the available evidence, to be stable and fairly uniform, so that assessment of palaeotechnic resource potential is relatively uncomplicated. If bronze age site hierarchies once existed, they should still be detectable, and in La Mancha better than in most regions of Europe.

Project history

Our survey team has brought together two independently developed lines of research on the Bronze Age of the Iberian peninsula. In their previous work in southeast Spain, Gilman and Thornes (1985) studied the placement of neolithic, copper, and bronze age settlements in relation to the agricultural resources in their vicinity. That research assumed that Argaric and earlier settlements were isolated, independent political and economic units, a necessary assumption given the incompleteness of the archaeological record. Survey work on the Bronze Age in La Mancha provides the opportunity to study the economic foundations of later prehistoric cultural change in the Iberian peninsula using the more realistic hypothesis that the political relations between settlements affected their size and placement.

Fernández-Miranda, Martín, and Fernández-Posse have worked on the Copper and Bronze Ages on the peninsula from a functionally informed culture-historical perspective. Their excavations at El Acequión [765/61] (Fernández-Miranda *et al.* 1988, 1990) and El Quintanar [764/49] (Martín Morales 1983, 1984) have provided necessary functional and temporal controls over the variability of bronze age assemblages in the study area.

Methods and progress

Our work aims to obtain evidence that will bear on two questions: 1. Did a site hierarchy develop in northern areas of the province of Albacete during the Bronze Age of La Mancha? If it did, the archaeological record should reveal a pattern of sites which are relatively large in proportion to the amount of prime arable land in their vicinity surrounded by sites that were small relative to the amount of such land. 2. Were sites functionally differentiated by their access to important non-agricultural resources, such as metal or salt? If they were, more sites and larger sites should be found next to scarce, restricted resources, such as ores or saline marshes. These goals required that we determine the relationship of sites of varying size both to the kinds and richness of the resources in their vicinity and to

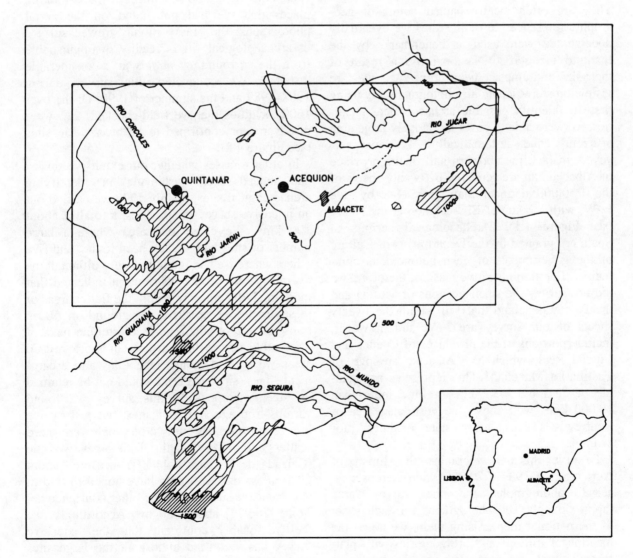

Figure 4.1   Location of Albacete province and the survey area within the Iberian peninsula.

one another. That is to say, we had to develop survey methods that would permit us to cover an area large enough to assure that it would encompass various polities with their central places (if these indeed existed) and that would do so systematically enough to assure that the distributional density of sites found in the present corresponded to their distributional density in the Bronze Age. These aims also required us to assess the distribution and productivity of relevant resources in bronze age times. We have implemented these tasks as follows:

Survey

Our main goal was to identify sites whose fortifications or defensive emplacements indicate that they were places of refuge and storage, that is to say possible political and economic centres. *Morras* and *castillejos* are frequently fairly large in size and prominently placed in the landscape. They are often locally named points of geographic reference: 26 of the sites we eventually documented were used as benchmarks by the Instituto Geográfico Nacional. As a result of their size and emplacement, bronze age sites are visible on stereoscopic air photographs. By using these to identify possible archaeological localities, we were able to cover a relatively large area efficiently and systematically. We have surveyed, in fact, the northern half of the province of Albacete, an area covered by twenty sheets of the 1:50,000 national map, four N–S by five E–W, with the site of El Acequión at the centre (see Figure 4.1). (Archaeological permits in Spain are granted by the Departments of Culture of the governments of each autonomous community. For administrative reasons, therefore, we did not survey the small portions of Murcia and the País Valenciano that fall within the twenty sheets of our survey area. We did, however, include portions of the provinces of Cuenca and Ciudad Real, which like Albacete are part of Castilla-La Mancha.)[1] This represents a rectangle of 72.6 by 143.2 km. (a little more than 10,000 km^2, well above the postulated area of Renfrew's (1975) 'early state modules,' for example).

To survey this area we obtained the Ministry of Agriculture's 1987 1:20,000 scale stereoscopic aerial photographs for the survey area (approximately 100 photographs for each sheet of the national map). Using them, we noted the location of hilltops and promontories with platforms suitable for occupation, of circular lumps that might be *morras*, and of other anomalies that

might be the result of ancient occupations. In other words, we identified localities that resembled what known bronze age sites looked like on the aerial photos, using stereoscopic viewing. All these places were then visited in the field. We also field checked all the official benchmarks and localities with suggestive place names. (Places called '*morras*' may be natural 'heads' of land, but often have archaeological sites on them. Localities named after '*el tesoro*' [the treasure], '*el moro*' [the Moor], or '*la encantada*' [the sorceress] often turn out to be associated with ancient occupations, as do various modifications of castle ['*castillico*', '*castellón*', etc.]). In addition, of course, we went to localities identified as belonging to the Bronze Age in publications and in the site register of the Museum of Albacete.[2] Finding all these places by vehicle and on foot involved criss-crossing the landscape, and in the course of these excursions we would see and visit likely-looking places that we had not noted on the aerial photographs: the grassy rubble-strewn surface of archaeological fill is readily distinguishable from the surrounding *maquis* at a considerable distance. We conducted this survey during 1988–1989 and the summer of 1990. Of the over 1600 localities that we field-checked, 272 were discovered or confirmed to be bronze age sites (see Figure 4.2).

In order to asses whether our extensive survey had indeed been systematic in identifying archaeological sites, in July 1990 we carried out an intensive survey in six areas, a total of about 100 km^2. We chose one area where a large number of sites had already been found, and five others where we had found few sites although the overall pattern of site distribution indicated that more might be present. Within the flatter areas of these tracts we covered the ground in 50 m transects except where crops or stubble made it impossible to see the surface. In more rugged areas we walked along ridge lines and escarpment edges (since material would not be retained on steeper slopes). In this survey we found various iron age and later sites, but just twelve bronze age ones, all but two of which were sherd scatters and/or very small. Of the other two, one (Calzada de Vergara [743/17]) measured about 1000 m^2, a size we would have hoped to find in our extensive survey, and the other (Barranco del Tollo [766/73] about 330 m^2. Accordingly, we feel reasonably confident that the extensive survey has identified almost all the large sites (over 1500 m^2) in northern Albacete. The effect of our survey has been to systematize

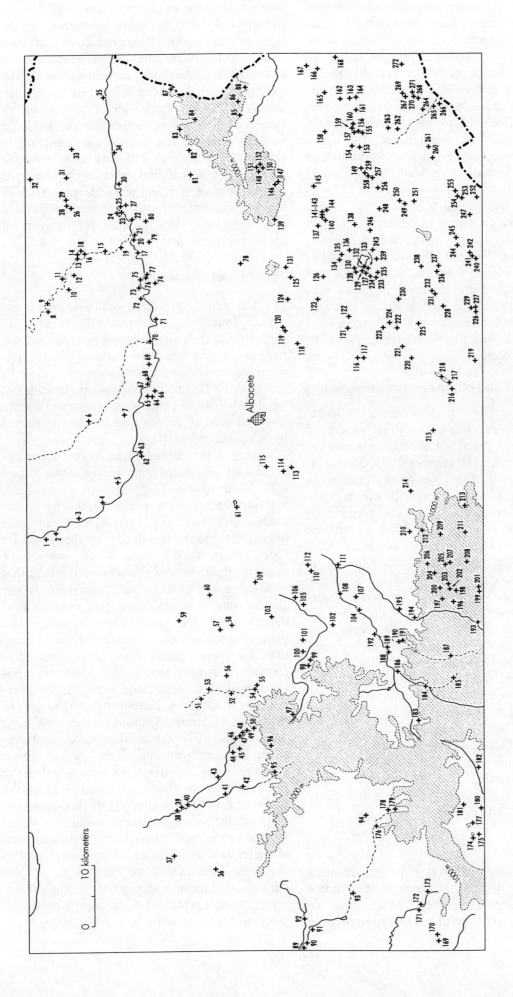

Figure 4.2   Distribution of bronze age sites within the survey area.

traditional site discovery methods across a region which had previously been investigated haphazardly. We have found sites that are salient. Thus, in areas which had received prior attention, we found relatively few new sites: for example, in the vicinity of El Quintanar, for a sector Martín had looked at during her excavations at the site, we added 11 localities to the 29 already known; in the portions of the municipality of Almansa that fell within our survey area, we found no sites that had not already been identified by Simón García (1987).

During our initial visits to the sites, we limited our descriptive fieldwork to collection of diagnostic materials (mostly pottery) from the surface. In July of 1991 and 1992 we revisited all of the sites, measuring them and preparing sketch plans of visible features where this was warranted. Our systematic description of the variability of the sites will provide, we hope, a basis for gauging the functional differentiation of the sites in our inventory.

Agricultural and other resource mapping

To determine the distribution of relevant resources, we are using a simplified version of the procedures worked out in detail in our earlier research (Gilman and Thornes 1985: 38–47). It must be understood that we do not propose to make a positive reconstruction of the resource potential of our study area. For the purposes of our analysis it is entirely sufficient to estimate the *relative* productivity of resource areas, since our intention is to compare these. This task is greatly facilitated, of course, by the relatively uniform climate and moderate erosion potential of the study area. It is also helped by the 1:50,000 maps of modern land use prepared by the Ministry of Agriculture for the survey territory. These can be adjusted to reflect traditional land use potential by the examination of photographs taken before recent agricultural modernization and the study of historical sources on agricultural land use. The 1956–1957 photographs taken by the U.S. Air Force precede the significant development of irrigation using artesian wells, for example, while the mid-18th century property register of Ensenada records an entirely palaeotechnic farming system.

Analysis

The object of the fieldwork is to prepare maps indicating the location and size of the Middle bronze age sites in the survey area against the distribution of agricultural and other resources in their vicinity. The existence of central places in a site hierarchy may be tested by comparing the sizes of sites against the productivity of their respective territories (the size of which may be estimated at various sizes in various trials). The basic approach has been developed by Steponaitis (1981), using the Valley of Mexico survey evidence. It should be noted that our evidence will improve on that which was available to Steponaitis in that we will have more sensitive measures of agricultural productivity than the simple measure of extent of arable land. Lack of any site hierarchy would, of course, support a non-managerial view of the development of social stratification in Europe.

Provisional assessments

The data we have collected in this survey are not yet developed to a point that will permit us to formally test the contrasting propositions on settlement patterns we have outlined above. The impressions we have formed over the course of our work so far are necessarily provisional, but we doubt that the conclusions suggested by the broad patterns of the evidence will be overturned by more detailed analysis.

It is clear, for example, that bronze age occupations are distributed quite unevenly (see Figure 4.2). Their location suggests, not surprisingly, that settlements were placed so as to secure access to land that could be cultivated intensively. Some two-thirds of the sites are found near lagoons and water courses or immediately above *cañadas* (low-lying land that receives moisture and sediment from surrounding slopes), that is to say, areas that would afford opportunities for short-fallow farming and permanent pasture. Site densities are low in areas that are only suitable for long-fallow dry-farming. It is also obvious that defensive considerations were extremely important in determining site locations. Nine-tenths of the sites are placed on escarpments, promontories, and steep hills. Where there is neither good land nor defensible emplacements, there are no bronze age sites. Thus, no sites at all were found in the two northwestern sheets (742 and 743) of the study area, which is uniformly of this character, and similar empty tracts existed in broad stretches of several other sheets. In the absence of better land or of locations providing natural defences, there would be no reason for the builders of bronze age sites to commit themselves to occupying (or fortifying) a particular place over the long term.

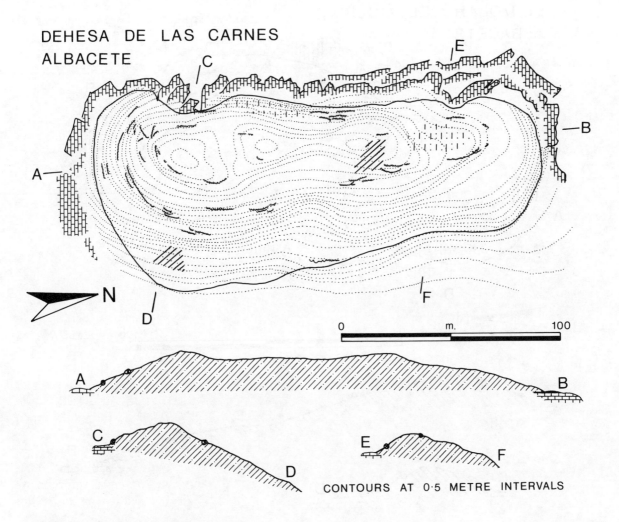

Figure 4.3   Sketch plan of Dehesa de las Carnes.

Our results make it clear that bronze age settlement patterns in our study are very different from those of subsequent periods. Of the 272 bronze age sites documented in our survey, only 21 have later occupations. It is also notable that of more than 1600 localities that we visited in our extensive survey, only eleven sites did *not* belong to the Bronze Age. In part, of course, these contrasts are a facet of our survey approach, which was oriented to finding places similar to known bronze age sites. That this approach was quite so efficient must indicate, however, that the makers of bronze age sites operated under social constraints that were very different from those encountered by their successors.

Our analysis of resource distributions has not progressed to the point that we can offer precise ratio estimates of site size to catchment productivity, but there is *prima facie* evidence that some contrasts do exist in this critical measure of set-

tlement hierarchies. Occupations placed at intervals along the same river valley must have approximately similar resources in their respective catchment areas, and in several cases some of these are much larger than others: thus, the site of Dehesa de las Carnes (789/108, Figure 4.3), at 3300 m^2, is much larger than sites further up the river Jardín (Castillico del Jardín [789/107], 160 m^2; Torre Vieja [789/104], 1250 m^2; Cabelluela [815/192], 480 m^2), although the width of the valley floor is quite similar in all four cases. Likewise, Bolinches [766/70] and El Quintanar [764/49] are much larger than other sites along their stretches of the rivers Júcar and Quintanar, respectively. A similar problem occurs with large sites at great elevations. El Molar del Molinar (816/211), for example, has the size (1750 m^2) and something of the layout of a small medieval castle, with a *morra* at its northern end, and two walls enclosing an inner and outer habitation spaces towards the south (see Figure

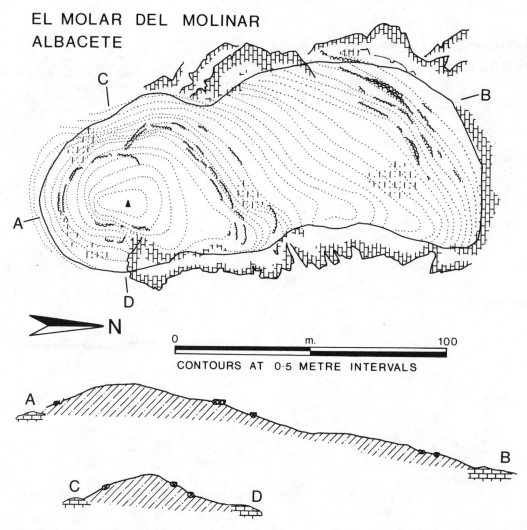

Figure 4.4   Sketch plan of El Molar del Molinar.

4.4). The nearest arable land of any quality is along a narrow *cañada* 1500 m to the north and 150 m lower in elevation than the site, which seems incongruously large for the agricultural resources in its immediate vicinity.

We find it difficult to interpret these differences as evidence of a hierarchy, however, because of the absolute site size ranges which are involved: large bronze age sites in northern Albacete, the putative centres of the system, fall between 0.15 and 1.2 hectares in size, while the mean size of sites is about 0.05 hectares. Both *morras* and *castillejos* cover the range from smaller to larger sites, and functional differences between sites of different sizes are not obviously apparent. Consequently, the size differences we observe could be the result of various factors which might have little to do with hierarchical social differences. Thus, the occasional hiving off of smaller social segments from larger ones would produce a settlement pattern of larger and

smaller sites, but this would reflect, not the greater power of the larger centres' inhabitants, but their relative weakness in being able to control dissidents. The main point to be made is that the range of sizes of bronze age site in northern Albacete does not reach the *oppidum* threshold: the coexistence fortified villages (of a few thousand square metres) with fortified farmsteads (of a few hundred square metres) cannot be considered an indication of the existence of higher order regulators, insurers of last resort, etc. We do not anticipate that the formal analysis of site sizes against available resources will support the managerialist accounts of emergent complexity in the European Bronze Age.

The commodity exchange approach cannot be supported in the metallurgical variants that have been proposed for the Iberian Bronze Age. There are small copper sources, not currently exploited, in the southwest of our study area (Carrasco Valor 1994), but there is no concentration of settlements in their vicinity, and evidence of copper smelting and casting is present at many sites, regardless of proximity to metal resources. That unreduced ores were transported over fairly long distances bears witness to the infinitesimal scale of metallurgical production, a circumstance confirmed by the paucity of metal taken out of circulation (and deposited in the archaeological record). It seems reasonable to suppose that a large-scale metallurgical industry would be organized cost-effectively, so that ores would be smelted in the mountains where they are to be found prior to long-distance transport. By contrast, it is characteristic of a domestic industry that economies of scale are unimportant. The metallurgical industry of the Bronze Age in La Mancha is far smaller in scale than that of the Argaric sector of southeast Spain, where its integration into a domestically organized economy is also supported by the available evidence (Montero Ruíz 1993, 1994; cf. Gilman 1987).

A better candidate for a resource the control of which might afford opportunities for exploitation is salt, a value-concentrated, divisible product that is limited in its availability and necessary to a human population and its livestock. The archaeological invisibility of salt has made systematic discussion of the development of its importance as a commodity difficult. La Mancha has a number of salt sources, some of which were in production until quite recently. A survey such as ours should be able to evaluate whether the existence of a salt source is associated with a greater density of sites than could be explained by the agricultural resources in their vicinity. It is certainly intriguing that the greatest concentration of sites in our study region (sixteen in an area of some 50 km^2, among them Cola Caballo [791/129], the largest in that region at 1.2 hectares) occurs near the saline lagoon at Pétrola. This concentration can only be assessed comparatively, however, and there are other salt sources in northern Albacete that do not appear to be associated with an unusual concentration of sites.

Conclusion

While we believe that the evidence we are gathering in our survey will be consistent with the view of incipient social complexity which we outlined earlier — that the petty gangsterism of incipient elites is permitted by intensified farming strategies — the principal merit of our work is to raise more questions than it answers. Thus, the chronological problems presented by smaller sites with presumably briefer occupations, or the possible functional distinctions between the various types of larger and smaller sites, are only some of the issues which must be addressed through excavations. What our survey makes clear, however, is that La Mancha is an area where many of the most important questions in studies of the European Bronze Age can be addressed and, perhaps, answered.

Acknowledgments

Our research in Albacete has been supported by the National Geographic Society, the Council of Albacete, the Ministry of Education and Science (Spain), the Program for Cultural Cooperation Between Spain's Ministry of Culture and United States Universities, the Combined Committee for Hispanic-North American Cultural and Educational Cooperation, the Fulbright Commission, and California State University, Northridge.

Notes

1 The sheets surveyed are Villarobledo (number 740 in the numbering of the Instituto Geográfico Nacional map series, number 22–29 of the Mapa Militar, Minaya (741, 23–29), La Roda (742, 24–29), Madrigueras (743, 25–29), Casas Ibáñez (744, 26–29), Sotuélamos (763, 22–30), Munera (764, 23–30), La Gineta (765, 24–30), Valdeganga (766, 25–30), Carcelén (767, 26–30), El Bonillo (788, 22–31), Lezuza (789, 23–31), Albacete (790, 24–31), Chinchilla de Monte-Aragón (791, 25–31), Alpera (792, 26–31), Villanueva de la Fuente (814, 22–32), Robledo (815, 23–32), Peñas de San Pedro (816, 24–32), Pozo Cañada (817, 25–32), and Montealegre del Castillo (818, 26–32).

2 At the beginning of our fieldwork, there were some 124 bronze age localities within our study area listed in the site register of the Museum of Albacete and/or mentioned in publications. (This number is necessarily approximate: many sites mentioned in the these sources are described in very general terms and are not given precise or accurate locations. Our estimate of 124 errs on the side of generosity). All of these were revisited over the course of the survey in order to verify their existence, to control our field procedures, to place the sites accurately on the maps, and to systematize information concerning their characteristics.

3 Mo = Morra; Ca = Castillejo; In = Sherd scatter.

4 Known = reported in publications or in the Albacete Museum site register prior to our survey; Survey = found during intensive survey in 1990.

5 Ib = Iberian (Iron Age); Ro = Roman; Me = Medieval.

Bibliography

Brumfiel, E.

1976   Regional Growth in the Eastern Valley of Mexico: A Test of the 'Population Pressure' Hypothesis. In K.V. Flannery (ed.), *The Early Mesoamerican Village*, 234–49. New York: Academic Press.

Carrasco Valor, J.C.

1994   Actividad Metalúrgica en Yacimientos de la Edad del Bronce en Alcaraz. *Al-Basit* 20: 151–59.

Chapman, R.

1982   Autonomy, Ranking and Resources in Iberian Prehistory. In C. Renfrew and S. Shennan (eds), *Ranking, Resource and Exchange: Aspects of the Archaeology of Early European Society*, 46–51. Cambridge: Cambridge University Press.

1990   *Emerging Complexity: The Later Prehistory of South-East Spain, Iberia and the West Mediterranean*. Cambridge: Cambridge University Press.

Díaz-Andreu García, M.

1990   La Edad del Bronce en el Noreste de la Submeseta sur: Un Análisis Sobre el Inicio de la Complejidad Social. Unpublished Ph.D. dissertation, Universidad Complutense.

Dupré Ollivier, M.

1988   *Palinología y Paleoambiente: Nuevos Datos Españoles, Referencias*. Servicio de Investigación Prehistórica, Serie de Trabajos Varios 84. Valencia: Servicio de Investigación Prehistórica.

Fernández-Miranda, M., M.D. Fernández-Posse and C. Martín Morales

1988   Caracterización de la Edad del Bronce en la Mancha: Algunas Proposiciones para su Estudio. *Espacio, Tiempo y Forma, Serie I, Prehistoria* 1: 293–310.

1990   Un Área Doméstica de la Edad del Bronce en el Poblado de 'El Acequión' (Albacete). *Archivo de Prehistoria Levantina* 20: 351–62.

1993   La Edad del Bronce en la Zona Oriental de La Mancha: El Acequión. In *El Acequión (Albacete) y El Tolmo de Minateda (Hellín): Síntesis de las Investigaciones*, 7–27. Albacete: Museo de Albacete.

Gilman, A.

1976   Bronze Age Dynamics in Southeast Spain. *Dialectical Anthropology* 1: 307–19.

1987   El Análisis de Clase en la Prehistoria del Sureste. *Trabajos de Prehistoria* 44: 27–34.

Gilman, A., and J.B. Thornes

1985   *Land Use and Prehistory in South-East Spain*. London: George Allen and Unwin.

Harrison, R.J., and A. Gilman

1977   Trade in the Second and Third Millennia B.C. between the Maghreb and Iberia. In V. Markotic (ed.), *Ancient Europe and the Mediterranean: Studies in Honour of Hugh Hencken*, 90–104. Warminster: Aris and Phillips.

Harrison, R.J., and G. Moreno López

1985   El Policultivo Ganadero o la Revolución de los Productos Secundarios. *Trabajos de Prehistoria* 42: 51–82.

Instituto Geológico y Minero de España

1931   *Mapa Geológico Escala 1:50.000: Memoria Explicativa de la Hoja N.° 790 Albacete*. Madrid: Tip. y Lit. Coullaut.

López Bermúdez, F.

1978   El Sector Pantanoso al Oeste de Albacete y su Desecación. *Al-Basit* 5: 69–90.

López García, P.

1977   Análisis Polínico de Verdelpino (Cuenca). *Trabajos de Prehistoria* 34: 82–83.

1978   Resultados Polínicos del Holoceno en la Península Ibérica. *Trabajos de Prehistoria* 35: 9–44.

1983a   Diagrama Polínico del Yacimiento de 'El Recuenco' (Cervera del Llano, Cuenca). In *Homenaje al Prof. Martín Almagro Basch*, 2: 45–48. Madrid: Ministerio de Cultura.

1983b   Análisis Polínico del Cerro del Castillejo (La Parra de las Vegas). *Noticiario Arqueológico Hispánico* 16: 215–17.

1986   Estudio Palinológico del Holoceno Español a Través de Yacimientos Arqueológicos. *Trabajos de Prehistoria* 43: 143–58.

Lull, V.

1983   *La 'Cultura' de El Argar*. Madrid: Akal Editor.

Martín Morales, C.

1983   Las Fechas del Quintanar (Munera, Albacete) y la Cronología Absoluta de la Meseta Sur. In *Homenaje al Prof. Martín Almagro Basch*, 2: 23–35. Madrid: Ministerio de Cultura.

1984   La morra del Quintanar. *Al-Basit* 15: 57–73.

Martín, C., M. Fernández-Miranda, M.D. Fernández-Posse and A. Gilman

1993   The Bronze Age of La Mancha. *Antiquity* 67: 23–45.

Martínez Navarrete, M.I.

1988   Morras, Motillas, y Castillejos: ¿Unidad o Pluralidad Cultural Durante la Edad del Bronce en La Mancha? In *Homenaje a Samuel de los Santos*, 81–92. Albacete: Instituto de Estudios Albacetenses.

Martínez Santa-Olalla, J.

1951   El 'Crannog' de la Laguna de Acequión en la Provincia de Albacete. *Anales del Seminario de Historia y Arqueología de Albacete* 1: 5–12.

Milisauskas, S.

1978   *European Prehistory*. New York: Academic Press.

Molina, F., and T. Nájera

1978   Die Motillas von Azuer und Los Palacios (prov. Ciudad Real): Ein Beitrag zur Bronzezeit der Mancha. *Madrider Mitteilungen* 19: 52–74.

Montero Ruiz, I.

1993   Bronze Age Metallurgy in Southeast Spain. *Antiquity* 67: 46–57.

1994   *El Origen de la Metalurgia en el Sureste Peninsular.* Almería: Instituto de Estudios Almerienses.

Nájera Colino, T.

1984   *La Edad del Bronce en la Mancha Occidental.* Unpublished PhD dissertation, University of Granada 458. Granada: Universidad de Granada.

Ramos Millán, A.

1981   Interpretaciones Secuenciales y Culturales de la Edad del Cobre en la Zona Meridional de la Península Ibérica: La Alternativa del Materialismo Cultural. *Cuadernos de Prehistoria de la Universidad de Granada* 6: 242–56.

Renfrew, C.

1973   *Before Civilization: The Radiocarbon Revolution and European Prehistory.* London: Jonathan Cape.

1975   Trade as Action at a Distance: Questions of Integration and Communication. In J.A. Sabloff and C.C. Lamberg-Karlovsky (eds), *Ancient Civilization and Trade*, 3–59. Albuquerque: University of New Mexico Press.

Ruíz Taboada, A.

1993   Producción y Explotación Económca en las Estribaciones Nororientales de los Montes de Toledo Durante la Edad del Bronce. *Complutum* 4: 311–20.

Sánchez Jiménez, J.

1947   La Cultura del Algar en la Provincia de Albacete. In *Actas, III Congreso Arqueológico del Sureste Español, Murcia 1947*, 73–89.

1948   La Cultura Algárica en la Provincia de Albacete: Notas para su Estudio. *Actas y Memorias de la Sociedad Española de Antropología, Etnografía y Prehistoria* 23: 96–110.

Savory, H.N.

1968   *Spain and Portugal: The Prehistory of the Iberian peninsula.* London: Thames and Hudson.

Simón García, J.L.

1987   *La Edad del Bronce en Almansa.* Albacete: Instituto de Estudios Albacetenses.

Steponaitis, V.P.

1981   Settlement Hierarchies and Political Complexity in Nonmarket Societies: The Formative Period of the Valley of Mexico. *American Anthropologist* 83: 320–63.

Appendix: List of Bronze Age Sites in the Survey

Number	Site Name	UTM Coord.	Type	OthOcc	Source
742/1	Villalgordo	579.2/4351.2	Mo[3]		Known[4]
742/2	Puente de Don Juan	580.0/4349.8	Ca		
742/3	La Hurona	582.8/4345.8	Mo		
742/4	El Carrasco	585.1/4341.6	Mo		
742/5	Atraca	588.3/4339.4	Mo		
742/6	Berli	598.8/4344.4	Ca	Ib[5]	Known
743/7	Vallejo del Gallo	599.5/4338.6	Ca		
743/8	Cenizate	616.5/4351.4	Ca		Known
743/9	Cerro Pelao	617.4/4350.7	Ca		Known
743/10	Derramadores	619.7/4347.6	Ca		Known
743/11	La Simona	621.4/4348.9	Ca		Known
743/12	Niño	621.9/4346.5	Mo		Known
743/13	Los Galayos Oeste	624.4/4346.0	Ca		Known
743/14	Los Galayos Este	624.7/4346.1	Ca		Known
743/15	Fuensanta (Abengibre)	625.8/4341.8	Ca		
743/16	Los Carboneros Sur	626.1/4345.3	Ca		Known
743/17	Calzada de Vergara	626.1/4336.5	Ca		Survey
743/18	Los Carboneros Norte	626.2/4345.4	Ca		Known
743/19	Arroyo de Abengibre	626.4/4339.2	Ca		Known
744/20	Castillo de Jorquera	627.9/4337.5	Ca	Ib,Me	
744/21	Frente Jorquera	628.4/4337.6	Ca	Ib,Me	Known
744/22	La Recueja	630.1/4337.3	Ca		Known
744/23	Cerro de la Reina	631.8/4339.2	In		Known
744/24	La Central	632.1/4339.6	In		
744/25	San Lorenzo	632.4/4338.9	Ca		Known
744/26	Cerro del Aguililla	632.9/4346.9	Mo		Known
744/27	Frasquito	632.9/4338.2	Ca		
744/28	Hoya Gualí	633.2/4347.9	Ca		Known
744/29	Cabezo del Judío	633.8/4348.1	Ca		Known
744/30	Mirador	636.5/4339.5	Ca		
744/31	Cerro Bermejo	637.7/4347.9	Mo		
744/32	Loma del Castillejo	639.9/4352.9	Ca		
744/33	La Pesadilla	642.3/4347.3	In		Known
744/34	Tranco del Lobo	644.6/4341.0	Mo		
744/35	Castillo de Ves	650.4/4341.8	Ca	Me	
763/36	Fuente del Espino	525.5/4324.1	Mo		Known
763/37	La Encantada (Villarobledo)	527.6/4330.5	Mo		
763/38	La Pasadilla Norte	535.0/4329.8	Mo		Known
763/39	La Pasadilla Sur	535.4/4329.3	Mo		Known
763/40	Los Castellones	536.0/4328.4	Mo+Ca	Ib	Known
763/41	Sotuélamos	537.4/4321.9	Mo		Known
763/42	Corral del Bombo	538.9/4319.4	Ca		
763/43	El Batán (El Bonillo)	540.3/4323.2	Mo		Known
764/44	Casares	544.2/4321.1	Ca	Me	Known
764/45	Marañas	544.6/4319.9	Mo		Known
764/46	San Telmo	546.0/4320.7	Mo		Known
764/47	La Ermita	546.5/4320.1	Mo		Known
764/48	El Toril	547.1/4319.4	In		
764/49	El Quintanar	547.2/4319.1	Mo		Known
764/50	Chavillo	548.4/4317.5	Mo		
764/51	El Pozo de Peralta	553.5/4325.9	Mo		Known
764/52	Corral de Piedra	554.3/4321.7	Mo		Known
764/53	Lechina	554.7/4324.8	Mo		Known
764/54	Lituero Suroeste	554.9/4317.6	Mo		Known

764/55	Lituero Noreste	554.9/4317.6	Mo		Known
764/56	Marigutiérrez	556.8/4322.1	Mo		Known
764/57	Casa del Moral	564.2/4323.0	Mo		
764/58	Tesoro de la Casilla	564.9/4321.1	Mo		
764/59	Viento	565.8/4329.5	Mo		
764/60	Barrax	569.9/4324.7	Mo		Known
765/61	El Acequión	584.2/4320.2	Mo	Ib	Known
765/62	La Encantada W (Albacete)	592.8/4336.0	Ca		
765/63	La Encantada (Albacete)	592.9/4336.0	Mo		Known
766/64	El Torcío	602.2/4334.3	Mo		Known
766/65	Cuevas del Salto	602.5/4334.9	Mo		
766/66	Fuentes de Mendoza	603.0/4333.5	Mo		
766/67	Barranco del Ciervo	604.5/4334.6	Ca		
766/68	El Mochuelo	605.0/4334.5	Mo		
766/69	Mahora	607.6/4334.8	Ca		Known
766/70	Bolinches	611.4/4334.2	Ca		
766/71	Valdeganga	614.8/4333.8	Ca		
766/72	Cumbres del Río	618.5/4335.6	Ca		Survey
766/73	Barranco del Tollo	620.1/4335.9	Ca		Survey
766/74	Los Bujes	620.3/4333.0	In		Survey
766/75	Malecones	620.9/4335.7	In		Survey
766/76	Cañahorro	621.6/4335.2	In		Survey
766/77	Cerro del Pollo	622.1/4335.1	Ca		
766/78	El Castillico (Pozo Higuera)	622.8/4319.6	Ca		Known
766/79	El Tornero	627.0/4334.6	Ca		
767/80	El Carrilero	630.6/4335.4	Ca		
767/81	Cerro del Pocico	638.3/4327.9	Ca		
767/82	Cerro Fino	642.2/4328.2	Ca	Me	
767/83	Peña Negra	645.6/4330.0	Ca		
767/84	Fuente Mayor	647.2/4327.0	Ca		
767/85	Asperones	647.9/4320.2	Ca		
767/86	Cerro Gallinero	649.9/4320.2	Ca		
767/87	Cerro Ramón	652.2/4331.1	Mo		
767/88	Bosque	652.3/4318.8	In		
788/89	Laguna Redondilla	513.0/4310.1	Ca		
788/90	El Almorchón (Ossa)	514.2/4309.3	Ca	Ib	Known
788/91	Laguna Concejo	516.1/4808.5	Mo+Ca		Known
788/92	Rochafrida	517.3/4309.3	Ca	Me	Known
788/93	Peñarrubia	521.2/4302.0	Ca		
788/94	Pajar de Marta	534.5/4299.5	In		Survey
788/95	Colmenar de Fulgencio	541.0/4314.3	Mo+Ca		
789/96	Casa de Riego	545.7/4310.9	Mo		
789/97	Calzadizo	550.6/4310.6	Mo		
789/98	Corazón Oeste	558.5/4308.3	Mo		
789/99	Corazón Este	559.1/4308.4	Mo		
789/100	Casa de Céspedes	560.6/4309.6	Mo		
789/101	Requena	562.5/4309.6	Mo		
789/102	Dehesa de Caracolares	564.9/4304.8	Mo		Known
789/103	Casas de Cuerva	566.4/4314.6	Mo		
789/104	Torre Vieja	567.5/4300.7	Ca	Me	Known
789/105	Vandelaras de Arriba	568.5/4309.6	Mo		Known
789/106	Vandelaras de Abajo	569.4/4310.9	Mo		Known
789/107	Castillico del Jardín	569.8/4300.9	Mo		
789/108	Dehesa de las Carnes	570.2/4303.7	Mo+Ca		Known
790/109	Casa de los Arboles	572.0/4317.3	Mo		Known
790/110	Casa de las Ideas Oeste	574.3/4308.3	Mo		
790/111	Balazote	574.4/4304.2	Mo		Known

790/112	Casa de las Ideas Este	574.5/4308.4	Ca		
790/113	Las Gorrineras		Mo		Known
790/114	Hoya Vacas	589.8/4313.2	Mo		Known
790/115	Ojos de San Jorge	590.6/4315.8	Mo		Known
791/116	Las Peñuelas Norte	609.1/4300.7	Mo		Known
791/117	Las Peñuelas Sur	609.1/4300.4	Mo		Known
791/118	Morrón de las Rozas	611.5/4310.8	Ca		Known
791/119	Los Hermanitos Oeste	613.4/4312.5	Ca		
791/120	Los Hermanitos Este	613.7/4312.5	Ca		
791/121	Doña Carmen	613.7/4302.5	Mo		
791/122	Gualda	615.4/4302.2	Mo		
791/123	El Judío	618.2/4307.3	Mo		Known
791/124	Rocinejos	618.4/4312.4	Mo		Known
791/125	Prado Viejo	621.8/4311.8	Mo	Ib	Known
791/126	Casa de Don Luis	622.0/4306.7	Mo		Known
791/127	La Torreta	622.8/4299.9	In		Survey
791/128	Los Castellares Oeste	623.0/4301.4	Mo		
791/129	Cola Caballo	623.1/4300.1	Mo+Ca		Known
791/130	Los Castellares Este	623.2/4301.4	Mo+Ca		
791/131	Fontanar de Arriba	623.4/4312.6	In		Known
791/132	Los Majuelos Norte	623.4/4299.8	Ca		
791/133	Los Majuelos Sur	623.4/4299.4	Ca		
791/134	Fuente del Cuerno	625.1/4303.8	Mo		
791/135	Fuente del Cuerno Este	625.3/4303.6	Ca		Survey
791/136	La Solana	626.2/4302.4	In		Survey
792/137	Las Charcas	629.8/4307.4	In		
792/138	Cerro de las Pilas	630.2/4301.7	Mo		Known
792/139	Oncebreros	630.9/4314.2	Mo		
792/140	Mompichel Mesa	631.0/4306.4	Ca	Me	
792/141	Mompichel Extremo Oeste	631.7/4306.3	Ca		
792/142	Mompichel Oeste	631.9/4306.4	Ca		
792/143	Mompichel Vértice	632.0/4306.3	Mo		Known
792/144	Mompichel Sureste	632.4/4306.3	Mo		
792/145	Cuarda	636.2/4308.2	Ca		
792/146	Tres Piedras	636.7/4314.2	Ca		
792/147	Fuente Navalón	637.3/4313.7	Ca	Ib	
792/148	Casa de las Breñas	639.3/4317.3	Ca		
792/149	Frontones	639.5/4300.2	Mo+Ca		
792/150	Mingo García	639.6/4316.6	Ca	Me	
792/151	Gira Valencia	639.7/4317.3	Ca		
792/152	Gira Valencia Este	639.9/4317.3	In		
792/153	El Amarejo	642.7/4301.3	Ca	Ib	Known
792/154	Hoya de la Torre	643.1/4302.3	Ca		Known
792/155	Chinar Sur	645.2/4300.9	Ca		Known
792/156	Chinar Extremo Sur	645.2/4300.4	Ca		Known
792/157	Chinar Vértice	645.4/4301.4	Ca		Known
792/158	Cerro de la Morrica	645.5/4306.9	Ca		Known
792/159	Chinar Noreste	645.8/4301.4	Ca		Known
792/160	Chinar Extremo Noreste	646.0/4301.5	Ca		Known
792/161	La Fuensanta (Almansa)	648.6/4301.5	Mo		Known
792/162	Cuchillo	650.3/4303.8	Ca		Known
792/163	Cuchillo Alto	650.6/4302.2	Ca		Known
792/164	Cuchillo Bajo	650.6/4302.0	Ca		Known
792/165	Cerrico de la Be	651.3/4306.4	Ca		Known
792/166	Puntal del Mugrón	655.3/4307.4	Ca		Known
792/167	Rambla Cueva del Pilar	655.7/4309.3	Ca		Known
792/168	Casa Cohete	657.0/4304.9	Ca		Known
814/169	Casa Silverio	515.4/4287.0	In		

814/170	Junta de las Cañadas	517.6/4286.5	In		
814/171	Piedras	519.1/4291.2	In		
814/172	Alejandrino	519.6/4290.6	Ca	Ib	
814/173	Angelón	521.9/4289.2	In		
814/174	La Gallega	531.3/4281.0	Ca		
814/175	La Mencia	530.6/4281.9	In		
814/176	Vado de Villanueva	533.1/4298.1	Ca		
814/177	Ermita del Picayo	533.2/4281.9	In		
814/178	Gredales	535.2/4295.8	Ca		
814/179	Arroyo de la Puerca	535.2/4294.5	In		
814/180	Gorgojí	535.2/4280.2	Ca	Ro,Me	
814/181	Cabezo Gonzalo	536.4/4283.6	Ca		
815/182	Los Álamos	542.0/4281.0	In		
815/183	Pradejón	549.9/4290.9	In		Survey
815/184	El Arquillo	555.5/4289.8	Mo		Known
815/185	Cilleruelo	556.7/4285.0	Ca		
815/186	Pesebre	557.7/4294.0	Ca		
815/187	Pico de Masegoso	560.1/4285.7	Ca		
815/188	Breñas	560.9/4296.1	Ca		
815/189	Cañada Honda	561.2/4295.9	Ca		
815/190	La Galdona Norte	562.1/4293.6	Mo		Known
815/191	La Galdona Sur	562.5/4293.1	Mo		Known
815/192	Cabelluela	563.5/4298.0	Mo		Known
815/193	La Tobica	565.5/4281.1	Mo		Known
815/194	El Batán (Casas de Lázaro)	566.3/4291.4	In		Known
815/195	Casa de la Quéjola	567.7/4293.9	Mo		Known
815/196	Cerro del Tesoro	569.0/4285.1	Ca		Known
815/197	El Castillico de la Rinconada	569.4/4286.9	Mo		Known
815/198	Peña del Guisaero	570.7/4284.7	Ca		Known
815/199	La Amada	570.8/4280.8	Mo+Ca		
816/200	Peña Galindo	571.0/4287.3	Mo		Known
816/201	La Amada Este	571.1/4280.7	Ca		
816/202	Peña la Mora	571.3/4285.6	Mo+Ca		Known
816/203	Peñica del Berro	572.0/4285.7	Mo		Known
816/204	Los Majanos	573.6/4288.3	Mo		
816/205	El Sahuco	574.7/4286.3	Mo+Ca		
816/206	Hariñuela	575.0/4289.3	Mo		
816/207	Atalaya del Sahuco	575.2/4285.6	Mo		
816/208	Corral de la Ventosa	575.7/4283.1	Mo		
816/209	Peña Roble	579.9/4287.1	Ca		Known
816/210	La Zarza	580.2/4296.6	Mo		
816/211	Molar del Molinar	580.3/4283.1	Mo+Ca		
816/212	El Madroño	580.6/4290.2	Ca		
816/213	El Royo	584.7/4283.3	In	Me	
816/214	El Castillico de Peñas	587.0/4292.1	In		
816/215	San Juan	597.2/4288.4	Mo		
817/216	Bellavista	604.1/4285.4	In		
817/217	Ontalafia Sur	605.2/4285.9	Ca		
817/218	Ontalafia Norte	605.8/4287.0	Ca		
817/219	El Berrueco	608.6/4281.6	Ca		
817/220	El Chortal	609.0/4292.1	Mo		Known
817/221	Mercadillos	610.6/4293.4	Mo		Known
817/222	El Campillo del Negro	613.8/4296.8	Mo		
817/223	Pardosa	614.0/4294.4	Mo		
817/224	Esparto	614.6/4295.7	In	Me	Known
817/225	'San Fermín'	615.7/4292.1	In		
817/226	Cuerdas del Cid Oeste	616.7/4281.4	Ca		

817/227	El Almorchón (Chinchilla)	616.8/4287.0	Ca		
817/228	Cuerdas del Cid Este	616.8/4281.5	Ca		
817/229	El Picorrón	617.0/4282.0	In		
817/230	Palomera	618.4/4294.3	Mo		
817/231	Olivares Sur	619.5/4288.3	Ca		
817/232	Olivares Norte	619.9/4288.5	Ca		
817/233	Las Camaricas	621.9/4298.1	Ca		
817/234	Horna	622.2/4299.3	Ca		
817/235	Camaricas Este	622.2/4298.0	In		Survey
817/236	Pinilla	622.9/4288.1	Mo		Known
817/237	Risca del Tío Pega	623.5/4288.0	Ca		Known
817/238	Montesinos	623.7/4290.6	Ca		
817/239	San Gregorio	624.9/4298.2	Ca		Known
817/240	Puntal de Conejeros	625.0/4281.5	Mo		Known
817/241	Candiles Suroeste	625.7/4282.1	Ca		Known
817/242	Candiles Noreste	625.9/4282.3	Ca		
817/243	El Mojón	626.5/4298.4	Ca		Known
817/244	Los Cerezos	627.1/4284.6	Mo		
817/245	El Jaraba	628.2/4284.7	Ca		Known
818/246	Pedriza	629.3/4299.4	Mo		
818/247	Colleras	632.1/4282.5	Ca		Known
818/248	Vista Alegre	633.2/4297.2	Ca		
818/249	Casa Nueva	633.9/4293.5	Ca		Known
818/250	Casa Nueva Norte	634.1/4293.7	In		
818/251	El Cepero	634.3/4291.8	Mo		Known
818/252	Mainetico	634.9/4281.5	Ca		Known
818/253	Los Cerricos Sur	635.1/4284.2	Ca		Known
818/254	Los Cerricos Norte	635.2/4284.5	Ca		Known
818/255	Cerro del Cementerio	636.1/4284.9	In		
818/256	La Paja	636.5/4297.6	Ca		
818/257	Buitre Sur	638.2/4298.8	Mo		
818/258	Buitre Centro	638.4/4299.6	Mo+Ca		
818/259	Buitre Norte	638.8/4299.4	Ca		
818/260	Cerro Moro	641.3/4288.9	In		Known
818/261	Arabinejo	642.8/4290.0	Ca		Known
818/262	Castillo de Montealegre	645.8/4294.9	Ca	Me	Known
818/263	Peña de la Mina	646.1/4296.3	Ca		
818/264	Cerrico Redondo	648.7/4290.6	Mo		Known
818/265	Zorreras	649.6/4288.5	Ca		Known
818/266	Tejera de Campillos	649.9/4287.5	Ca		Known
818/267	Cegarrón	650.7/4293.1	Ca		Known
818/268	Media Barba Sur	650.8/4291.1	Ca		
818/269	Cegarrón Este	651.0/4293.2	Mo		Known
818/270	Media Barba	651.1/4291.6	Ca		Known
818/271	El Castillico (Montealegre)	651.4/4291.6	Ca		Known
818/272	Zurridores	656.1/4293.6	Ca		Known

5. The Development of Cultural Complexity in the Western Mediterranean: A New Approach

Almudena Hernando Gonzalo

Introduction

The study of the prehistory of the Iberian peninsula has been traditionally approached from a historicist point of view. Now, however, we are beginning to see a move away from this approach in favour of others which see culture as an inter-related whole. I consider this a better way of reflecting on and understanding the operation of historical process. The study of the cultural development of the southeast of the Iberian peninsula comprises a paradigmatic test-case in this respect (Hernando 1988).

Every version of historicism has been applied in this area; from theories of 'culture' to theories of colonization. The present state of knowledge on the processes of change experienced in this region is a result of all this, since the inherently subjective selection of information makes it difficult to compare hypotheses generated from different theoretical positions.

For some time now, a better understanding of how cultural complexity began has been developing, based mainly on functionalist (Chapman 1982, 1984; Mathers 1984a, 1984b) or materialist (Gilman 1987a, 1987b; Gilman and Thornes 1985) interpretations. In addition, research projects such as the one undertaken by the University of Granada at the site of Los Millares have provided interesting information. As a result we are beginning to be able to explain developmental conditions in southeast Spain without turning to 'colonizations' which cannot be proved, or to mysterious 'migrations'. We can instead make a greater acknowledgement of the possibility that the development of social complexity on the Iberian peninsula was an indigenous phenomenon.

In this paper I aim to stress this view of the origin of complexity in southeast Spain. With regard to this, Waldren (1984: 915) made an interesting remark when he suggested that "the islands can contribute greatly to our knowledge of the prehistoric events that occurred in the adjacent continental areas" and even that "in some respects they are capable of reflecting those prehistoric events more reliably." Indeed, islands demand extreme measures of adaptation which, since they are often more visible, can help us to understand the processes followed and experienced in other areas.

Regional patterns

I intend to make a comparison between three areas in which the processes of cultural development are, in my opinion, particularly interesting: the islands of the central Mediterranean (Sardinia in particular), southeast Spain, and La Mancha in Spain. The undeniable appeal of the architectural structures in each of the three areas has encouraged the development of much speculation about the ideological and social structure of the groups that built them, with each area being treated as an isolated entity, and this has hindered the advance of our knowledge. However, I think there are objective conditions which make these regions comparable. In their points of similarity, elements can be found for an argument that would contribute to a better understanding of the processes of transformation in the three areas. In Corsica, Sardinia and the Balearic Islands, and in the southeast of the Iberian peninsula, development from the Neolithic to the Late Bronze Age was remarkably similar.

The available information gives no definite indication of settlement in any of the Mediterranean islands before the Neolithic, although there is evidence of previous movement between the islands that could go back a considerable time: the presence of Sardinian obsidian in Corsica from the sixth millennium BC is proof of this (Cherry 1990). The Sardinian economy was based on hunting, fishing and gathering during the Early Neolithic (the Filiestru, Su Carroppu and Grotta Verde Cultures) and was accompanied by Cardial Ware (fifth millennium BC). Domesticated animals are present from the beginning, but not cereals (Chapman 1985: 145), so it would appear that an agrarian economy was not consolidated until the time of the Ozieri Culture, dated to the transition from the fourth to the third millennium BC (Atzeni 1985: xxvii; Trump 1984: 513; Chapman 1985: 145). In view of the characteristics of the remains recovered, Trump (1984) argues that Sardinian prehistory can be divided into three periods: the Ozieri Culture and its predecessors, the various pre-Nuraghic complexes and the Nuraghic. However, I believe that this pattern characterized a wider geographical area, and it is this which makes the sequence comparable with the Iberian peninsula.

The Ozieri Culture still relied on hunting and fishing as subsistence activities, but at the same time it can be defined as a farming and stock-raising economy, in which there are also some indications of the beginning of mining. It is at this point that settlement locations begin to be become differentiated (plain and coast, hills and mountains) (Atzeni 1985: xxix), indicating a notable population increase. Tombs and places of worship also make their appearance at this time. Collective burials with both primary and secondary deposits are observed in numerous natural caves and, more particularly, in artificial, rock-cut tombs. These are scattered throughout the island, and on occasion are enormously complex. They sometimes reproduce the houses of the living to a surprising degree, with different rooms, and what appear to be doors with lintels cut into the rock. Some even appear to be sanctuary-tombs, in view of the complexity and proportions of their chambers (Atzeni 1985: xxi–xl) and the evident ritual activity that took place there. Sanctuaries such as the one at Monte d'Accoddi (Tinè and Traverso in press) represent the opposite extreme, all of them reflecting the need of the living to demonstrate — to themselves and to others — a link with the dead.

There has been lengthy discussion on whether the Ozieri should be classified as Late Neolithic or Early Copper Age, since some metal artefacts have also appeared here. For the following period, traditional research has tried to distinguish between different 'cultures' (the Abealzu/Filigosa, Monte Claro 'cultures', etc.), but as Lewthwaite (1986: 21) indicates these may simply be functionally differentiated manifestations of the same cultural phenomenon.

At the beginning of this copper age phase the first defended settlements began to appear in the Sardinian countryside, as well as some constructions that precede the *nuraghi*, the most distinctive architectural structures on the island in later periods. The so-called proto-nuraghi of Sa Korona is linked with the Abealzu Culture (Lewthwaite 1986: 27), while other structures of the same type are associated with the Monte Claro Culture. A little later, Bell Beakers appeared, followed by what is referred to as the 'Bonnanaro Culture' (1850–1650 BC), ascribed to the traditional Early Bronze Age, whose final facies of Sa Turricula seem to be contemporary with early *nuraghi*. At this point, perhaps around 1850 BC, what has been called the Nuraghic Culture begins; it was contemporary with the Talayotic and Torrean Cultures and together they constitute the foci of attention of traditional studies.

In the arid southeast of the Iberian peninsula there is almost no sign of evidence of settlement during the Early and Middle Neolithic. As Molina (1988: 258–59) points out, initial settlement of the Almerian lowlands would have begun during the Late Neolithic, with a sharp increase in the number and size of settlements from the beginning of the Copper Age. The Late Neolithic population lived in open settlements, some of which were permanent. The temporary camps that constitute the majority of habitation sites in the Late Neolithic were larger than the small seasonal camps documented in upland Andalusia during the Middle Neolithic. The material culture of these societies displays middle neolithic traditions. Most of the megalithic cemeteries, the *Rundgräber* and megalithic cists belonging to Phase I of the Almerian Culture according to the Leisners' (1943) periodization, must belong to this period (Molina 1988: 262). This phase would date to the second half of the fourth millennium BC.

The first copper age sites are dated at the beginning of the third millennium BC. Although few of them are known, Molina (1988: 262) believes that they display "a clear continuity with the earlier period". The site at Los Millares would have been founded about 2500 BC, and went through various phases of occupation until about 1800 BC when it was abandoned, but not before the development of a complex system of defence (between 2400 and 2000 BC) and the creation of its own Bell Beaker style, characteristic of the southeast of the Iberian peninsula (Molina 1988: 262). The *tholos* cemetery surrounding it constitutes one of the most complex funerary groups known in the region.

Around 1900/1800 BC the copper age settlements seem to have been abandoned. They gave way to a new mode of occupation of the region, with sites located in places where access was difficult, individual tombs, and the first indications of what could constitute a class society. This is the El Argar Culture.

Finally, it is extremely difficult to produce a synthesis of the development of settlement in La Mancha (province of Albacete and Ciudad Real in the southern Meseta of Spain), an area bordering on the Spanish southeast and of interest for the purpose of this paper. Because there are few notable structures, either domestic or funerary, belonging to the Copper Age, there has been little research relating to this period, while it is precisely the monumental character of some bronze age settlement sites that has attracted archaeological attention to the region. However, the limited data available for the Copper Age suggests the existence of sites of the 'hut floor' type (subsurface settlement features truncated by the plough zone), relatively ephemeral occupations on "slopes and low hills ... and small elevations which scarcely rise above the plain ... without defensive constructions" (Nájera Colino 1984: 22), while funeral customs are represented in collective cave burials, a practice common in the Spanish Levant and the Meseta in general (Galán Saulnier 1988). However, the 'Mancha Bronze Age' (Martín *et al.* 1993) is very different, although some archaeologists recognize "an indigenous substratum" (Galán Saulnier 1988: 193). Most of the sites are now villages, in a few of which burials like those on the Argaric Culture appear. Traditionally oriented archaeologists have distinguished two 'cultural facies', each represented by various styles of settlement: on one hand, the 'motillas culture' and, on the other, the 'highland village culture' (Nájera Colino 1984: 23). As Martínez Navarrete (1988) points out, these are better interpreted as functionally different manifestations of a single cultural group. The first would be characterized by sites on flat, low and generally marshy land, where a central tower would be built, surrounded by one or two concentric circular walls. Around it, the houses are spread out in irregular fashion (Nájera Colino 1984: 8–10). The hilltop villages are situated, as their name suggests, on craggy hill tops in the mountain ranges which surround and cross La Mancha, and are similar in appearance to villages of the El Argar Culture, with fortifications on the perimeter (Nájera Colino 1984: 19). La Mancha settlements are preferentially located along water courses and in swampy zones, which together with other economic data (Martín *et al.* 1993) suggests that this new, defensive and hierarchical settlement pattern was associated with the introduction of

Mediterranean farming systems into an environment characterized by climatic uncertainties

Discussion

We find that, in the islands of the central Mediterranean as well as in southeast Spain, Early Neolithic groups, although they had pottery, still pursued a way of life largely centred on hunting and gathering. This gradually became an agricultural existence, a phenomenon that occurred in the Middle and Late Neolithic. In Sardinia this is clearly demonstrated in the Ozieri Culture. This is when the land becomes systematically occupied, and marginal areas like southeast Spain, are exploited for the first time.

Sardinia and southeast Spain are high risk areas for a subsistence farming way of life, defined by Vicent (1990: 275) as "the various forms of production and social organization that arise when primary producers interact with nature through a full commitment to agriculture." Thus "what characterizes the subsistence farmer is that his immediate connection with the land derives from the social labour he invests in transforming it into the means of production" (Vicent 1990: 276), so that the investment becomes sufficiently large to deter its abandonment.

Both the southeast of Spain and the Mediterranean islands are regions that could be classified as marginal in their different geographic contexts. Southeast Spain, given its geographic position in the rain shadow of the Betic mountain chains, is the most arid part of Europe. Rainfall conditions in the fourth millennium BC were more favourable than at present, but in any case, as Gilman and Thornes (1985: 13) point out, it should be assumed that regional differences would have been the same. This means that southeast Spain offered fewer incentives to human settlement than did upland Andalusia or the Spanish Levant, adjacent areas with very different climatological characteristics. A detailed analysis of the arid region of southeast Spain, which was only systematically occupied in the Late Neolithic, indicates that its fundamental difference from the humid region is the lower proportion of arable land (Hernando and Vicent 1987), so that subsistence farmers must have invested greater effort, energy and labour than in neighbouring, more humid regions in order to obtain a similar output. Likewise, an island environment, in itself, on top of the particular characteristics of each area, implies a risk for survival, in view of the absence of alternatives, of other areas to move to or other resources to exploit in the case of climatic disaster. La Mancha also presents, albeit to a lesser extent, a risky climate for an agricultural economy [Martín *et al.* 1993: 31]: it has a semi-arid continental Mediterranean climatic regime, with annual precipitations of 350 to 450 mm, concentrated in the winter, and strong seasonal contrasts in temperature. It would thus seem that we can apply Cherry's (1990: 201) observation, "that to these regions the absence of settlement in the 'hunting-gathering' phases seems more the result of voluntary avoidance than lack of knowledge or inability to establish it."

But it is precisely the attachment of villagers to their means of production that distinguishes the subsistence farming way of life from that of the hunter-gatherer: the land ceases to be conceived of as an object of labour and becomes a means of production (Vicent 1990: 271). This means that, once this process began in the Late Neolithic (when the archaeological record indicates that livestock raising and crop growing became established), the land became an essential element for the survival of human communities, despite the fact that commitment to the particular area that furnished the necessary means of production might eventually become the main source of concern of any community, should it be threatened. Undoubtedly the well-watered continental areas (in the climatic and geographical sense of the word) felt this risk to a much lesser extent. On one hand, the investments in energy to obtain a satisfactory output were much less costly, which means, on the other, that attachment to the land takes on different characteristics in continental regions than it does in arid regions. In this respect, both arid southeast Spain and the islands are high risk regions, the latter because their territory is intrinsically limited and cannot be extended, and the former because of its unfavorable climatological conditions and a shortage of arable land (see above). Once again, La Mancha may also be seen as an area that is risky for farmers (see above), although to a lesser extent than either Sardinia or southeast Spain.

Thus, it would be expected that in these regions, the attachment of a group to the land would be a matter of life and death and territory would be strongly delineated. As Vincent (1990: 284–85) points out:

> the archaeological phenomenon most clearly related with the institutionalization

of the permanent appropriation of the means of production is the beginning of permanent funerary practices, except in a system in which the figure of the 'ancestor' is important for regulating access to the means of production, funerary practices can only be sporadic. The turning point is, therefore, the formation of funerary traditions, rather than the mere fact that burials occurred.

As we have seen, this is the first feature which stands out both in the Sardinian sequence and in southeast Spain: firstly in the form of the *domus de janas* and other types of tomb belonging to the Ozieri Culture which have always been the features of the Late Neolithic which have attracted most attention, and secondly, in the case of what is referred to as Almerian Culture, which is defined almost exclusively in terms of its funerary types. However, the beginning of the burial tradition always manifests itself in collective tombs which, according to the ideas of Criado (1989) on megaliths, imply not a display of death but rather the concealment of the dead. In other words, it is not the individual that is important in this society, but the ancestor, the dead person belonging to the other world of the dead. The legitimacy of appropriation of the land derives, basically, from continuity of occupation, so it does not matter precisely which individual is buried, but which particular group is buried. Again, according to Vicent, "collective burial is, by its nature, a result of long-term occupation of a region by part of a group of descendants" (1990: 285–86) whose investment in the land will presumably be greater the more competition there is to occupy that land. Undoubtedly, more stable settlements than those of earlier phases would similarly be expected.

During the first half of the third millennium both features were consolidated in the two regions although, as we saw at the beginning of this chapter, ritual activity in Sardinia and in the islands in general (e.g., the temples of Malta or the *taulas* of Menorca) seems even more intense than in the southeast of the Iberian peninsula. Thus, ritual activity in connection with the dead seems to constitute a fundamental factor in the social reproduction of these subsistence farmers, who were obliged to radically restructure their social and economic organization. Tombs came to be represented as houses of the ancestors, their places of residence, thus definitively tying the land to the lineages that exploited it.

Sardinia and Mallorca are islands with a risk-prone Mediterranean environment, which must have created competition for ownership of the land even more intense than that experienced in the Iberian peninsula. By 3000 BC this situation seems to be reflected in the archaeological record. However, as the new social and cultural order was established and accepted as inherent in the functioning of the competing groups, we may suppose that claims to land were no longer founded in ancestral legitimization, but in the actual balance of power established among the living. At this point, the investment of energy in building fortified settlements would make manifest the 'political map' of ownership within a region, as we have seen in the Bronze Age of La Mancha. Thus we see that towards 2500 BC, when the building of collective tombs reached its apogee and began to decline, walled settlements began to appear.

In the second half of the third millennium BC (or even earlier in some areas) the investment of labour in settlements continued to increase. The inhabitants of the open settlement of Son Ferrandell Oleza – Old Site (SFO-OS) (Valldemosa, Mallorca), for example, built a rectangular enclosure which included, among other structures, a water reservoir adjoining the outside of the enclosure, which, by means of an elaborate stone channel, brought water to the inhabitants of the village (Waldren 1984) who raised stock and grew crops in the area. Both in Los Millares (Santa Fe de Mondújar, Almería), and in the Cerro de la Virgen (Orce, Granada), similar channels are recorded for the same period, which would seem to confirm the increasing investment in the land from which social groups derived their sustenance. In fact, Waldren considers that the SFO-OS wall would not have been used for defensive purposes, in view of the characteristics of its construction, but rather that it would have constituted a declaration of the 'the investment of capital' expressed in the organization and construction of permanent areas of operation, in the control of resources such as water and land, and in activities such as the raising of stock. The continuous occupation of the site for six hundred years would seem to testify to the consolidation of the new order. (In La Mancha the long continuous occupation of *morras*, *motillas* and *castillejos* is indicative of the same pattern [Martín *et al.* 1993: 40]).

The relations of power between the various communities would seem then to be represented in the fortifications which now appeared in all the regions discussed. They gradually became more complex, until they became as effective as those of the Argaric villages, the Sardinian *nuraghi*, the Corsican *torri* or the villages of La Mancha (where the 'motillas' are reminiscent of the Sardinian constructions).

It is argued that, from approximately 1800 BC in the three regions discussed, competition between groups of subsistence farmers struggling for survival led to the construction of sophisticated settlement buildings, which usually included tombs of individuals whose wealth demonstrates the emergence of economically differentiated classes. The dead now represent one more stage in the life of the living, and maintain the characteristics of the latter in real life. In contrast with the past, a distinction no longer exists between the two worlds, since the fundamental conflict now occurs between individuals and not between social groups. For this reason, in Spain the abandonment of most of these fortified settlements at the end of the Middle Bronze Age (about 1300 BC) could well be explained by the consolidation of control over persons and resources by the emergent elite (Martín *et al.* 1993: 41): once the relations of power were firmly established, the large and costly defensive emplacements were no longer required and were replaced by more convenient, but archaeologically less visible, living places.

Finally, it should be remembered that in the Tagus estuary of Portugal, in southern France and also in the greater part of Italy, a somewhat similar initial development would seem to occur in less competitive conditions than those displayed in the areas we have discussed. These are regions that are much more favourable for agriculture and where there is less pressure for space. It would therefore seem unwise to use phenomena such as emigration or colonization to explain the similarities in the lifeways of early subsistence farmers in the islands of the western Mediterranean and southeast Spain. These similarities were generated as responses to the heightened risks for such a way of life that these regions had in common.

In this respect, Chapman's timely observations (1990: 260–62) should also be remembered. On one hand, the winds of the Mediterranean meant that the best route between two points was not always the shortest; in fact it is easier to reach the southeast of Spain by sailing along the coast from Sardinia than by sailing directly. On the other hand, Sardinia is not visibly connected with the Balearic islands, and therefore even less so with the Iberian peninsula, which reduces the chance that 'temptations to colonize' might have arisen amongst their inhabitants.

Conclusion

To sum up, it can be said that the tripartite sequence suggested by Trump (1984) for the cultural development of Sardinia could also be applied to the arid southeast of Iberia or to the La Mancha area, but interpreted in a new way: 1) a hunting-gathering way of life (into which animal and plant domesticates had been incorporated without a substantial transformation of the socio-economic organization) prior to the development of the Ozieri Culture in Sardinia, the Almerian Culture in the southeast and at an indeterminate point, but which would be around the fourth millennium, in La Mancha; the beginning of a subsistence farming way of life in all the 'cultures' traditionally included in the Late Neolithic and the Chalcolithic (which would correspond with the pre-Nuraghic, pre-Talayotic phase, etc.); and consolidation of the subsistence farming way of life with the beginning of class society in the Bronze Age in each of these regions.

Acknowledgments

I should like to thank J. M. Vicent and J. Lewthwaite for their helpful comments on the original draft of this paper. Any errors are the sole responsibility of the author.

Bibliography

Atzeni, E.

    1985   *Ichnussa: La Sardegna dalle Origini all'Età Classica*. Milan: Scheiwiller.

Chapman, R.

    1982   Autonomy, Ranking and Resources in Iberian Prehistory. In C. Renfrew and S. Shennan (eds), *Ranking, Resource and Exchange: Aspects of the Archaeology of Early European Society*, 46–51. Cambridge: Cambridge University Press.

    1984   Early metallurgy in Iberia and the Western Mediterranean. In W.H. Waldren, R. Chapman, J. Lewthwaite and R.C. Kennard (eds), *The Deya Conference of Prehistory: Early Settlement in the Western Mediterranean Islands and their Peripheral Areas*, 1139–61. British Archaeological Reports International Series 229. Oxford: British Archaeological Reports.

    1985   The Later Prehistory of Western Mediterranean Europe: Recent Advances. *Advances in World Archaeology* 4: 115–87.

    1990   *Emerging Complexity: The Later Prehistory of South-East Spain, Iberia and the West Mediterranean*. Cambridge: Cambridge University Press.

Cherry, J.F.

    1990   The First Colonization of the Mediterranean Islands: A Review of Recent Research. *Journal of Mediterranean Archaeology* 3: 145–221.

Criado, F.

    1989   Megalitos, Espacio, Pensamiento. *Trabajos de Prehistoria* 46: 75–98.

Galán Saulnier, C.

    1988   Los Enterramientos del Calcolítico y el Bronce Inicial de la Submeseta sur. In *Actas, I Congreso de Historia de Castilla-La Mancha*, 2: 193–97. Toledo: Junta de Comunidades de Castilla-La Mancha.

Gilman, A.

    1987a El Análisis de Clase en la Prehistoria del Sureste. *Trabajos de Prehistoria* 44: 27–34.

    1987b Unequal Development in Copper Age Iberia. In E.M. Brumfiel and T.K. Earle (eds), *Specialization, Exchange and Complex Societies*, 22–29. Cambridge: Cambridge University Press.

Gilman, A., and J.B. Thornes

    1985   *Land Use and Prehistory in South-East Spain*. London: George Allen and Unwin.

Hernando, A.

    1988   Evolución Interna y Factores Ambientales en la Interpretación del Calcolítico del Sureste de la Península Ibérica: Una Revisión Crítica. Unpublished Ph.D. dissertation, Universidad Complutense.

Hernando, A., and J.M. Vicent

    1987   Una Aproximación Cuantitativa al Problema de la Intensificación Económica en el Calcolítico del Sureste de la Península Ibérica. In *El Origen de la Metalurgia en la Península Ibérica*, 23–39. Madrid: Instituto Universitario José Ortega y Gasset.

Leisner, G., and V. Leisner

    1943   *Die Megalithgräber der Iberischen Halbinsel*. I. *Der Süden*. Römisch-Germanische Forschungen 17. Berlin: Walter de Gruyter.

Lewthwaite, J.

    1986   Nuraghic Foundations: An Alternate Model of Development in Sardinian Prehistory, ca. 2500–1500 B.C. In M.S. Balmuth (ed.), *Studies in Sardinian Archaeology II: Sardinia in the Mediterranean*, 19–37. Ann Arbor: University of Michigan Press.

Martín, C., M. Fernández-Miranda, M.D. Fernández-Posse and A. Gilman

    1993   The Bronze Age of La Mancha. *Antiquity* 67: 23–45.

Martínez Navarrete, M.I.

1988   Morras, Motillas y Castillejos: ¿Unidad o Pluralidad Cultural Durante la Edad del Bronce de la Mancha? In *Homenaje a Samuel de los Santos*, 81–92. Albacete: Instituto de Estudios Albacetenses.

Mathers, C.

1984a   Linear Regression, Inflation and Prestige Competition: 2nd Millenium Transformations in Southeast Spain. In W.H. Waldren, R. Chapman, J. Lewthwaite and R.C. Kennard (eds), *The Deya Conference of Prehistory: Early Settlement in the Western Mediterranean Islands and Their Peripheral Areas*, 1167–96. British Archaeological Reports International Series 229. Oxford: British Archaeological Reports.

1984b   Beyond the Grave: the Context and Wider Implications of Mortuary Practices in Southeastern Spain. In T.F.C. Blagg, R.F.J. Jones and S.J. Keay (eds), *Papers in Iberian Archaeology*, 13–44. British Archaeological Reports International Series 193. Oxford: British Archaeological Reports.

Molina, F.

1988   El Calcolítico en la Península Ibérica: el Sudeste. *Rassegna di Archeologia* 7: 255–62.

Nájera Colino, T.

1984   *La Edad del Bronce en la Mancha occidental.* Tesis Doctorales de la Universidad de Granada

458. Granada: Universidad de Granada.

Tiné, S., and A. Traverso

1992   Relazione Preliminare. In V. Tiné and A. Traverso (eds), *Monte d'Accoddi: 10 Anni di Nuovi Scavi*, iv–xl. Genoa: Istituto Italiano di Archeologia Sperimentale.

Trump, D.

1984   The Bonu Ighinu Project: Results and Prospects. In: W.H. Waldren, R. Chapman, J. Lewthwaite and R.C. Kennard (eds), *The Deya Conference of Prehistory: Early Settlement in the Western Mediterranean Islands and their Peripheral Areas*, 511–32. British Archaeological Reports International Series 229. Oxford: British Archaeological Reports.

Vicent, J.M.

1990   El Neolítico: Transformaciones Sociales y Económicas. In J. Anfuns and E. Llobet (eds), *El Canvi Cultural a la Prehistòria*, 241–93. Barcelona: Columna.

Waldren, W.H.

1984   Chalcolithic Settlement and Beaker Connections in the Balearic Islands. In: W.H. Waldren, R. Chapman, J. Lewthwaite and R.C. Kennard (eds), *The Deya Conference of Prehistory: Early Settlement in the Western Mediterranean Islands and their Peripheral Areas*, 911–65. British Archaeological Reports International Series 229. Oxford: British Archaeological Reports.

6. Aspects of Talayotic Culture

Manuel Fernández-Miranda

The Talayotic Culture developed in the islands of Mallorca and Menorca (Balearic Islands, Spain, Figure 6.1) from the middle of the second millennium BC to about the turn of the era, when the islands became fully and effectively Roman. The name derives from the Catalan word for a particular kind of tower construction, the *talayot* (watchtower), that is supposed to characterize the architecture of the islands throughout the period in question. The term presents some difficulties, however, since there are a variety of structures of differing types and functions that are called by this name, and a number of other types of structures, both domestic, habitational and funerary, were probably also in use during that time.

The term 'Talayotic Culture' is used on both Mallorca and Menorca, but this should not lead one to the mistaken supposition that there were homogeneous, synchronic, and archaeologically similar cultural developments on both islands. Current research makes it clear that the two islands were quite different, both in the contents of their material cultures and in the processes of change which each underwent. There are, nevertheless similarities between Mallorca and Menorca, and there is no doubt that, unlike their relationship to neighbouring Ibiza, the two islands clearly maintained close mutual ties. It may be concluded, in other words, that there was a certain degree of shared identity between Mallorca and Menorca in spite of their differences, some of which may be the result more of the contrasting research that has been carried out on each island than of their particular histories.

For reasons at times reinforced by chronological and other arguments, the Talayotic Culture has been linked not infrequently with the Nuraghic Culture of Sardinia and the Torrean Culture of Corsica. Undoubtedly, a preliminary, or superficial, analysis may make it seem that these are all interrelated phenomena, but in reality, there is little that is similar between them beyond a partial (albeit prolonged) degree of synchrony and a common propensity for building towers (something that, as well may be understood, inevitably occurs for exclusively external reasons). Apart from these two traits, there is no other realistic point of comparison other than those elements that are common to the entire western Mediterranean area and that, in various specific forms, repeat themselves over all of the last millennium throughout the region (such as, for example, certain bull cults, or the exchange of particular luxury or prestige goods).

The beginning of the Talayotic Culture in Mallorca (the island that, for the moment, has the most complete radiocarbon record) is datable to the fourteenth century BC on the basis of uncalibrated radiocarbon dates, which correspond approximately to the middle of the sixteenth century BC in a (QL system) calibrated chronology.

The latest date comes from an isolated *talayot* at Pula (Son Servera) which places the abandonment of its chamber there at 3260±60 BP (P-1404: 3260±60 BP) (Locations of sites in Mallorca are indicated in Figure 6.1). *Talayot*-type ceramics appear in the stratigraphies of the rock-shelter of Son Matge (Valldemossa) at about 1250 bc, likewise based on an uncalibrated radiocarbon determination (Y-2667: 3200±100 BP), and of the settlement of S'Illot in 1130 BC (HV-1715: 3080±75 BP), the latter, as at Pula, being a *talayot* in use (all these dates are based on charcoal samples). This means that it seems most likely that the construction of the first *talayots* in Mallorca occurred around these dates, which in a calibrated radiocarbon chronology would mean the second half of the sixteenth century BC, a period rather more recent than that proposed for the origins of *torri* and *nuraghi* in Corsica and Sardinia. As we shall see later, in the case of Menorca the earliest dates calculated for *talayots* do not display the same antiquity as those in Mallorca.

The appearance of Talayotic architecture involves an innovation with respect to some of the structural types (in particular the *talayot* itself), but not with respect to the technology of construction (which has clear precedents in earlier periods) or the settlement patterns that can be inferred from a geographic analysis of the habitat. Thus one may propose, at least as a hypothesis, a clear continuity in which the

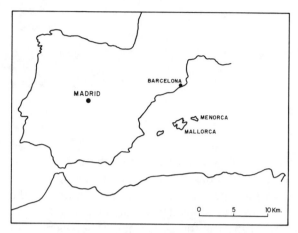

Figure 6.1   Location of Mallorca and Menorca in the western Mediterranean.

appearance of a new architectural type would be nothing other than a consequence of changes which, at least at first, can be seen with little clarity with respect to causes, but with greater precision with respect to consequences.

The pre-Talayotic Period

Both in Mallorca and in Menorca, the term 'Pre-Talayotic Culture' refers to archaeological manifestations which immediately precede the *talayots* in time but are later than groups with Beaker pottery. In Mallorca they are dated between 1670 and 1400 bc, using an uncalibrated radiocarbon chronology, although one may suppose that they have a somewhat older origin and that they are probably linked with settlements characterized by artefacts of Beaker typology. The dwelling place of this period is the habitational *naveta*, a long structure with an apse at one end and an entrance at the other. These are fairly similar, and not just in formal terms, to the *Fontbouisse*-type huts of the Chalcolithic of southern France. These *navetas* occur singly, in pairs or in threes, and sometimes form small groups of two or three units, but they never constitute whole villages of any great size. The only exception is Bóquer (Pollença), but this is a survival which is dated considerably later than the period to which I am referring.

The distribution of habitational *navetas* seems to indicate the existence of small population centres in which a few families lived, each of them occupying living spaces which rarely exceeded 50 m². Although several of these constructions have been excavated, in one case only it has been possible to ascertain their internal arrangements without problems posed by super-

positions or looting prior to the excavation. In this case, the *naveta* of Alemany in Magaluf (Calviá), there was an interior living space of about 70 m², making it the largest *naveta* known (Enseñat 1971). Its function as a domestic establishment seems clear: it had a hearth in the middle, stone querns, and a considerable amount of pottery for daily use, some utilized as a table service and others as storage receptacles.

In Menorca there are two well-excavated sites of the same type: Son Mercer de Baix and Clariana. Son Mercer de Baix (Rita *et al.* 1987) consists of two main *navetas* as well as other, complementary structures, one of them a small copper-smelting workshop. The whole site, including the open spaces between the buildings, covers some 3000 m², which suggests it was a small village with two habitational units with an interior area of about 30 m² apiece. At Clariana (Plantalamor 1975, Plantalamor and Anglada 1978) two *naveta*-type structures were also identified, one close to the other. The *navetas* were possibly associated with other buildings, but the continuous use of the site in subsequent periods and the absence of an extensive area excavation make it difficult to be sure. The better-preserved *naveta* at Clariana has a usable internal area of about 35 m².

The spatial distribution of the Menorcan *navetas* indicates an intelligent exploitation of natural resources (Locations of sites in Menorca are indicated in Figure 6.2). The sites are near ravines or other places where it would be possible to obtain drinking water. The faunal remains found at Son Mercer de Baix indicate a food-procurement strategy based on the exploitation of sheep and goats, with a considerable amount of pigs. No signs of agriculture were found, but some querns and a number of storage vessels may provisionally be considered indirect evidence of its existence.

The excavations carried out in recent years at Torralba d'en Salort (Alaior) have contributed some facts that help us better understand the origins of the Talayotic Culture of Menorca. The earliest construction on the site is a hut with Pre-Talayotic pottery dated to the end of the second millennium. This hut was subsequently used as the base for the construction of a *talayot*, which in turn fell into ruins some centuries later, not long before the construction of a *taula* precinct at the site. This stratigraphy, partly vertical and partly horizontal, is confirmed by radiocarbon dates and permits one to analyze the evolution of a Talayotic settlement from its origins until well into the Romanization of the island.

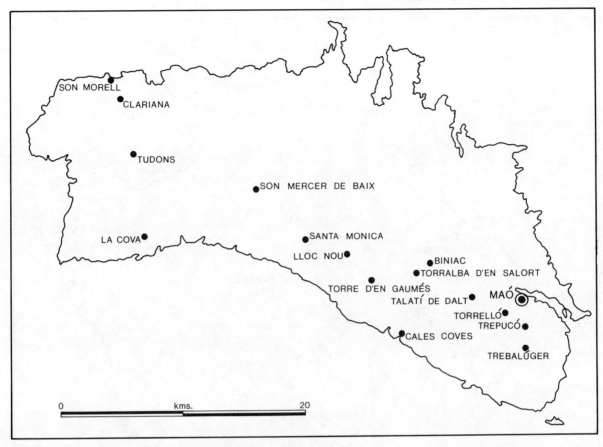

Figure 6.2   Location of the principal Talayotic sites on Menorca.

The pre-Talayotic hut at Torralba d'en Salort has a more or less oval floor plan, with a usable interior space of about 20 m² and a probable doorway oriented to the north-west. Of the pottery recovered from the hut the most interesting item was a storage vessel containing carbonized grain. Most of the grain consisted of barley (39% hulled, 33% naked) with just 4% being wheat (*Triticum dicoccum*); 24% consisted of uncultivated barley that can be gathered as fodder for livestock. Faunal remains with a predominance of ovicaprids were also recovered. Three radiocarbon samples of charcoal, ovicaprid bones, and barley provided dates for the occupation of 2970±70 BP (QL-1433A), 3020±60 BP (QL-1433B), and 3030±90 BP (QL-1433C), respectively, using the Libby half-life. The combined calibration of these three determinations using the QL system suggests a 55% probability that date falls between 3268 and 3200 BP (that is to say, the first half of the thirteenth century BC).

The *talayot* was erected on top of the ruined hut after 2860±54 BP (BM-1697), the end of the tenth century in uncalibrated terms. This was obtained from a layer in which the hut was torn down to form a kind of fill to prepare the site for the erection of the *talayot*. This date is confirmed by radiocarbon samples obtained in a nearby stratigraphic sequence which permits us to observe the first remodelling of the village. This renovation was also characterized precisely by the destruction of some pre-Talayotic huts in order to build the above-mentioned *talayot*.

Another site that provides interesting information about the origins of the Talayotic Culture in Menorca is Trebalúger (Es Castell), which is as yet unpublished, but about which I have some information thanks to the kindness of the excavator, Plantalamor, with whom I had the opportunity to visit the site. Two architectural structures were discovered at Trebalúger, the older dating to the pre-Talayotic, the younger to the Early Talayotic. The so-called *talayot* of Trebalúger is, in fact, a natural elevation that rises a little above the surrounding arable land. The hill is defended by a wall with a surface similar to those of *talayots*, but which does not strictly speaking, constitute a tower. The site is interesting because it permits us to demonstrate continuity of settlement at a single locality, but with clear differences in the size of the occupation in the successive periods, the pre-Talayotic settlement being much smaller (no more than one or two huts in all) than its successor.

Other Menorcan localities confirm the continuity of settlement between the two periods. A

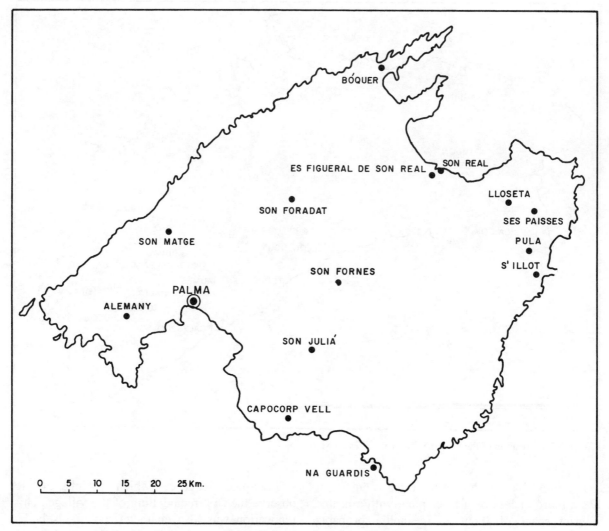

Figure 6.3   Location of the principal Talayotic sites on Mallorca.

typical example is Lloc Nou d'es Fasser (Alaior). This is a small hamlet that is also surrounded by good arable land. Its *talayot*, around which some other buildings are erected, was built upon an earlier edifice, perhaps an oval hut like that of Torralba, and the layout of the *talayot* is influenced by its predecessor. At the settlement of Santa Mónica (Es Migjorn Gran) one can also see how the remains of a habitational *naveta* serve as part of the foundations for a building of the Talayotic period.

On the island of Mallorca the transition from the pre-Talayotic period to the Talayotic period is also documented at a number of settlements where buildings of the domestic *naveta* type serve either as foundations for later structures, as at Son Juliá (Llucmajor), or remain in use during the Early Talayotic, as at Es Figueral de Son Real (Santa Margalida). The absolute chronology suggests the existence of a 400 year transitional period between the earliest dates for the first *talayots* and the final abandonment of the last

navetas. This confirms the idea of a progressive replacement of architectural types and at the same time contradicts the hypothesis that the *talayot* appeared as a consequence of an abrupt transformation in the indigenous society which would have led inevitably to the adoption of the new type of structure as a matter of urgent necessity.

Clear evidence that this change involved a slow process of transformation is found at Es Figueral de Son Real (Rosselló Bordoy and Camps Coll 1972), a group of *navetas* which constituted a small village in the northern part of Mallorca. One of these was still in use at the end of the eleventh century (Y-1856: 2960±120 BP) and was abandoned 40 years later (Y-1857: 2920±80 BP), with both dates coming from archaeological levels associated with Talayotic ceramics. There are some *talayots* near the *navetas* which controlled a nearby ravine and a level area suitable for herding livestock. The *talayots* do not constitute a homogenous, integrated settlement, but rather are individual settlement units that happened to be close to one another: this pattern of settlement probably typifies the beginning of the Talayotic period. The above-mentioned case of Pula shows the same distribution, and the subsequent origin of a relatively extended settlement from a *talayot* with some adjoining rooms can likewise be observed at Son Fornés (Montuiri), during a phase earlier than the growth and remodelling of the first area of occupation (Gasull *et al.* 1984).

The Talayotic Period

On both Mallorca and Menorca it seems clear that the first *talayots* followed the same settlement pattern that characterized the preceding phase (Fernández-Miranda 1991). Setting aside those cases in which use of *navetas* persisted, the *talayot* with a few roughly quadrangular houses built against it constitutes a small village-type occupational unit apparently similar to those of pre-Talayotic times. There was, however, one difference which must be taken into account. The construction of a *talayot* involves a much greater effort, no doubt of a collective nature, that was furthermore intended to erect a building that was

not used as a dwelling place (as at Torrelló, Plate 6.4). Such an enterprise requires that one have available a certain number of individuals who would live next to or near the *talayot*, who would share certain interests, and who would build it either as a symbol of their possession of a particular territory or as a centre for observation and for the protection of the group. This process of settlement nucleation can be seen, for example, in the cases of Clariana in Menorca and Es Figueral de Son Real in Mallorca, but it is not so clear at Son Mercer de Baix or in many cases where there is no break from the phase characterized by *navetas* (e.g., the above-mentioned case of Alemany). It is apparent that certain conditions determined the subsequent development of pre-Talayotic occupations, with some of them remaining in use, and others being abandoned. Perhaps the explanation should be sought in the capacity of the local environment to support the subsistence needs of an appreciably increasing population.

We have little information about the subsistence strategies of the Early Talayotic. The archaeological record suggests a predominance of livestock keeping, but it is also apparent that evidence of this is detected more easily than evidence of plant cultivation as a result of

taphonomic factors. All the same, an analysis of the environment in which sites are located (not only the first Talayotic villages, but also the larger settlements of later times, such as Torre d'en Gaumés in Menorca or Capocorp Vell in Mallorca) suggests a predominately livestock-oriented economy, supplemented by dry farming. Only in a few cases can we suppose that a form of agriculture involving irrigation was practised: the inhabitants of Torralba d'en Salort in Menorca, for example, may have watered the plain of a small valley using a natural spring at the valley's head.

Much of Mallorca and Menorca is not suitable for agriculture, so that a subsistence pattern based on livestock-keeping may have constituted the base of economic development over the course of the pre-Talayotic and the Early Talayotic periods. In such a setting communities consisting of a small number of individuals could have made a good living on the basis of livestock, the gathering of some uncultivated products, and perhaps some incipient dry farming. The distribution of pre-Talayotic hamlets in Mallorca and Menorca suggests, furthermore, that the population density was low, so that conflicts between neighbors must have been practically nonexistent. In such a setting it is perfectly feasible that a process of transformation could have developed which gave rise to the appearance of the Talayotic Culture without any need for outside influences or abrupt social changes.

Whatever the timing and circumstance of its origin on each island, the Talayotic Culture unfolds over the course of the first millennium until it is overtaken by the Roman occupation. Romanization gradually brings about the decline of the native culture, although cultural elements of indigenous character persist for some time as is demonstrated, for example, by the names cited in Roman funerary epigraphy in Mallorca (Veny 1965). Throughout this period the native culture goes through transformations due in part to its own internal dynamic, but also to the growing influence of external elements, particularly towards the middle of the millennium. All the same, the image of Talayotic Culture is that of societies which are fairly closed, because the area does not display the culture as a uniform entity but rather it is manifested slightly differently on each of the islands of Menorca and Mallorca.

Various factors, both internal and external, suggest that the Talayotic Culture in Mallorca should be divided into two major periods (Fernández-Miranda 1978): these are differentiated by funerary rites, by the greater concentration of population in certain settlements, by the increase of external cultural influences, and by the appearance of iron metallurgy. On Menorca there is less evidence on which to base a judgment, but a two phase division can also be proposed, taking into account that neither the timing of the two phases on the two islands nor the factors which bring about their development need coincide.

On Mallorca as much as on Menorca it seems certain that use of an isolated *talayot* with adjoining rooms is the mark of the primary architectural model at the beginning of the Talayotic period. Gradually these simple units incorporate additional elements until they form, over the course of the Early Talayotic, groupings of considerable importance that undergo substantial spatial remodelling. The abandonment of the *navetas and* the houses that are refurbished at Ses Paisses at around 950 bc (Gif-1247: 2900±110 BP) are proof of this process, and which involved a significant increase in settlement size that continued until around 800 bc.

The stratigraphy at Son Matge clearly reflects a change in funerary ritual beginning in the eighth century BC, a change which constitutes one of the clearest markers to date of the two phases in the development of the Mallorcan Talayotic Culture (Fernández-Miranda and Waldren 1979). Simple inhumations (the characteristic form of what few burials there are in the Early Talayotic) are replaced by a collective burial ritual with lime. This involves the cremation of the corpses to a certain degree and the subsequent collection of the bones which are then arranged in an apparently disorganized manner, inside natural and or partially modified caves. It may be that the first walled settlements made their appearance at this time (although as yet we lack completely convincing proof of this). This would imply an increase in the number of people living in one place and a corresponding reorganization of the territories of economic exploitation. At the above-mentioned site of Son Fornés this process is well documented at a slightly later time: the initial *talayot* with its adjoining room is supplemented by new buildings which stay in use until the sixth century BC.

The available evidence for Menorca largely confirms this pattern, but with some peculiarities. At the settlement of Torralba d'en Salort the *talayot* built on top of the pre-Talayotic hut falls into ruin in about 600 bc, as is demonstrated by some fragments of Ionic pottery found in the destruction levels of the building. This area of the settlement is remodelled, and years later the *taula* precinct is built. That precinct is the centre of a large walled settlement that is in full operation in the fourth century BC. The central and prominent placement of the *taula* precinct can also be seen at localities like Torre d'en Gaumés, Talatí de Dalt, Trepucó, and others. As in Mallorca, the concentration of the population is apparent, although use of small installations which are dependent on the main sites and whose functions are not well defined in all cases continues. On occasion these medium-sized and small sites seem to be located in areas that are particularly suitable for farming, but others give the impression that they also served as points of control and observation in relation to the larger, more important centres.

Studies of the funerary structures on Menorca yield good information about the evolution of the Talayotic Culture. In the late pre-Talayotic period and throughout the early phase of the Talayotic, the prevailing burial pattern is a collective one in structures that, because of their shape, have also been termed *navetas*. These stand alone and are dispersed throughout the island. From a chronological point view they replace the dolmens and the elongated artificial caves (rock-cut tombs) that characterized the funerary ritual during the height of the pre-Talayotic. The *navetas* are collective ossuaries into which secondary inhumations were placed in no apparent order. The number of burials must often have been more than a hundred individuals.

The excavation of the *naveta* of La Cova has permitted Veny (1982a) to determine the chronology of the structures with considerable precisionse. Its lower level was dated to the late pre-Talayotic period by the pottery which formed part of the grave goods, the decorative types and vessel shapes being very similar to those found in the hut at Torralba d'en Salort. The suceeding level contained Talayotic ceramics, in some cases with decorative elements similar to the types that are considered to be the earliest in the group of burials attributed to the later phase of the culture. This means that these collective tombs were in use until the eighth to seventh centuries BC, when the use of the more recent Talayotic necropoli began.

The burial *navetas* are generally located at a certain distance from settlements. One has the impression that each village was formed by a small group of families which slowly became more numerous from the time of the *navetas* to

that of the *talayots* and which used the same *naveta* as a burial place for a fairly long time. If this were confirmed, it would constitute good proof of the existence of strong kinship ties between settlements, to the extent that a single *naveta* could equally well have been used by more than one of the villages that were close to one another; this would have been an egalitarian society, at least with respect to funerary ritual. The communal character of the construction is indisputable, above all in the most prominent architectural examples, such as the well-known Nau d'es Tudons (Ciutadella). Likewise, it could be suggested that population increase in a particular territory would sometimes provoke the partition of this basic kinship tie and would give rise to the appearance of a second burial *naveta* near an already existing one, as in the cases found at Biniac-L'Argentina (Alaior). The demographic increase reflected in the funerary structures would be equivalent to that which can be plausibly inferred in cases where the first *talayots* are built singly but near to one another, as well as in cases where rooms are gradually added on to the fortified nucleus.

About the eighth and seventh centuries BC the Menorcan burial *navetas* are replaced by a new funerary ritual: corpses are deposited in natural, partially modified or completely artificial caves on the sides of ravines or sea cliffs, the caves sometimes being found in groups of considerable size. In other words, ritual use of an isolated mausoleum, isolated and clearly visible in the landscape, is substituted by large necropoli in places chosen deliberately for discretion. An individual social unit may, however, continue to share a common burial in one particular cave within the cemetery group. The best known necropolis of this type is Cales Coves (Veny 1982b), which was in use from about 800–600 bc until the time of the Roman Republic.

The necropolis of Cales Coves, from which nearly a hundred burial caves are known, has no large settlement in its vicinity, although there are some small- and medium-sized occupations within a few kilometres. The same occurs in other cases where a considerable number of tombs are concentrated, as at Son Morell (Ciudatella). In contrast, smaller tomb groupings are found close to settlements. The large tomb concentrations must have been used by several different settlements, perhaps by individuals with differing status, given that some of the artificial caves exhibit a monumentality which would seem to reflect social distinctions. This feature is not found in Mallorca, where groups of large tombs are unknown in the Late Talayotic until Roman funerary patterns are introduced. The exception is the necropolis of Son Real (Tarradell 1964), which seems to have been a cemetery reserved for persons of outstanding social importance, at least at the beginning.

The external relations of the Talayotic Culture are problematic and need to be better understood. The archaeological record suggests that the society was fairly isolated, with outside contacts that seem to have been neither frequent nor intense, at least throughout the Early Talayotic phase. This does not mean, of course, that such contacts did not exist, because some technological changes, particularly those observed in certain metallurgical processes, indicate outside links. All the same, what we might term the domestic inventory of the Talayotic reflects scant foreign influence. Only broad similarities can be observed, such as the fact of building *talayots* in the first place (if their general form is considered the result of relations with other western Mediterranean islands).

An important element of the earliest Talayotic is the bronze sword of Son Matge type, dated at that site to the thirteenth century BC (Delibes and Fernández-Miranda 1988). Some examples are known from Mallorca, occasionally forming part of hoard-like caches. From a technological point of view, these pieces mark the consolidation of bronze metallurgy on the island, since the majority of metal pieces dated to the pre-Talayotic period are made of copper. The swords also reflect the introduction of certain kinds of metallurgical know-how, such as the 'casting on' process, that would be difficult to arrive at by simple experimentation. On the islands there are, furthermore, no tin sources, so that the use of this metal in alloys necessarily implies that it has been imported.

From a typological point of view, Talayotic swords on Mallorca seem to be inspired by Central European types which may have reached the central Mediterranean by way of northern Italy. They clearly have no similarity to the western sword types which were prevalent at this time in the Iberian peninsula. From a functional perspective, these weapons, like the necklaces and pectorals which appear in hoards such as those of Son Foradat or Lloseta, seem to indicate the emergence of groups or individuals that were socially differentiated, since a detailed analysis tends to suggest they were more objects of personal prestige than weapons to be used in the literal sense of the term.

It is apparent that, over the course of the development of Talayotic Culture, Mallorca and Menorca underwent a process of increasing social complexity. The import of prestige metal goods, no doubt technologically reproduced on Mallorca, is an argument in favour of this. So too is the construction on Menorca of funerary *navetas* of considerable size, which implies a significant concentration of the work force, and the progressive increase in the number of domestic structures in the vicinity of one or more *talayots*. This increase was based on a livestock-oriented economy that was probably developed to the fullest. The analysis of the faunal remains recovered at Son Fornés (Gasull *et al.* 1984: 83) suggests a farmstead type of agrarian economy based on a mixed flock that would guarantee dietary stability, but would also provide other goods and services such as milk, wool traction etc. The concentration of people would necessitate an increase in the size of the herds, which would in the end create conflict between the main settlements, with all the consequences that such a situation implies. One must, however, take into account the capacity of the Balearic environment to support a relatively large population using minimum technology. This is demonstrated in historical times up until the eighteenth century bc and can be seen in earlier periods, to judge by the large number of settlements that belong to the final phase of the Talayotic Culture and must be broadly contemporaneous.

From the eighth century bc on there are appreciable changes both in the funerary rites (which we have already mentioned) and in the internal organization of settlements. Over the course of a couple of centuries the structure of the settlements undergoes modifications in two respects: new domestic units are added to existing ones, and the distribution begins to change. This new model lasts into the Roman period with different responses at particular localities to the conditions first of the conquest, then of the process of acculturation. The new model does not involve a regulated urban system, since the various buildings are placed next to one another without any apparent plan. In some cases it appears that population increase leads to the progressive adding on of dwellings, but one of the occupational areas at Torre d'en Gaumés in Menorca, for example, shows a regular distribution of houses, so-called 'circles' because of their external appearance, consisting of several rooms arranged around a *compluvium* of modest size. In other cases, such as Capocorp Vell in Mallorca, various rooms are placed following along principal axis of construction. At some sites, such as Ses Paisses (Artá) in Mallorca, there seem to be separate habitational units that form part of a single walled settlement. The most distinctive characteristic, however, is the appearance of the concept of a central place in the interior of the settlement, a feature which is common in Menorca. The *taula* and its precinct is built near the centre of settlements, sometimes taking advantage of a place slightly higher than the surrounding area; the precinct is accompanied by a *talayot* with its adjoining rooms and by some other public building, such as the hypostyle hall at Torralba d'en Salort. On the basis of the information obtained in the only excavation to date in one of these central areas (Fernández-Miranda *et al.* 1980), it is tempting to suggest that this arrangement bears witness to the existence of a hierarchical society, in which the *talayot* with adjoining houses would be the place of residence and symbol of the chief; the *taula* precinct obviously would be the area devoted to religious worship and offerings; and the hypostyle hall would be a communal storehouse for surplus production.

From the fifth century on contacts with the outside world increase appreciably, particularly commercial relations with Punic Ibiza, which according to various sources of evidence, reach their maximum intensity during the second century, prior to the Roman conquest. These contacts are marked in the archaeological record by the appearance of wheel-turned pottery and amphoras inside the native villages, but they do not involve the establishment of settlements inhabited by foreigners on the islands. In just a few cases the presence of foreigners can be detected some islets near the coast; one of these, Na Guardis south of Mallorca (Guerrero 1985), has a factory (sometimes erroneously called a 'colony') devoted to commerce and metal smelting. In other cases, Cales Coves in Menorca for example, what one sees is the continued, but temporary use of an anchorage site where boats paused during long-distance voyages.

These relations greatly influenced fairly intensely certain aspects of indigenous life, particularly those of religious character. Cults, rituals, and even representations of divinities are imported from Sicily, southern Italy, Ibiza, and perhaps other places. Examples of this include the so-called Balearic Mars figurines, the evidence of a symposium ritual carried out in the *taula* precincts, the imitations of fire altars, the offerings of dismembered animals, and so on. It is even possible that the remodelling of the interior arrangements of the settlements, with the place of worship situated in the centre, may also be a consequence of such outside influences, the principal carriers of which were probably returning Balearic mercenaries.

The Roman conquest of the islands at the end of the second century marks the beginning of the end of the Talayotic Culture. However, it appears that what took place was not a violent annihilation, but rather a slow process of acculturation which unfolded over more than a century and still had not been completed around the turn of the era, when there were still some survivals of Tayolitic Culture to be found. In both Mallorca and Menorca it is striking, for example, that the pattern of occupation and exploitation of the landscape barely underwent changes of importance as far as the native population was concerned. Of course, new cities were built in strategic locations, taking advantage of natural harbours, into which colonists brought from Iberia were installed, but life went on unchanged in many of the native settlements and no villas were established (with all that would have implied about the Romanization of territory). The persistence of Talayotic Culture is best seen in the continuity of funerary practices and use of places of worship. In the stratigraphy at Son Matge, for example, lime burials continue into Augustan times; at the necropolis of Son Real/Illa dels Porros, a radiocarbon date demonstrates that the site, half cemetery half sanctuary, was still in use in AD 100 (I-4524: 1850±95 BP). In Menorca the use of *taula* precincts as places of worship stops in some cases, but in others, Torralba d'en Salort for example, sacrifices continued to be made following the native rite until well after the turn of the era. It appears that some native settlements declined while others became fairly important enclaves within the system of Roman territorial occupation. At Torralba d'en Salort, this persistence might be explained by the fact the settlement was placed on the road that linked the two Roman cities on the island, Mahón and Ciutadella.

Bibliography

Delibes, G., and M. Fernández-Miranda

1988   *Armas y Utensilios de Bronce en la Prehistoria de las Islas Baleares*. Studia Archaeologica 78. Valladolid: Universidad de Valladolid.

Enseñat, C.

1971   Excavaciones en el Naviforme Alemany, Magaluf (Calviá, Mallorca). *Noticiario Arqueológico Hispánico* 15: 37–73.

Fernández-Miranda, M.

1978   *Secuencia Cultural de la Prehistoria de Mallorca.* Bibliotheca Praehistorica Hispana 15. Madrid: Consejo Superior de Investigaciones Científicas.

1991   La transición Hacia la Cultura Talayótica en Menorca. *Trabajos de Prehistoria* 48: 37–50.

Fernández-Miranda, M., P. Bueno, F. Piñón and A. Rodero

1980   Torralba d'en Salort (Alayor, Menorca): La Sala Hipóstila. *Noticiario Arqueológico Hispánico* 10: 137–82.

Fernández-Miranda, M., and W. Waldren

1979   Periodificación Cultural y Cronología Absoluta en la Prehistoria de Mallorca. *Trabajos de Prehistoria* 36: 349–77.

Flaquer, J.

1910   La Naveta de Cotayna. *Revista de Menorca* 5: 142–48.

Gasull, P., V. Lull, and M.E. Sanahuja

1984   *Son Fornés 1: La Fase Talayótica.* British Archaeological Reports International Series 209. Oxford: British Archaeological Reports.

Guerrero, V.

1985   *Indigenisme i Colonització Púnica a Mallorca.* Ses Salines: Ajuntament de Ses Salines.

Plantalamor, L.

1975   La Naveta de Clariana. *Mayurka* 14: 231–45.

Plantalamor, L., and J. Anglada

1978   Excavació a la Naveta d'Habitació de Clariana (Ciutadela, Menorca). *Fonaments* 1: 205–08.

Rita, M.C., L. Plantalamor and J. Murillo

1978   *Guía Arqueológica de la Zona de Son Mercer (Ferreries).* Maó: Consell Insular de Menorca.

Roselló Bordoy, G., and J. Camps Coll

1972   Excavaciones en el Complejo Noreste de 'Es Figueral de Son Real' (Santa Margarita, Mallorca). *Noticiario Arqueológico Hispánico, Prehistoria* 1: 109–76.

Tarradell, M.

1964   *La Necrópolis de Son Real y la Illa dels Porros, Mallorca.* Excavaciones Arqueológicas en España 24. Madrid: Ministerio de Educación Nacional.

Veny, C.

1965   *Corpus de las Inscripciones Baleáricas hasta la Dominación Árabe.* Rome: Consejo Superior de Investigaciones Científicas, Delegación de Roma.

1982a   La Naveta de la Cova. *Trabajos de Prehistoria* 39: 73–136.

1982b   *La Necrópolis Protohistórica de Cales Coves, Menorca.* Bibliotheca Praehistorica Hispana 20. Madrid: Consejo Superior de Investigaciones Científicas.

7.   Prehistoric Subsistence and Monuments in Mallorca

Robert Chapman and Annie Grant

The last two decades have witnessed a resurgence of interest in, and research on, the prehistoric cultures of Mediterranean islands. While the Minoan palaces of Crete, the neolithic 'temples' of Malta and the monuments of Sardinia (*nuraghi*), Corsica (*torri*) and the Balearic islands (*talayots*, *taulas*, and *navetas*) have been known to the archaeological world throughout this century, it is the earlier cultures of these and other islands which have been the foci of major discoveries through fieldwork in recent years. Such fieldwork, coupled with changing theoretical perspectives, has led to a comparative analysis of the earliest human colonization of Mediterranean islands using the conceptual framework of island biogeography (e.g. Cherry [1981, 1990] for seminal and synthetic papers; Shackleton, van Andel and Runnels [1984] for reconstruction of prehistoric coastlines; and, most recently, Broodbank and Strasser [1991] for the colonization of Crete). The pre-bronze age archaeological records of islands such as Sardinia (e.g. Trump 1984), Corsica (e.g. Lewthwaite 1983) and Mallorca (e.g. Waldren 1982) have been created largely by stratigraphic excavations since the 1960s, and the combination of cultural and economic data has provided the basis for discussion of issues such as the adoption of agriculture and the origins of social inequality (e.g. Lewthwaite 1981, 1982, 1983, 1985a, 1986, 1989).

For the second and first millennia BC cultures of the west Mediterranean islands, archaeological research has progressed at a less dramatic rate. Regional synthesis using monument typology remains the basis of much research (e.g. Camps 1988 for Corsica; Pericot 1972 and Rosselló 1973 for the Balearic islands). Analyses of settlement patterns using field survey are rarer (e.g. on the Marghine plateau in west-central Sardinia [Michels and Webster 1987]), as are reconstructions of social hierarchies from spatial patterning in settlement data (e.g. Lewthwaite 1985b for Mallorca) or from intra-site patterning in structural, artefactual and economic data (e.g.

Lanfranchi, cited in Lewthwaite [1984: 508], for Corsican *torri*; Webster [1988] for Sardinian *nuraghi*; Gasull *et al.* [1984a, 1984b, 1984c] for Mallorcan *talayots*), calculations of the costs of monument construction through time in relation to the available human labour (for Sardinia, see Webster 1991) and measurement of human interaction with the landscape as a consequence of the need to provide subsistence and an economic base for social mobilization and control in the second and first millennia BC (e.g. for economic data, the work of Vigne 1988 on animal exploitation on Corsica is exemplary and a long way from being equalled on the other west Mediterranean islands).

The occurrence of monuments of varying types, sizes and densities on west Mediterranean islands has been the basis for the inference of social stratification in the Bronze and Iron Ages. To understand the reasons why such complex societies emerged, we need to evaluate various general models which specify relationships between variables such as subsistence intensification, environmental change, social differentiation, scale, interaction and integration (for the cross-cultural relevance of these variables to such models, see discussion in Chapman [1990: 10–15]). The measurement of change in these variables in time and space should be central to research strategies. As Binford (1989: 36) has written, "to be productive, theories must be directed towards anticipating relationships among variables, and such relationships must be monitored by scientists." Furthermore, it must be remembered that it is the emergence of complexity in island ecosystems that is being studied and that the processes which promote similarities and differences between the cultures inhabiting such islands must be central to research. Hence it is argued that the theoretical perspective which has begun to structure research on island colonization in the Mediterranean should serve the same function for later periods of prehistory.

Fosberg (1963: 5) lists nine significant characteristics of island ecosystems:

1. relative isolation
2. size limitation
3. resource limitation
4. limited organic diversity
5. reduced interspecies competition
6. protection from outside competition, leading to the preservation of archaic, bizarre or ill-adapted forms
7. tendency to climatic equability
8. extreme vulnerability, and a tendency to instability when isolation is broken down,
9. tendency to rapid increase in entropy after change

Such characteristics are not invariable, as indeed islands are not invariable, but they indicate the problems posed for human societies in trying to colonize such ecosystems and maintain viable populations. These problems have been discussed elsewhere (e.g. Cherry 1981, 1990) and it may be safely predicted that the expansion of populations subsisting on agricultural systems will contribute to reduced variability (e.g. through clearance, extinction of indigenous fauna). But these problems did not continually result in failure and extinction for island populations. The comparative archaeological and anthropological record from the Mediterranean to Polynesia show many examples of cultural complexity, even reaching the level of state systems, and continuous occupation over thousands of years, while in other cases colonization was only a short-lived process.

This observation requires us to structure our research on island societies so that similarities and differences (e.g. in terms of complexity, formal characteristics such as monument construction, unique cultural forms, etc.) are understood in terms of long-term interaction between human populations and their island habitats. In their study of the evolution of Polynesian societies, Kirch and Green (1987: 440–43) have proposed five processes which led to divergence, and three processes which promoted convergence in human societies through time in this region. Leading to divergence were:

1. isolation
2. the founder effect (operating culturally and biologically)
3. colonization processes (behavioural and technological innovation as part of the process of successful colonization)
4. long-term environmental selection (e.g. the effects of deforestation, faunal depletion, erosion)
5. external contact.

Processes leading to convergence through time were:

6. demographic trends (initially high growth to enable successful colonization, then later on switching to density-dependent cultural controls on growth)
7. intensification of production (both as a response to selective pressures such as population growth and environmental circumscription, and as a product of social competition in a hierarchical system)
8. competition (between social groups, in the form of rivalry, territoriality, warfare, etc.).

To isolate such processes does not imply the determination of cultural evolution by nature, nor does it deny historical sequences specific to individual islands. Rather, a comparative approach to the analysis of island cultures serves as a heuristic device to structure research on long-term changes in the archaeological record and not just on the initial stages of colonization. For example, when did intensification of production take place, what form did it take, where did it occur, and what was its relationship to change in other variables, such as demography? At the same time, it has to be stressed that the theoretical framework proposed by Kirch and Green is not without its problems: for example, we find it difficult to understand why 'external contact' is included among processes leading to divergence rather than convergence in island societies.

As has been pointed out already, we know that more complex societies developed on Mediterranean islands several thousand years after their initial colonization. Such complexity varied from the state and urban forms of large, eastern islands such as Crete and Cyprus respectively, to the monument-building 'chiefdoms' of the west (e.g. Webster 1991), although here more urban-like forms can be claimed to have emerged in the first millennium BC. Similarities between the forms of monuments constructed on Sardinia, Corsica, and the Balearic islands have long been noted, and there are also differences in the specific forms, in their rates of change, etc. It would be fair to observe that the dominant research on these monument-building cultures has focused on their mutual interactions, on their external context rather than their internal evolution, whether conceived in terms of formal diffusion or increasingly well documented trade between mainland and islands. For example, the degree to which islands are advantageously located in relation to trade routes has received attention (e.g. Lewthwaite [1985b] on the Balearic islands and Chapman [1990: 260–65]; cf. Knapp 1986). Our ability to measure demographic change, intensification of production, social evolution, and other key variables within these islands during the last two millennia of prehistory still lags behind our understanding of external contact.

Given these observations on island societies in general, and in the Bronze and Iron Ages of the west Mediterranean in particular, it is our intention to present new data on subsistence on one island, Mallorca, and to use these data as the basis for a wider discussion of research into the archaeological record of monument-building societies on the Balearics.

Monuments on the Balearic islands

The construction of monuments on the Balearic islands of Mallorca and Menorca began in the later second millennium BC. Widespread on both islands are *talayots* ('watchtowers') and their associated domestic structures (for examples, see Mascaró Pasarius [1968], Pericot [1972], Rosselló [1973], and Waldren [1982]). In what is thought to be later, first millennium BC contexts, such *talayots* may be incorporated into defensive walls as part of more nucleated settlements. In addition to *talayots*, other monuments include megalithic tombs (e.g. CaNa Costa, on Formentera, Topp *et al.* 1976), *taulas* and *navetas*. *Taulas* ('tables') are restricted to Menorca and consist of T-sha¸ ⁻ᵈ standing stone pillars, one to four metres in height, located within a horseshoe-shaped enclosure. Excavation supports their ritual function (e.g. Torralba den Salort [Waldren and van Strydonck 1992: 9–10]) within the first millennium BC. Lastly, *navetas* are also restricted to Menorca and have the form of upturned boats. They are stone-built and may be up to 20 m long, 6 m wide and 4 m high. They were used for communal mortuary rituals (e.g. Els Tudons [Grinsell 1981]) and date to the late

second and early first millennia BC. Similarly-shaped and often less well preserved structures (*navetiformes*) on Mallorca are argued to have had a more domestic function.

Current archaeological evidence suggests that a degree of vertical social differentiation may have begun to emerge in the later pre-Talayotic period, in the second half of the third millennium BC, as seen, for example in a possible settlement hierarchy consisting of enclosed settlements such as Son Ferrandell Oleza (Waldren 1987) associated with open, more isolated navetiformes (Lewthwaite 1985b). A millennium later, at Son Fornés, in the middle of Mallorca, the presence of social hierarchy has been inferred on the basis of intra-site spatial analysis (Gasull *et al.* 1984a, 1984b, 1984c). Taken together with the investment of communal energy in the construction of monuments such as *talayots*, *taulas* and *navetas*, the data suggest an increase in complexity. The distribution of monuments such as *taulas* on Menorca suggests that supra-community rituals played a role in social integration.

Research analysis on *talayots* has also focussed on their social context, using intra-site analysis to think about their function(s) within the community (Gasull *et al.* 1984a, 1984b, 1984c; Chapman and Grant 1989). The construction of such monuments must have represented an intensification of production among the communities whose surplus labour was being exploited. Was this, as might be expected, accompanied by an intensification of subsistence production which supported the populations living around these monuments and/or the elite members who organized the construction of the monuments for their own gain? Was monument construction and use a continuous or discontinuous activity? Were construction rates responsive to local or regional factors? To what extent was social competition expressed through the construction of these monuments? Such questions, along with others about changing population sizes and densities in the islands, are difficult to answer at present due to lack of relevant data. It was one of the aims of the Reading University Son Ferrandell Oleza project to collect such data, especially that relating to the chronology of the monuments and the subsistence of their builders. It is the subsistence data which forms the focus of this chapter.

The Son Ferrandell Oleza project

Son Ferrandell Oleza is a multi-period site located at the foot of a limestone ridge immediately to the west of Valldemossa in northern Mallorca (Waldren 1982, 1984, 1986, 1987). Succeeding a pre-Talayotic enclosed settlement is a linear, Talayotic settlement which includes five *talayots* and traces of other, domestic structures, some of which have been excavated. *Talayots* 1, 2, and 3 have been excavated by Waldren, while the excavation of *talayot* 4 formed the main activity of the 1984–85 excavation seasons of the Son Ferrandell Oleza project (see Chapman and Grant 1989; Chapman and Grant in press). Within *talayot* 4 (T4), seven alternating phases of use and disuse were distinguished, while outside the monument, in structures 1 and 2 and in neighbouring refuse dumps, only three broad occupation phases could be identified within shallower deposits (for site location and layout, as well as excavation plans and fuller details of phasing, see Chapman and Grant 1989; in press). Radiocarbon dates from T4, as well as T1 and T2, support the inference that the monuments were constructed and in primary use within the period *c.* 1200–900 BC, and abandoned and filled in by *c.* 600–400 BC. This gives a maximum 'life-span' of 500–800 years for the monuments, with occupation continuing in many of the surrounding domestic structures until the Roman period (Chapman *et al.* 1993).

The faunal assemblage from talayot 4

Nearly 10,000 animal bones were recovered from the excavation of T4 and its exterior structures. The majority of the bone (Figure 7.1) was found inside T4 in the deposits that accumulated during disuse (phase 4) or during the structure's final abandonment (phase 7). Little material was found in the initial occupation (phase 1), and none at all in the subsequent re-use phases 3 and 5. On the basis of sherd size data (Chapman and Grant 1989) and radiocarbon dating (Chapman *et al.* 1993), we argue that refuse from the external structures was being dumped inside T4 during its phases of disuse.

The fragmented nature of the animal bone assemblage was immediately apparent from the fact that only 40% of it was identifiable. The proportion of loose teeth compared with the total number of identified bones provided further quantitative support for the effects of physical and chemical stress on the assemblage (Table 7.1, Figures 7.2–7.3). The higher proportion of loose teeth and the lower proportion of identifiable bone found in contexts outside T4 suggests greater weathering and trampling than occurred in the deeper, more rapidly accumulated and protected deposits inside the monument (Chapman and Grant 1989). As we have argued elsewhere, the nature of the assemblage restricts our ability to make inferences on the basis of skeletal part representation, but where there were data available (for sheep and goat bones in phase

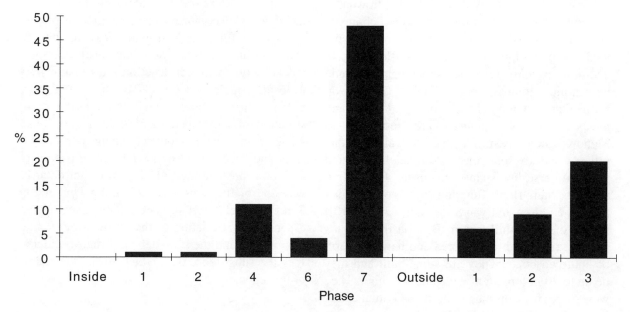

Figure 7.1   Percentages of total weight of animal bone inside and outside T4, Son Ferrandell Oleza.

Phase	% loose teeth	% ident. bone
Interior		
1	0	61
2	9	36
4	30	46
6	28	18
7	26	44
Exterior		
1	36	26
2	52	35
3	37	40
Top Soil	41	32
Total Interior	26	41
Total Exterior	41	35

Table 7.1 Percentages of loose teeth from different phases at T4, Son Ferrandell Oleza.

3 deposits outside, and phase 7 deposits inside T4), there was not support for spatial differentiation of the butchery and consumption of species (Chapman and Grant 1989: 66–67). Finally, the low incidence of gnawing on bone, in spite of the presence of dog in the assemblage, suggests that the bone had not been left lying about occupation areas long before it was covered over. This observation supports the relatively rapid accumulation of deposits, especially inside T4.

Given these limitations, we can now proceed to examine the evidence for animal husbandry provided by the bone assemblage. Table 7.2 shows the numbers and percentages of bones identified per phase for each of the species represented at T4. The vast majority of the identified bones were from the domestic species, sheep, goat, cattle, pig, and dog. There were only four contemporary bones from wild species, all from fallow deer. The condition of a small number of cat, bird and lizard bones found in contexts close to the ground surface was so demonstrably better than the rest of the bones that they must be considered intrusive.

If the relative proportions of bones give us an accurate impression of the composition of the domestic flocks and herds, it can be seen that while in all periods a mixed animal husbandry was practiced, the raising of sheep and goats was the most important element in that husbandry. In many instances it was not possible to separate sheep from goat bones, but where such a distinction could be made the proportion of goat bone was between 20% and 50%. Unless any indication is given to the contrary, throughout this discussion 'sheep' implies 'sheep and/or goat'. The different methods used to calculate the relative proportions of animals (see Grant 1975: 379) each give slightly different results, but overall suggest that more pigs than cattle were kept in most periods. Figure 7.4 summarizes the changing proportions of sheep, cattle and pig.

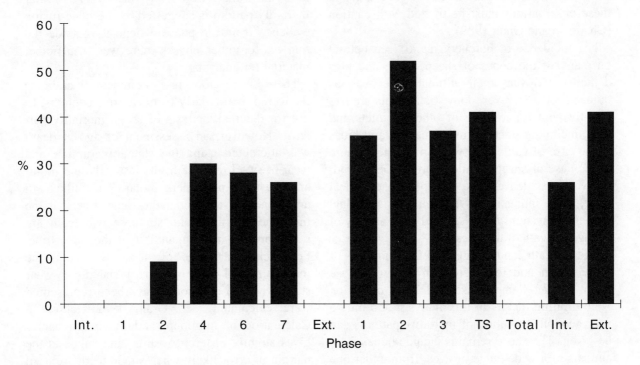

Figure 7.2 Percentages of loose teeth by phases inside and outside T4, Son Ferrandell Oleza (see Table 7.1).

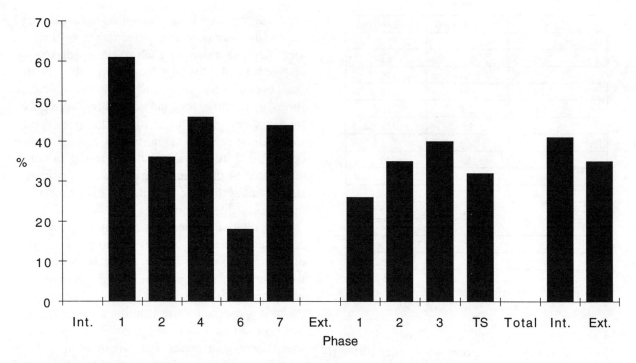

Figure 7.3   Percentages of identified bones by phases inside and outside T4, Son Ferrandell Oleza (see Table 7.1).

The clearest change over time appears to be the decline in the importance of pigs from phase 2 to phase 7 inside the *talayot*. There are also differences in proportions of these species in internal and external contexts, most clearly seen in the slightly increased proportion of sheep and lower numbers of pig bones outside the structure. However, there are likely to be biassing effects in the different sample sizes and bone condition and these observations must be treated with caution (Chapman and Grant 1989).

The incidence of butchery marks (see below) on many of the bones of sheep, cattle and pigs demonstrated that their ultimate use was as human food. However, domestic animals are frequently kept for a range of other products and uses, including traction, milk, manure and hides in the case of cattle; and wool, milk and manure in the case of sheep. While many of these products or uses leave little or no archaeological trace, some indication of the aims of individual husbandry systems can be gained from a study of the age at death of the livestock.

Age at death can be suggested from analysis of bone fusion and tooth eruption and wear (see Grant 1982). Sample size and bone condition were limiting factors in this analysis, and only a very general indication of mortality patterns can be given. The sheep remains include bones from animals of a wide range of ages, from under one year to over three to four years. Bone survival is better for animals killed when they are mature than for those killed when they are very young, and thus calculated proportions of young animals are likely to be underestimates. The bone fusion evidence (Table 7.3) suggests that a significant number of the sheep whose bones were found in phase 7 deposits were killed as juveniles, perhaps around two years of age, but many were kept at least until they were fully mature. A similar mortality pattern is suggested by the bone fusion evidence from the phase 3 deposits outside the *talayot*; for other phases there was insufficient material for analysis.

There were too few complete mandibles recovered, particularly from exterior contexts, to use for detailed analysis of sheep mortality patterns. However, an assessment of age at death was attempted using the state of eruption and wear of two lower teeth, the last milk and molar and the third permanent molar. The milk teeth are usually lost at about the same time that the third molar erupts, and so these two teeth are rarely present in the mandible at the same time. For each wear stage of these two teeth, the minimum and the maximum mandible wear stages (MWS) that could have been represented were calculated (see Grant 1982: table 3). Calculation of minimum and maximum values gives slightly different results, and suggests the margin of error likely when single teeth are used to estimate MWSs. Both loose teeth and teeth

| | Inside Talayot 4 | | | | | | | | | | Outside Talayot 4 | | | | | | | |
| | Phase 1 | | Phase 2 | | Phase 4 | | Phase 6 | | Phase 7 | | Phase 1 | | Phase 2 | | Phase 3 | | Top Soil | |
	N	%	N	%	N	%	N	%	N	%	N	%	N	%	N	%	N	%
Species																		
Epiphyses only																		
Sheep/goat	5	83	6	55	68	64	29	64	262	54	58	91	48	71	147	79	34	67
Cattle	1	17	1	9	7	6	2	4	31	6	4	6	13	19	14	7	7	14
Pig			3	27	14	13	6	13	29	6	2	3	7	10	22	12	5	10
Dog			1	9	18	17	8	18	165	34					3	2	2	4
Fallow Deer																	3	5
Total	6		11		107		45		527									
Fragments																		
Sheep/goat	11	85	26	76	199	58	71	56	803	54	160	89	222	75	524	84.9	148	82
Cattle	1	8	2	6	32	9	6	5	110	7	12	7	57	19	45	7	20	11
Pig	1	8	2	6	30	9	23	18	95	6	7	4	18	6	42	7	6	3
Dog			4	12	83	24	26	21	489	33					6	0.97	4	2
Fallow Deer									1								3	2
Total	13		34		344		126		1498		179		297		617		181	

Table 7.2 Frequencies of animal species by occupation phase at T4, Son Ferrandell Oleza.

found still in place in mandibles were used. Figure 7.5 summarizes the results for phases 1–3 outside the *talayot*, and phases 4, 6 and 7 inside the *talayot*.

This method can only be used to give a very general indication of sheep mortality, and the sample sizes vary considerably for the five phases analyzed. However, we may be justified in drawing some interesting conclusions from the analysis. Despite the apparently poorer survival of bone in the exterior deposits, there are more teeth from young sheep (those with lower MWS values) than in the interior deposits. In fact we may suggest an increase in the proportion of old sheep over time, with the highest proportion of old animals in the phase 7 deposits. In all phases except phase 1, the peak in mortality seems to have occurred between MWSs 26 and 34 (using minimum MWS calculations). Maximum MWS calculations suggest peak mortality between MWSs 30 and 37 in phases 2 to 4. In phase 7, the peak age at death appears to occur slightly later than in phases 2–6, at between MWSs 38 and 46, but very similar numbers of animals also seem to have been in the MWS 23 to 29 and the MWS 30 to 37 age groups.

Assigning absolute ages to these calculations of relative age is problematic, but tentatively we may suggest that many of the sheep were over three years old at death. While the killing of a proportion of juvenile animals suggests that some animals were raised specifically for meat, many of the Son Ferrandell sheep and goats were kept beyond the optimum age for meat produc-

tion, indicating that wool or hair and perhaps milk may have been important products of the husbandry of these animals. The increase in the proportion of older animals in the latest phases of use of the site suggests that there may have been a greater concentration on wool production by the middle of the first millennium BC. It may also reflect improvements in the crop husbandry, allowing animals to be fed for a longer period before slaughter. However, there was still a sufficiently high proportion of juvenile animals found in phase 7 deposits to suggest that meat production may also have had some importance.

The small numbers of cattle bones recovered made assessment of the cattle husbandry very difficult. The evidence, such as it is, suggests that although a very small number of bones and teeth were from juvenile animals, the majority were from animals that were skeletally mature at death, with well worn third molars. Cattle are extremely important draught animals in many primitive agricultural systems, particularly when, as seems to be the case on Mallorca at this period, there are few horses (see below). The presence of a large proportion of mature animals is consistent with their primary use for traction. The climate and topography in this part of Mallorca are not particularly suitable for cattle rearing — this is reflected in the rather small proportion of cattle bones recovered (Table 7.2; Figure 7.4). Their relatively high nutritional requirements may have made considerable demands on the crop husbandry system, and in periods of drought, when grass was in short

	N.F.	N.U.F	%F	N.F.	N.U.F	%F
Radius	5	0	100	17	3	85
Humerous D	19	0	100	19	5	79
Scapula D	3	1	75	8	0	100
Pelvis	4	0	100	7	1	89
2nd Phalange	5	0	100	7	0	100
1st Phalange	9	2	81	11	4	73
Tibia D	10	2	83	11	3	79
Metacarpal D	2	2	50	6	7	46
Metatarsal D	2	1	67	3	2	60
Calcaneum	2	2	50	2	3	40
Ulna P	1	1	50	1	5	17
Femur P	3	5	38	1	4	20
Femur D	2	1	67	1	2	33
Radius D	2	2	50	6	5	55
Tibia P	3	1	75	4	2	67
Humerous P	0	1	0	1	1	50

Table 7.3   Sheep bone fusion data for phase 3 (outside) (columns 1–3) and phase 7 (inside) (columns 4–6) at T4, Son Ferrandell Oleza. NF = numbers of fused bones; NUF = numbers of unfused bones.

supply, they are likely to have required supplementary feeding. However, those cattle that were kept may have been of great value to the farmers, only to be killed when sickly or at the end of their useful lives.

Pig keeping, like cattle keeping was clearly an important but secondary aspect of the animal husbandry system. Pigs have little economic value except as producers of meat, although their manure may be utilized as good quality fertilizer. The majority of the pig bones and teeth recovered were from juvenile animals, which is consistent with a husbandry that concentrated on the production of meat. They are omnivorous feeders, and will eat rough grass and scrubland vegetation, but if there are insufficient natural resources they may have to be fed with cereal products that could otherwise be used for human food. The natural environment on Mallorca is likely to have effectively limited the number of pigs that could be kept.

The rearing of animals for meat alone does not seem to have been the major aim of the animal husbandry practiced at Son Ferrandell, and this suggests that vegetable food may have made the main contribution to the diet. However, while sheep, goats and cattle may have been raised for a range of products, butchery marks on the bones of even elderly animals indicate that most, if not all, animals were eaten at the end of their useful lives. The traces left on the bones by the tools used for butchery, can suggest the butchery techniques employed, and these have been shown to be culture specific to a certain extent(Grant 1987). The majority of the cut marks observed on the bones of all four food animals had been made by fine knives, and suggest the careful separation

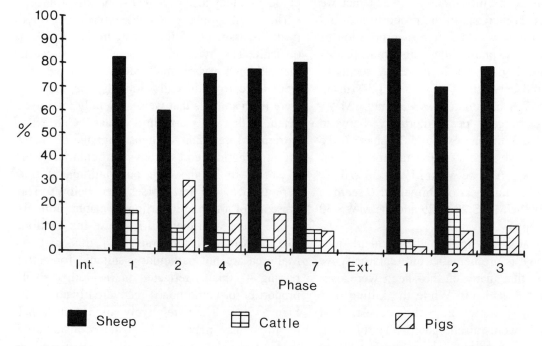

Figure 7.4   Percentages of sheep, goat, and cattle by phases inside and outside T4, Son Ferrandell Oleza.

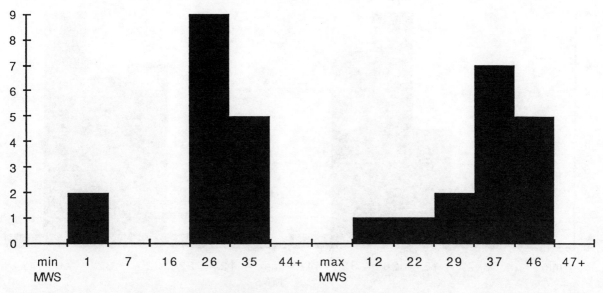

Figure 7.5a Tooth eruption data for sheep from phase 4 interior, Son Ferrandell Oleza.

of the bones by cutting through the ligaments around the joints. A small number of cattle bones indicated the use of heavier chopping tools. There were quite remarkable similarities between the butchery practiced here and that seen in the Iron Age in Britain. Grant (1987) suggested that this was a tradition of careful disarticulation and subsequent removal of the flesh that was largely dictated by anatomical considerations.

The poor condition of most of the bone remains limited the extent of any metrical analysis. Very few long bones were complete, and so calculation of the heights of withers was not possible. The measurements that were obtained are listed in Chapman and Grant (in press) and suggest that the domestic animals were rather small. Most measurements fall within

range for southern British Iron Age livestock (for example, see Grant 1984: 506, 514, 517) although two pig bones were from smaller animals than have been found at Danebury.

Dog bones were found in all phases except phase 1 inside, and phases 1 and 2 outside the *talayot*. In the latest deposits inside the structure they amounted to between 21% and 33% of the bone identified. It has already been suggested that the *talayot* was used as a dump for the carcasses of dogs — the absence of cut marks on their bones and their relatively complete condition rule out their use as food (Chapman and Grant 1989: 69). While it is unlikely that the percentages of dog bones found in the *talayot* reflect the true proportion of dogs kept relative to the other domestic animals, it does suggest that

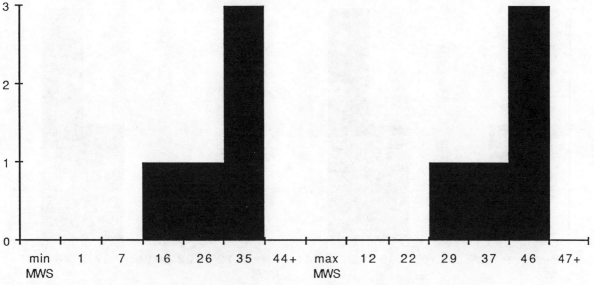

Figure 7.5b Tooth eruption data for sheep from phase 6 interior, Son Ferrandell Oleza.

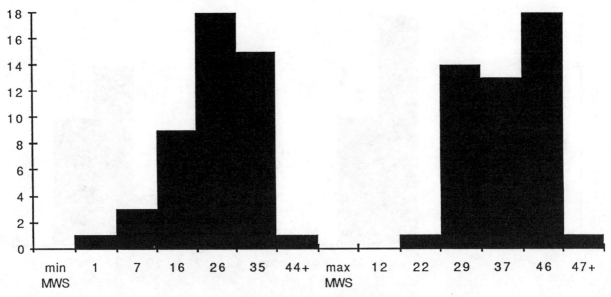

Figure 7.5c Tooth eruption data for sheep from phase 7 interior, Son Ferrandell Oleza.

dogs may have been common animals, perhaps used in particular for controlling the herds of sheep and goats. The majority of the dogs were mature, with all bones fully fused, but the remains of a small number of younger animals were found too. Again, almost all the measurable dog bones fell within the range of sizes found in British iron age sites, but the rather low coefficients of variation calculated for the Son Ferrandell dogs suggests that the dog population here was rather less varied than in Britain at the same period (Chapman and Grant, in press).

The only wild animal remains were a fragment of antler in phase 7 deposits, and three fallow deer bones in the top soil outside the *talayot*, which are of uncertain date. The subsistence economy at Son Ferrandell was clearly a farming economy, and there seems to have been little need to supplement the diet by hunting. There may in any case have been only a relatively small population of large wild animals on the island, as the only indigenous large mammal was *Myotragus balearicus* which is believed to have become extinct by the middle of the third millennium BC (Burleigh and Clutton Brock 1980). The other large wild (and domestic) animals were introduced to the island.

Animal husbandry at Son Ferrandell *talayot* 4 in its wider context

Interest in prehistoric economy and subsistence on Mallorca is a recent aspect of archaeological investigation on the island, and the faunal assemblage from Son Ferrandell *talayot* 4 is one

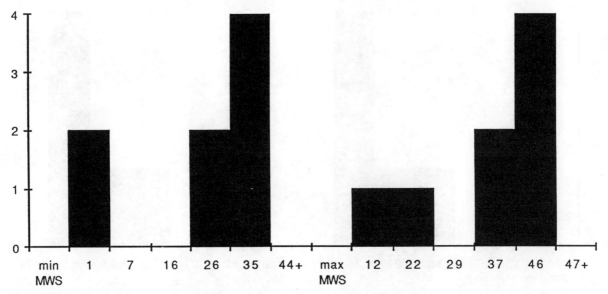

Figure 7.5d Tooth eruption data for sheep from phase 1 exterior, Son Ferrandell Oleza.

of only four published modern collections. Two come from Talayotic settlements, S'Illot and Son Fornés (Uerpmann 1971; Estévez 1984), and the other from the pre-Talayotic Settlement at Son Ferrandell (Clutton-Brock 1984). The radiocarbon dates from Son Fornés suggest broad contemporaneity with the Son Ferrandell *talayots*, although perhaps beginning a little later (Gasull *et al.* 1984b, 1984c), while the S'Illot material is divided into two groups; A being 'Pre-Roman' and having two radiocarbon dates of 1113±75 and 727±60 bc, while B is described as 'Transitional' to the Roman period; the 'Old Settlement' is an earlier settlement with radiocarbon dates in the first half of the second millennium bc (Waldren 1984). Figure 7.6 gives the percentages of the bones of the four main domestic animals for these sites and for the two phases at Son Ferrandell which produced the largest numbers of animal bones. The figures are all based on counts of the total number of fragments. The predominance of the remains of sheep and goats at all sites is striking, but not surprising given the natural environment. Comparisons between sites excavated by different workers, with varying conditions of bone survival and different sample sizes must be made with caution, however some observations can be made. While Son Ferrandell has the highest percentages of sheep and goats, its domestic animal faunal assemblage is very similar to that found at the 'Old Settlement' and the earliest phase at S'Illot. In the latest phase at S'Illot there was an increased percentage of cattle bones, with a slight decline in the proportion of sheep, but this

was not matched at Son Ferrandell. However, it is in comparison with the bones found at Son Fornés that the clearest differences are seen. Here, although the bones of sheep and goats together are the most abundant, the proportions of cattle and in particular of pig bones are significantly higher than at any of the other locations. There is no clear reason at present for such differences in species representation, which may relate to environment, economy or both. One suggestion is that the area immediately around Son Fornés was more favourable for cattle pasture as there were marshy areas there until drainage by the Arabs (Ferrés, in Gasull *et al.* 1984a: 132).

At all these Mallorcan sites the ovicaprid remains include a fairly high proportion of goats, although sheep seem to have been kept in greater numbers in all locations except at the old settlement of Son Ferrandell Oleza.

Estévez suggests that the animal husbandry at Son Fornés was very similar to that deduced for Son Ferrandell, with many of the cattle and sheep being kept until they were adult, when they were able to supply traction, wool and milk. The pigs were mostly killed when juvenile here too. At S'Illot a slightly higher proportion of the cattle seems to have been killed when juvenile and Uerpmann has suggested that they were kept for meat. The husbandry systems for pigs and sheep and goat however seem similar to those at the other sites.

The measurements taken on the Son Ferrandell bones mostly fall within the range of sizes already established from the other sites, although

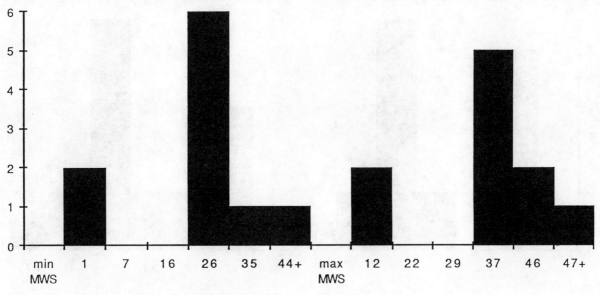

Figure 7.5e Tooth eruption data for sheep from phase 2 exterior, Son Ferrandell Oleza.

in some instances the range has now been extended slightly. With the very small number of measurable bones found so far from all sites, it is not yet appropriate to make any definitive statement about the size and range of variation in the domestic animals. Both Estévez (1984) and Uerpmann (1971) note the small size of the Mallorcan domestic fauna in comparison to that found on roughly contemporary sites in continental Europe, but we have already noted the similarity in the size of the Son Ferrandell domestic animals to the British animals of the second half of the first millennium BC. There is clearly much more research to be done on the form and size of domestic animals in relation to their geographical distribution in Europe at this time.

Some of the most obvious differences to be found between the four settlements are in the occurrence of the less common species. Dog bones, found in fairly large numbers in the later phases at Son Ferrandell, are present, but rather rare, at the other three sites. The dates for the occupation at Son Fornés and the first phase of occupation at S'Illot are rather earlier than the later phases at Son Ferrandell, but the later occupation at Son Fornés is at least partly contemporary, and only 3 dog bones were found at this site.

Horse bones were absent from all sites except Son Fornés, where 15 were found, thought to be the remains of one animal. When the use of an animal is other than as food, its bones may be under-represented in archaeological contexts. Although the horse may be, and indeed has been eaten and still is eaten, it is nonetheless not uncommon to find cultures that use horses, but

do not eat them. The absence of horse bones at S'Illot and Son Ferrandell T4 may be explained in this way, however the later deposits at the latter site included large numbers of bones from dogs, that do not seem to have been eaten. It is thus quite possible that the scarcity of horse bones does reflect a scarcity of these animals on the island. On the other hand, sampling factors may have played a part in this patterning, as a large number of horse teeth have been found in a non-monumental structure between and to the north of *talayots* 2 and 3 at Son Ferrandell (Waldren, pers. comm.). Cultural material and radiocarbon dates suggest that this structure was in use at the same time as T4 and subsequently into the Roman period, although it is not known whether occupation was continuous.

There was a wider range of wild animals found at both Son Fornés and S'Illot than at Son Ferrandell but this may be due to differences in the conditions for preservation — many of the wild animal bones were those of small creatures such as birds, hare, rabbits and mice whose bones may not have survived at Son Ferrandell. The bones of the larger wild animals were rare at all sites. One red deer bone was found at Son Fornés, none at all at the 'Old Settlement', and 24 red and 16 fallow deer bones at S'Illot.

Current knowledge of the colonization of the Mediterranean islands by wild and domestic animals introduced by man has been summarized by Vigne and Alcover (1985). Red deer have been found on Corsica and Sardinia at least as early as the beginning of the first millennium BC, but fallow deer seem to have been introduced later on Sardinia, and have not been found

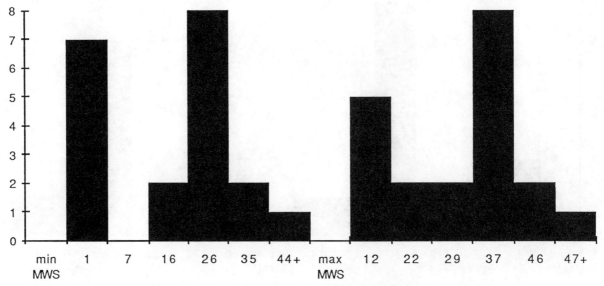

Figure 7.5f   Tooth eruption data for sheep from phase 3 exterior, Son Ferrandell Oleza.

in prehistoric or early historic contexts on Corsica. Menorca has a very restricted fauna without large wild animals. On Mallorca the earliest find of a red deer bone is at Son Fornés and of fallow deer at S'Illot. These animals were introduced much later than the domestic species and the reasons for their introduction are not clear. If they were introduced for food, they do not seem to have been at all intensively exploited, and it is possible that the impetus for their importation may have been as much social and cultural as economic.

Cereal exploitation and economic reconstruction

The discussion so far has centred upon the evidence for the animal husbandry practiced by *talayot* builders in Mallorca. What part did cereal exploitation play in the subsistence of the island's population at this time, and what kind of reconstruction can be proposed for the economic system as a whole?

There is no direct evidence for the exploitation of plant foods from *talayot* 4 or from the structures attached to it. Examination of flotation samples yielded no carbonized seeds, but grinding stones were found inside and outside the monument. A fragment of a flint sickle blade, a type occurring in large numbers in association with the earlier pre-Talayotic settlement at Son Ferrandell (e.g. Waldren *et al.* 1984), was found in phase 2 (first phase of disuse) deposits within T4. In addition to the technology for plant exploitation, we also suggest that the high proportion of mature animals amongst the cattle remains from T4 may be used to support the view that cereal production was sufficiently established to produce a surplus, or at least enough waste products for supplementary feeding for these animals. The cattle themselves may have been major contributors to any crop growing regime as providers of traction. The association of the Son Ferrandell Oleza Talayotic settlement, and its pre-Talayotic predecessor, with the fertile Pliocene marls of the Pla del Rei (the focus for modern farming in the Valldemossa region) adds further support to the inference that cereal agriculture played an important role in the economic system.

The paucity of data on plant remains is a wider problem for Mallorcan prehistory, and seems to be as much a problem of collection methods as it is choice of contexts (e.g. monumental/domestic) for sampling. Evidence for cereal exploitation going back to the pre-Talayotic period does exist, but there is at present no evidence for tree crop cultivation before the Punic period (Lewthwaite 1985b). At Son Fornés olive charcoals were found, but it is argued that beams were used as roofing material (Gasull *et al.* 1984a). Where studied, the location of both pre-Talayotic and Talayotic sites on the island argues in favour of the integration of cereal cultivation in the economy. For the pre-Talayotic period, Lewthwaite (1985b: 216) observes that "the naveti-formes are invariably located beside small marly basins and alluvial valleys offering limited areas of deep, humid soil, and a system of permanent cultivation, particularly one integrated with animal husbandry is likely." The association of Talayotic settlements in the municipal territory of Alcudia (northeast Mallorca) with cultivable land (and with more defensive locations than in the preceding pre-Talayotic period) has been discussed by Coll Conesa *et al.* (1984). On a larger scale, Mota Santos (1988) has statistically analyzed the distribution of Talayotic settlements on Mallorca in relation to seven variables (altitude, distance from the coast, rainfall, distance from seasonal water courses, soil type, geology, land use) and concludes that "the main factor, from all the considered ones, influencing *talayot* location is distance from seasonal water courses" (*ibid*: 20), with land use in second or third place, depending upon the data used. Mota Santos (1988: 20) comments on the "remarkable emphasis on *talayots* setting on land that nowadays is used for the growing of fruit trees", while land used for dry cereal cultivation occupied second place. Of course, an association between settlements and land use categories does not necessarily imply a predominant role for one sector of the economy: it has been argued that stockbreeding formed the focus of the economy in the Talayotic, given the on-site evidence, but that the increased production of storage vessels in the Post-Talayotic signifies a greater emphasis upon cereal agriculture (e.g. Mayoral Franco 1984).

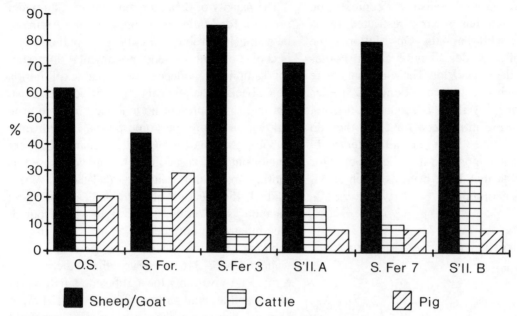

Figure 7.6   Percentages of the main domesticated animals from excavated faunal assemblages on Mallorca. O. S. = Old Settlement (pre-Talayotic), Son Ferrandell Oleza; S. For. = Son Fornés; S. Fer 3 = Son Ferrandell Oleza, *talayot* 4, phase 3 (exterior); S'Ill. A = S'Illot group A ('Pre-Roman'); S. Fer 7 = Son Ferrandell Oleza, *talayot* 4, phase 7 (interior); S'Ill. B = S'Illot group B ('Transitional' to Roman period).

For the pre-Talayotic period, Lewthwaite (1985b: 216–17) has proposed the existence of a mixed farming economy.

> Each species could have performed a complementary and essential function: small stock would have maintained arable productivity through manuring, cattle could have supplied traction and pigs could convert sundry vegetable produce into high quality protein. For such a system to function, an extensive zone of pasture and open forest would have been required to complement the arable sector. Since the islands are only slightly differentiated ecologically, there is no reason to suppose that transhumance was ever systematically practiced in order to exploit complementary resources.

This reconstruction is not inconsistent with the evidence from Son Ferrandell Oleza *talayot* 4, nor, in general terms, from the other sites discussed above. At Son Ferrandell, the hills and ridges around the basin of the Pla del Rei contain both pasture and open forest.

While the small degree of ecological variability within Mallorca and the other Balearic islands (when compared with Corsica and Sardinia) helps us to understand the similarities between the four faunal assemblages from sites in the north (Son Ferrandell Olzea), centre (Son

Fornés) and east (S'Illot) of the island, it would be a mistake to assume an unchanging economy through three thousand years of prehistory and without regard to location. Even with only this small sample (less than 18,000 bones) variability can be observed. We have commented on the increase in wool and/or milk production inferred for Son Ferrandell Oleza *talayot* 4 by the middle of the first millennium BC, and on the higher proportions of cattle and pig represented at Son Fornés as compared with the other assemblages. In the case of the latter site, locational factors were suggested as reason for this variability, although it should be remembered that cattle traction is argued by the excavators to have been used for transporting the building material (limestone) to the site (Gasull *et al.* 1984a). Depending upon the distances between sources and sites, we would expect the need for cattle traction to vary. In the case of the increase in wool and/or milk production at Son Ferrandell Oleza *talayot* 4, this could be a purely localized factor within the Talayotic settlement (and hence, perhaps, have implications regarding the organization of production within the community), or it could be related to wider changes in an economy which was now brought into irreversible contact with economic systems from outside the Balearic islands, in this case Punic colonization.

Even with the limited sample of faunal material, there is clearly variability in time and space, and we need to consider the reasons (environmental, social) which lie behind this. At the level of the community, differences relating to population size (itself a vital factor in considering investment of energy in monument construction) and/or position within the regional settlement hierarchy would be expected to underlie differences in animal and crop exploitation, while at the level of individual households within these communities, differences in access to basic production also require explanation in terms of the wider social framework. A good example of the latter is Lewthwaite's (1985b: 218–19) argument about the costs of cattle maintenance on Mediterranean islands and the inability of all households to maintain draught oxen, hence affecting their ability to enter successfully into agricultural production. We would also expect variability in faunal assemblages, and presumably also in evidence for cereal agriculture, in functionally different kinds of sites, such as the more ritualistic *taulas*, the Talayotic settlements, and the funerary *navetas*. Such an emphasis on degrees of variation in the economy, and on the understanding of its causes (not solely internal, nor environmental nor demographic), provides a focus for future research into later prehistoric economic strategies.

Mallorca; monuments, islands and archaeological research

The construction of monuments on the Balearic islands, and specifically Mallorca, was an activity which climaxed in the later second and early first millennia BC. Given the labour requirements of the mixed farming economy, and the inability of all households to have access to the main labour-saving device, cattle-traction, it is clear that the requirement of surplus labour for construction (e.g. calculated at Son Fornés as either 20 people working for one and a half years, or 40–50 individuals working for two months [Gasull *et al.* 1984a]) would have posed problems for local productive systems. Either individuals would have to be removed in small numbers from production over a long period of time, or, perhaps more likely, larger numbers would cooperate during the agriculturally slack times of the year. However this was organized, there are implications for food production: not only do the 'workers' have to eat, but the 'organizers', the monument builders, have to convince the population of the need for such monuments. One method by which both these needs may be fulfilled, especially if the monument construction is carried out by larger numbers over a shorter period of time, is by ritual feasting, which also provides a focus for competition between rival elite groups. Such feasting is hypothesized for the Talayotic settlement of Son Fornés (Gasull *et al.* 1984a).

Intensification of production is also made likely by the nucleation of population in Talayotic walled villages (Rosselló 1973), which have traditionally been dated to the first millennium BC. The competitive nature of social relations at this time is not only supported by the burst of monument construction, but also by observations such as the 'killing' of artefacts (e.g. the Atlantic bronzes found in the final abandonment deposits of T4 [see Chapman *et al.* 1993] or the weaponry deposited with the Son Matge lime burials [see Waldren 1982]). The destruction of artefacts and the construction of monuments are both means by which competition between groups and individuals can be expressed in material terms (Bradley 1990). In this case, the deposition of the artefacts occurred when the monuments were being abandoned. If it is not stretching an inference too far, can we suggest that the material medium through which social competition was expressed was, in fact, changing?

This all occurred after nearly two millennia of agricultural exploitation on Mallorca (a critical reading of the currently available data suggests that agriculture had been introduced by the first half of the third millennium BC [Enseñat 1993], but Waldren [1982] takes this dating back to *c.* 3500 BC). Given the predictions of island biogeography, we would expect instability in such an ecosystem with the arrival of full-scale agricultural colonization and a further reduction of ecosystem diversity with vegetational clearance and faunal extinctions. After the extinction of *Myotragus balearicus* by the mid-third millennium BC, there were no large, wild mammals until the introduction of deer, thus denying local populations some of the flexibility enjoyed by mainland agricultural communities (e.g. see Chapman [1990: 118, 139, table 11] for discussion of the role of wild animals in subsistence strategies in the later prehistory of southeast Spain). The effects of prehistoric agricultural exploitation upon the landscape of Mallorca and Menorca are still largely unknown, but in the case of Son Ferrandell Oleza it is clear that erosion resulting in the deposition of at least one metre of colluvium in the Pla del Rei occurred before medieval times, when the landscape was stabilized by the construction of terraces (Fisher in Chapman and Grant, in press). It would be purely speculative, but an interesting starting point for future research, to propose that parts of the landscape were 'running down' just as social competition and stratification were 'speeding up'. Indeed, what would the causal relationship have been between such changes in landscape and society?

When we return to the study of Polynesian societies by Kirch and Green (1987), we note that most of this concluding discussion has centred on the three processes which they claim led to convergence through time between different islands: demographic trends, intensification of production and competition. A further point to be made here is that predictions for demographic trends in islands are for initially high growth rates, and then, later on, a transition to density dependent controls, including greater competition. The archaeological record for Mallorca would suggest that this transition was complete by the second half of the second millennium BC, when *talayot* construction began.

The inclusion of the factor of external contact to processes leading to divergence between Polynesian island societies (Kirch and Green 1987) would seem unlikely when transferred to the Balearic islands, or indeed to the other islands of the west Mediterranean where monuments were constructed. As pointed out earlier in this paper, much greater attention has been devoted to external contact or interaction as a variable leading to convergence between the islands and their monuments than has to internal variables such as demography and production. A role for external contact is not ruled out by the discussion in this paper (e.g. the references to Punic colonization and its relationship to local competition, monument abandonment, and expansion in wool production). Rather the strategy employed has been to focus on the internal variables for which current data is inadequate and to which our work can make a contribution.

Finally, let us return to the points from which this paper 'kicked off'. The archaeological sequences for later prehistory on west Mediterranean islands reveal both similarities and differences in their records of monument construction. In the last decade, archaeologists have found the adoption of a theoretical framework derived from island biogeography to be useful for the study of island colonization in the Mediterranean basin as a whole. We contend that this framework should be extended to focus our research on later prehistory, when the Balearic islands, as well as Corsica and Sardinia, in the west Mediterranean show signs of more complex, stratified societies emerging prior to their being drawn into more broadly-based colonial political and economic networks. This means the construction of research strategies designed to measure such variables as intensification of production, demographic change, and interaction/competition. It also means an emphasis on variation in time and space, and attention must be paid to the relationships between these variables, and to the relationships between these variables and changes in the landscape as the island ecosystem responds to increasingly intense human exploitation. We have presented new data on subsistence from one site in northern Mallorca, and allowed ourselves the luxury of both reason and speculation in discussing the implications of that data. We look forward to further research which will yield data relevant to this and the other variables discussed in this paper, and to an increase in our understanding of monument construction on west Mediterranean islands.

Acknowledgments

We thank the National Geographic Society, the British Academy, the Society of Antiquaries, the Prehistoric Society and the University of Reading for the financial support which enabled the excavations of *talayot* 4 at Son Ferrandell Oleza to take place. We also thank Drs. William and Jacqueline Waldren for their support and hospitality in Deya.

Bibliography

Binford, L.R.

    1989   *Debating Archaeology*. New York: Academic Press.

Bradley, R.

1990   *The Passage of Arms*. Cambridge: Cambridge University Press.

Broodbank, C., and T.F. Strasser

1991   Migrant Farmers and the Neolithic Colonization of Crete. *Antiquity* 65: 233–45.

Burleigh, R., and J. Clutton Brock

1980   The Survival of Myotragus Balearicus into the Neolithic of Mallorca. *Journal of Archaeological Science* 7: 385–88.

Camps, G.

1988   *Préhistoire d'une Île: Les Origines de la Corse*. Paris: Éditions Errance.

Chapman, R.W.

1990   *Emerging Complexity: The Later Prehistory of South-East Spain, Iberia and the West Mediterranean*. Cambridge: Cambridge University Press.

Chapman, R., and A. Grant

1989   The Talayotic Monuments of Mallorca: Formation Processes and Function. *Oxford Journal of Archaeology* 8: 55–72.

in press   Talayot 4, Son Ferrandell Oleza: Problemas de los Procesos de Formación, Función y Subsistencia. *Revista d'Arqueologia de Ponent*.

Chapman, R., M. Van Strydonck and W. Waldren

1993   Radiocarbon Dating and the Talayots: the Example of Son Ferrandell Oleza. *Antiquity* 67: 108–16.

Cherry, J.F.

1981   Pattern and Process in the Earliest Colonization of the Mediterranean Islands. *Proceedings of the Prehistory Society* 47: 41–68.

1990   The First Colonization of the Mediterranean Islands: A Review of Recent Research. *Journal of Mediterranean Archaeology* 3: 145–221.

Clutton-Brock, J.

1984   Preliminary Report on the Animal Remains from Ferrandell-Oleza with Comments on the Extinction of *Myotragus Balearicus* and on the Introduction of Domestic Livestock to Mallorca. In W.H. Waldren, R. Chapman, J. Lewthwaite and R.C. Kennard (eds), *The Deya Conference of Prehistory: Early Settlement in the Western Mediterranean Islands and their Peripheral Areas*, 99–118. British Archaeological Reports International Series 229. Oxford: British Archaeological Reports.

Coll Conesa, J., L. Mazaira Cabana-Verdes and S. Riutort Mir

1984   Evolución del Hábitat Durante la Prehistoria y la Antigüedad en el Término Municipal de Alcudia (Mallorca). *Arqueología Espacial* 2: 111–29.

Enseñat, J.

1993   The Balearic Copper Age in the Context of West Mediterranean Archaeology. Unpublished

D.Phil. dissertation, University of Oxford.

Estévez, J.

1984   Restos Alimentarios e Industria Ósea de Son Fornés (Mallorca). In P. Gasull, V. Lull and M.E. Sanahuja, *Son Fornés 1: La Fase Talayótica*, 139–70. British Archaeological Reports International Series 209. Oxford: British Archaeological Reports.

Fosberg, F.R. (ed.)

1963   *Man's Place in the Island Ecosystem: A Symposium*. Honolulu: Bishop Museum Press.

Gasull, P., V. Lull and M.E. Sanahuja

1984a   *Son Fornés 1: La Fase Talayótica*. British Archaeological Reports International Series 209. Oxford: British Archaeological Reports.

1984b   Estudio Comparativo de los Talaiots no. 1 y 2 de Son Fornés (Montuiri-Mallorca). In W.H. Waldren, R. Chapman, J. Lewthwaite and R.C. Kennard (eds), *The Deya Conference of Prehistory: Early Settlement in the Western Mediterranean Islands and their Peripheral Areas*, 1239–57. British Archaeological Reports International Series 229. Oxford: British Archaeological Reports.

1984c   La Habitación no. 5 de Son Fornés (Montuiri, Mallorca): Modelo de una Vivienda Talayótica. In W.H. Waldren, R. Chapman, J. Lewthwaite, and R.C. Kennard (eds), *The Deya Conference of Prehistory: Early Settlement in the Western Mediterranean Islands and their Peripheral Areas*, 1259–97. British Archaeological Reports International Series 229. Oxford: British Archaeological Reports.

Grant, A.

1975   The Animal Bones. In B. Cunliffe, *Excavations at Porchester Castle*, 1: 378–408. London: Society of Antiquaries.

1982   The Use of Tooth Wear as a Guide to the Age of Domestic Ungulates. In B. Wilson, C. Grigson and S. Payne (eds.), *Ageing and Sexing Animal Bones from Archaeological Sites*, 91–106. British Archaeological Reports British Series 109. Oxford: British Archaeological Reports.

1984   The Animal Husbandry. In B. Cunliffe, *Danebury: An Iron Age Hillfort in Hampshire*, 496–548. London: Council for British Archaeology.

1987   Some Observations on Butchery in England from the Iron Age to the Medieval Period. In J.D. Vigne (ed.), *La Découpe et le Partage du Corps à travers le Temps et l'Espace*, 51–58. Paris: Anthropozoologica.

Grinsell, L.

1981   The Naveta of Els Tudons (Menorca). *Antiquity* 55: 196–99.

Kirch, P.V., and R.C. Green

1987   History, Phylogeny and Evolution in Polynesia. *Current Anthropology* 28: 431–56.

Knapp, A.B.

1986   Production, Exchange and Socio-political Complexity on Bronze Age Cyprus. *Oxford Journal of Archaeology* 5: 35–60.

Lewthwaite, J.G.

1981   Ambiguous First Impressions: A Survey of Recent Work on the Early Neolithic of the West Mediterranean. *Journal of Mediterranean Anthropology and Archaeology* 1: 292–307.

1982   Cardial Disorder: Ethnographic and Archaeological Comparisons for Problems in the Early Prehistory of the West Mediterranean. In R. Montjardin (ed.), *Le Néolithique Ancien Méditerranéen: Actes du Colloque International de Préhistoire, Montpellier 1981*, 311–18. Sète: Fédération Archéologique de l'Hérault.

1983   Why Did Civilization Not Emerge More Often? A Comparative Approach to the Development of Minoan Crete. In O. Krzyszkowska and L. Nixon (eds), *Minoan Society*, 171–83. Bristol: Bristol Classical Press.

1984   Sardinia and Corsica. In W.H. Waldren, R. Chapman, J. Lewthwaite and R.C. Kennard (eds), *The Deya Conference of Prehistory: Early Settlement in the Western Mediterranean Islands and their Peripheral Areas*, 499–508. British Archaeological Reports International Series 229. Oxford: British Archaeological Reports.

1985a   From Precocity to Involution: the Neolithic of Corsica in its West Mediterranean and French Contexts. *Oxford Journal of Archaeology* 4: 47–68.

1985b   Social Factors and Economic Change in Balearic Prehistory, c. 3000–1000 bc. In G. Barker and C. Gamble (eds), *Beyond Domestication in Prehistoric Europe*, 205–31. London: Academic Press.

1986   The Transition to Food Production: A Mediterranean Perspective. In M. Zvelebil (ed.), *Hunters in Transition: Mesolithic Societies of Temperate Eurasia and their Transition to Farming*, 53–66. Cambridge: Cambridge University Press.

1989   Isolating the Residuals: The Mesolithic Basis of Man–Animal Relationships on the Mediterranean Islands. In C. Bonsall (ed.), *The Mesolithic in Europe*, 541–55. Edinburgh: John Donald.

Mascaró Pasarius, J.

1968   *Prehistoria de las Baleares*. Palma de Mallorca: Gráficas Miramar.

Mayoral Franco, F.

1984   La Fase Post-talayótica Mallorquina: Periodización y Dinámica Económico-social. In W.H. Waldren, R. Chapman, J. Lewthwaite, and R.C. Kennard (eds), *The Deya Conference of Prehistory: Early Settlement in the Western Mediterranean Islands and Their Peripheral Areas*, 1299–1313. British Archaeological Reports International Series 229. Oxford: British Archaeological Reports.

Michels, J.W., and G.S. Webster (eds.)

1987   *Studies in Nuraghic Archaeology*. British Archaeological Reports International Series 373. Oxford: British Archaeological Reports.

Mota Santos, P. da

1988   Torres and Torrentes: A New Approach to the Settlement Patterns of Mallorcan Talayots. Unpublished M.A. Dissertation, Department of Archaeology, University of Reading.

Pericot, L.

1972   *The Balearic Islands*. London: Thames and Hudson.

Roselló, G.

1973   *La Cultura Talayótica en Mallorca*. Palma de Mallorca: Ediciones Cort.

Shackleton, J.C., T.H. van Andel, and C.N. Runnels

1984   Coastal Palaeogeography of the Central and Western Mediterranean During the Last 125,000 Years and its Archaeological Implications. *Journal of Field Archaeology* 11: 307–14.

Topp, C., J.H. Fernández and L. Plantalamor

1976   Ca Na Costa: a Megalithic Chamber Tomb on Formentera, Balearic islands. *Bulletin of the Institute of Archaeology, University of London* 13: 139–74.

Trump, D.H.

1984   The Bonu Ighinu Project: Results and Prospects. In W.H. Waldren, R. Chapman, J. Lewthwaite, and R.C. Kennard (eds), *The Deya Conference of Prehistory: Early Settlement in the Western Mediterranean Islands and their Peripheral Areas*, 511–32. British Archaeological Reports International Series 229. Oxford: British Archaeological Reports.

Uerpmann, H.P.

1971   Die Tierknochenfunde aus der Talayot Siedlung von S'Illot (San Lorenzo, Mallorca). *Studien über frühe Tierknochenfunde von der Iberischen Halbinsel* 2: 1–110.

Vigne, J.D.

1988   *Les Mammifères Post-Glaciaires de Corse: Étude Archéozoologique*. Paris: C.N.R.S.

Vigne, J.D., and J.A. Alcover

1985   Incidence des relations historiques entre l'homme et l'animal dans la composition actuelle du peuplement amphibien, reptilien et mammalien des iles de la Méditerranée Occidentale. *Actes, XI Congrès National des Sociétés Savantes, Montpellier 1985*, 2: 79–91.

Waldren, W.H.

1982   *Balearic Prehistoric Ecology and Culture*. British Archaeological Reports International Series 149. Oxford: British Archaeological Reports.

1984   Chalcolithic Settlement and Beaker Connections in the Balearic islands. In W.H. Waldren, R. Chapman, J. Lewthwaite and R.C. Kennard (eds), *The Deya Conference of Prehistory: Early Settlement in the Western Mediterranean Islands and their Peripheral Areas*, 911–65. British Archaeological Reports International Series 229. Oxford: British Archaeological Reports.

1986　*The Balearic Pentapartite Division of Prehistory.* British Archaeological Reports International Series 282. Oxford: British Archaeological Reports.

1987　A Balearic Beaker Model: Ferrnadell-Oleza, Valldemossa, Mallorca, Spain. In W.H. Waldren and R.C. Kennard (eds), *Bell Beakers of the Western Mediterranean*, 207–66. British Archaeological Reports International Series 331. Oxford: British Archaeological Reports.

Waldren, W.H., E.A.C. Sanders, and J. Coll Conesa

1984　The Lithic Industry of the Balearic islands. In W.H. Waldren, R. Chapman, J. Lewthwaite, and R.C. Kennard, (eds), *The Deya Conference of Prehistory: Early Settlement in the Western Mediterranean Islands and their Peripheral Areas*, 859–909. British Archaeological Reports International Series 229. Oxford: British Archaeological Reports.

Waldren, W.H., and M. van Strydonck

1992　*A Radiocarbon Analysis Survey Dating the Activity Sequences of the Prehistoric Sanctuary of Son Mas.* Oxford: Baden-Powell Quaternary Research Centre.

Webster, G.S.

1988　Duos Nuraghes: Preliminary Results of the First Three Seasons of Excavation. *Journal of Field Archaeology* 15: 465–72.

1991　Monuments, Mobilization and Nuraghic Organization. *Antiquity* 65: 840–56.

8. A Thorny Problem: Was there Contact between the Peoples of the Sea and Tartessos?

Manuel Bendala Galán

The possibility of contact between the Peoples of the Sea and Tartessos was defended and discussed by the German scholar Schulten (1922, 1930) in his famous studies on this problematic period of protohistory. Schulten maintained that the foundation of Tartessos was the result of an immigration of Tirseni, who arrived from Lydia in Asia Minor at around 1200 BC. Like the Etruscans, the Tirseni were one of the Peoples of the Sea referred to in Egyptian sources. The previous, megalithic culture of the Copper Age would have been the result of an older immigration of Cretans, during a period which Schulten called pre-Tartessos, even though there was no demonstrable connection between these two waves of people.

Schulten's thesis was completely discredited because of its many weak points. It was one-sided and ignored the limitations of the philological evidence he used — toponyms, ethnonyms and anthroponyms, — which are open to question and without archaeological validation. Archaeologists criticized, or simply scorned, his theories, when it became clear that only archaeological exploration could accurately answer many of the questions Tartessos posed. Garcia y Bellido, without rejecting the value of the old literary sources and the contributions of philology, discredited Schulten by saying that the archaeology did not support the 'ingenious theory' of the German researcher:

> All these hypotheses and many others are proof of how little we know about the dark period at the end of the second millennium BC. The Mediterranean was characterized by the moving to and fro of the people, mass migrations, invasions, in brief, a gigantic ethnic upheaval ... that preceded the entry of the Iron Age and prepared the first flourishing of the so called Western (Greek-Roman) culture (García y Bellido 1931: 128).

As archaeological studies in Spain advanced, Schulten's thesis sank into oblivion. But it was not completely forgotten, and without a detailed discussion of his position, it is fair to say that some scholars have suspected that Schulten's ideas could help explain the complex reality of Spain's protohistory. As Blanco (1967: 170) put it:

> Schulten's thesis has not found scientific credit even though there are certain aspects of the Tartassos question (such as the alphabet, the pre-Hellenic name the Greeks gave the city, etc.) which invite one to consider that, in the diaspora that took place in the Mediterranean as a result of the last Indo-European invasions and the upheaval caused in the Orient by the Peoples of the Sea, some waves of new groups may have reached the coast of the peninsula and efficaciously contributed to the formation of the new world that was soon to be visited and colonized by Phoenicians and Greeks.

Blanco's reflection provides a good example of a marginal allusion to a very difficult subject that research has just begun to touch on. Not so cautious, in contrast, was Montenegro's (1970) defence of the arrival of the Peoples of the Sea in Spain. (Montenegro is not an archaeologist and uses a text-based, philological methodology like Schulten's; his ideas have had little influence on the scientific community.)

Other than these exceptions, a discreet silence has surrounded the Peoples of the Sea, largely because it did not even seem necessary to discuss the matter. Archaeological studies have been increasingly successful at increasing our understanding of prehistoric and protohistoric Spain. Furthermore, the discarding of the Peoples of the Sea hypothesis was influenced by a growing aversion to diffusionism, encouraged by a better understanding of prehistoric Spanish cultures. The diffusionism (often hyperdiffusionism) of earlier theorists, was countered by a strong focus on indigenous development that remains an important component of current prehistoric and protohistoric studies.

As far as Tartessos is concerned, archaeological studies of the last decades have paid increasing attention to the Celtic and indigenous contributions to Tartessos, as well as to later, less problematic periods. Conventional wisdom viewed Tartessos as a civilization that was associated with the diffusion of orientalizing trends, in which decisive roles were played by the Pheonicians, and later, by the Greeks. Tartessos became a link to the East to the extent that it became exclusively identified with it (a good example of this is Blázquez's [1975] work, which owes much to the studies of orientalization carried out by by Blanco, García y Bellido, Maluquer, and others.) It made sense, when dealing with a civilization about which everything was unknown, to explore it by paying attention to a more approachable archaeological period. From the eighth century BC, the material culture of the Mediterranean is connected by accurately dated materials that can be found everywhere, thus allowing firmer chronologies and conclusions than for the preceding period. In brief, this means that one could work on the firmer ground of a complex structure that spread by means of the consolidation of urban life, with its ongoing commercial and cultural contacts, and high level of literacy.

But the establishment of historical realities in those periods where archaeological evidence and the written texts have cast more light would not last long. The development of research on earlier cultures and advances in archaeology raised questions about the obscure formative stages from which we could gain a better understanding of the subsequent periods, periods which could not be wholly understood when contemplated merely in their stages of optimum development. It was necessary to look back again, this time using the new understanding of the earlier periods generated by archaeological research.

It was discovered, for instance, that the Phoenicians' expansion was preceded by a very significant expansion on the part of the Mycenaeans. Exactly what this meant should not be underestimated. It was akin to a scientific revolution: the information provided by the contacts between Italy and the Mycenaean world gave a better understanding of the 'historic' Etruscan and Latin cultures that developed at the core of the Italian peninsula. It also contributed to our understanding of important island cultures, such as the Nuraghic of Sardinia. One of the surprises of modern archaeology has been the verification that a large amount of the ancient documents that refer to the formative stages of classical cultures (documents that archaeological positivism ignored on principle) can be read as a fictionalized reflection of a cultural reality that archaeology is only now beginning to reveal (cf. Bendala 1985, 1990, 1991).

In Italian research the scorn for the legends outlined in the documents was replaced long ago by a more balanced position that is more willing to recognize a connection between what can be inferred from archaeological information and what the texts suggest. In an important systematization of Roman and Latium protohistory, Colonna (1974: 282) referred to the legends about the founding of Rome and the saga of Aeneas and his descendants, and showed that the total scepticism of the modern critic towards this sort of scholarly reconstruction could not be maintained in light of the archaeological discoveries of the last few years. Some components, such as the connection with the Mycenaean world alluded to in the legend or the idea that Aeneas was a real person, match archaeological evidence, which also shows clear signs of the concentration of power (Bendala 1977, 1986).

The Aeneas legend takes one back to the Trojan cycle and, above all, to the famous *nostoi*, the tales about the homeward return of the Greek and Trojan war heros who travelled the whole Mediterranean. Furthermore, the former scepticism is being replaced by a modern critique that regards the *nostoi* as testimony of the migrations that followed the crisis of the Mycenaean world in the poorly understood period known accurately as the Dark Age.

Recent scholars have made archaeological discoveries that suggest that there is some historical truth behind Greek myths about the presence of Achaean and Trojan heroes in the western seas. Marazzi (1976) for example, establishes three stages in the relations between the Aegean sea and the west: Mycenaean penetration, the precolonial stage and the historic colonization. All three stages have distinct characteristics but are causally linked. The second stage corresponds to the reality that is reflected in the tales of the *nostoi* in which, according to Marazzi, a memory of real events can be perceived: the fact that these tales are the result of a later elaboration does not rule out the possibility of their being the result of a conscious historical appraisal of past events. Some recent authors (e.g. Luzón Nogué and Coín Cuenca 1986) are conducting a respectful appraisal of traditional accounts.

With regard to the Tartessian civilizations something similar has begun to take place. Archaeological research has demonstrated the existence of a long Tartessian stage that predates the Phoenician colonization. This precolonial stage has a definite character and played a determinant role in the configuration of Tartessos as a civilization. In this period, dating from the end of the second millennium to the mid-eighth century BC (when Phoenician civilization began to experience an important cultural change), Tartessos became defined: settlement patterns emerged, territory was organized, and forms of social and economic organization developed. The material culture of this period, on which the archaeological and historical interpretation of the culture is based, is of great richness and character, as demonstrated by the burnished ceramics (especially revealing are those decorated with painted geometric motifs) and by the stelae carved with depictions of warriors. Distributed throughout a large area of southwest Iberia, about 100 examples of these stelae have been catalogued. The archaeological literature on this subject is broad and represents one of the more attractive and widely-debated areas of the archaeological historiography of ancient Spain (cf. discussions and references in Bendala 1990, 1991).

The problem lies in the interpretation of this material culture. Here, the positions are divided among scholars, with a wide variety of proposals and counterproposals, the details of which are beyond the scope of this paper. Briefly, in the post-war years the Celtic hypothesis has been defended by Almagro Basch and Blanco. This theory involves the idea that both the ceramics and the stelae reflect the arrival of people of Celtic origin from central Europe, who imposed themselves on the native population as a dominant caste, and built a thriving economy and culture that eventually became Tartessos.

Once established, Tartessos was soon to benefit from Phoenician acculturation, favourable sea routes, and an economic prominence based on the demand of its production of metal. Also important are the indigenous elements that give priority to the process of cultural maturation in southern Spain from the Chalcolithic onwards. These cultures would have experienced the Phoenician colonization as a stimulant immediately prior to the period when Tartessos flourished. Thus, when external factors are examined, theories on the potential influence of the Atlantic cultures on Taressos gain new prominence.

As for my own position, in the last few years I have maintained that substantial aspects of the archaeological reality of the early stages of Tartessos were due to an important human and cultural impulse of Mediterranean origin, previous to the Phoenician colonization. I favour ideas close to those Schulten proposed, but my argument is now based on archaeological evidence, the richness of which opens up new possibilities.

To begin with, Mediterranean seafaring, trade, and human migration at the end of the second millennium and the beginning of the first millennium BC appear to have been more important than was previously suspected (cf. Sandars 1985; Deger-Jakotzy 1983; Bunnen 1986). Their representation in the literature indicates that the historical reality of the myths is more than hypothetical. Possible contacts with Spain had been suspected but the archaeological data did not provide unquestionable proof until Mycenaean materials began to be recovered in the deposits of the Tartessian world (Martín de la Cruz 1988).

It is hard to know who exactly the agents of these Mediterranean contacts were, even though all evidence seems to point to people of the Aegean and eastern Mediterranean seas, most probably Mycenaean Cypriots (Bendala 1989, 1990, 1991; Lo Schiavo et al. 1985). With regard to the mode of navigation used in the precolonial period, recent studies (e.g., Bunnes 1986; Vagnetti 1985; Knapp 1992) identify sailors in search of fortune as an important catalyst to the Mediterranean ferment in the years of the Dark Age.

As far as the *nostoi* are concerned, it must be remembered that Iberia is also a part of the geographic realm of the adventures associated with those voyages. This is indicated in the accounts gathered mainly by Strabo, and also contained in works by Silius Italicus and Justinus. Modern Spanish scholars have always doubted the historical accuracy of the tales. García y Bellido (1948), who studied the texts which link the western Mediterranean with the *nostoi*, considered them to be a collection of old myths and legends written by poets and unscrupulous historians. Another Spanish author, García Iglesias (1979), carried out a more recent study of the *nostoi* and other Greek legends refering to Iberia.

He concluded that the Greek mythical traditions that refered to the west are late fabrications that do not indicate contact with the Greek world before the actual colonization. But generally speaking, these legends have been forgotten or dismissed, largely as a result of a legacy of pseudoscientific story-telling which used them as the basis of arguments for fantastic historical claims (such as the notion that the Greeks reached Galicia [Bermejo 1982]).

Nevertheless, as in the case of the legends associated with Italy, we should perhaps moderate our criticism and take the stories of the *nostoi* that refer to Iberia as accounts of actual voyages. Asklepiades of Myrlea, Strabo's main source of information on this subject, was perhaps not a frivolous inventor of stories during his stay in Betica, but rather a compiler of oral traditions that could have been distorted over the centuries since precolonial times. In much the same way, it is generally accepted that there is some historical truth in the story that Posidonius reports that the people of Gadir told about the founding of their city and the three trips the people from Tyre made prior to establishing themselves.

It is necessary to examine both the extent of movement in the Mediterranean in the period between the Mycenaean collapse and the historical colonizations, and the influence of that movement on the west side of the Mediterranean. This means, in other words, that we pay due attention to the phenomena accurately referred to as 'precolonization,' to its characteristic migrations, and the important consequences of these migrations in the Mediterranean as a whole, including the lands of its western border.

Now is the time to ask the main question of this discussion: if there were contacts with the Aegean realm in the first stage of Tartessos, is it possible to consider the actions of the Peoples of the Sea as one of the components of that contact? The issue can be discussed not only in terms of the arguments once used by Schulten, but also using archaeological evidence. The warriors depicted on the Tartessian stelae of the southwest have many of the characteristics of some of the Peoples of the Sea and, in particular, of the *Sherden* or *Shardana*: helmets with horns, swords and round shields. Even if the Peoples of the Sea were present, it is as yet difficult to determine whether they were present in sufficient quantity to have had an effect among the ranks of the agents who intervened in the formation of the early period in Tartessos.

Even without taking Tartessos into consideration, it is difficult to establish certain facts about the Peoples of the Sea, who have generated a rich bibliography in their own right (e.g., Alvar 1989; Bunnes 1986; Dothan 1983; Sandars 1985). It seems that, in general, the Peoples of the Sea came from regions situated west and south of Asia Minor and north of Syria, without any important settlements in Crete and Cyprus. Some of them could be the Achaeans themselves, if one accepts the correlation between the Achaeans and Danaans of the Greek tradition and the *Eqwesh* and *Danuna* referred to by the Egyptians. However, any attempt at identification encounters problems. For example, it is not clear whether one of the groups that is most often discussed, the *Sherden* (documented from the time of Rameses II to that of Rameses III), arrived in Sardinia from the east, as some suspect (e.g., Sandars 1985), or whether they originated in Sardinia, an idea that I personally find improbable.

The possibility of a migration toward the western Mediterranean of groups of Peoples of the Sea, including the thought-provoking etymological relationship between the *Shardana* and Sardinia, is not to be dismissed, even if there are still problems to be solved (Knapp 1992; Tykot 1994). A different question is whether, following the same trend, groups of Peoples of the Sea also arrived in the Iberian peninsula. The question raised by Deger-Jakotzy (1983) of the relationship between the Peoples of the Sea and the use of 'handmade burnished ware' begs the question about Tartessian pottery, which is very similar in the precolonial period. It will be important to continue a careful investigation of this kind of pottery, which also is present in the Nuraghic Culture. In numerous places affected by destruction caused by the Peoples of the Sea it is also noted that, immediately afterwards, cremations suddenly replace inhumations in burial practice (Karkemish, Alalakl Hamat). That could also feasibly have taken place in Iberia where it is possible to associate the emergence of the funerary rite of cremation with the first stage of the development of Tartessos.

On the other hand, the Mycenaean component that is ascribed to the early Tartessian period could be explained by direct contacts with Myceneans, who were, in my view, one of the Peoples of the Sea. With regard to this, what is known about the Peleset-Philistines, and their characteristic material culture (Dothan 1982) should be borne in mind. Perhaps the cultural process which is discernible in Tartessos will find useful parallels in Palestine. Considering all the archaeological indications, and the warriors of the stelae in particular, which are closest in appearance to the Shardana above all, one is tempted to agree with authorities such as Pingel (1980), who argued that, despite the problems of interpretation that exist, the similarities between Sardinian warriors and those represented in Tartessian stelae are such that it cannot be denied that there is some relation between them.

Bibliography

Alvar, J.

1989   *Los Pueblos del Mar y Otros Movimientos de Pueblos a Fines del II Milenio*. Historia del Mundo Antiguo 7. Madrid: Akal.

Bendala, M.

1977   Notas Sobre las Estelas Decoradas del Suroeste y los Origenes de Tartessos. *Habis* 8: 321–30.

1985   Tartessos. In *Historia General de España y América*, 1: 595–642. Madrid: Rialp.

1986   La Baja Andalucía durante el Bronce Final. In *Homenaje a Luis Siret, 1884–1934*, 530–36. Sevilla: Consejería de Cultura, Junta de Andalucía.

1990   Tartessos Hoy a la Luz de los Datos Arqueológicos y Literarios. *Cuadernos Emeritenses* 2: 11–27.

1991   Tartessos. *Boletin de la Asociación Española de Amigos de la Arqueología* 30–31: 99–110.

Bermejo, J.C.

1982   *Galicia y los griegos*. Santiago: Salvora.

Blanco, A.

1967   La Colonización de la Península Ibérica en el Primer Milenio Antes de Cristo. In J.M. Gomez-Tabanera (ed.), *Las Raíces de España*, 167–97. Madrid: Instituto Español de Antropología Aplicada.

Blázquez, J.M.

1975   *Tartessos y los Orígenes de la Colonización Fenicia en Occidente*, 2nd ed. Salamanca: Universidad de Salamanca.

Bunnes, G.

1985   I Filistei e le Invasioni dei Popoli del Mare. In D. Musti (ed.), *Le Origini dei Greci, Dori e Mondo Egeo*, 227–56. Rome: Laterza.

Colonna, G.

1974   Preistoria e Protostoria di Roma e del Lazio. In M. Pallotino, G. Mansuelli, A. Prosdocimi and O. Parlangeli (eds), *Popoli e Civiltà dell'Italia*

Antica, 2: 273–346. Rome: Biblioteca di Storia Patria a Cura dell'Ente per la Diffusione e l'Educazione.

Deger-Jalkotzy, S.

1983   Das Problem der 'Handmade Burnished Ware' von Myk. IIIC. In S. Deger-Jalkotzy (ed.), *Griechenland, die Ägäis und die Levant während der 'Dark Ages' vom 12. bis zum 9. Jahrhundert v. Chr.*, 161–68. Sitzungberichte der Österreichischen Akademie der Wissenschaften 418. Mykenische Forschungen 10. Vienna: OAW.

Dothan, T.

1982   *The Philistines and their Material Culture*. New Haven: Yale University Press.

1983   Some aspects of the appearance of the Sea Peoples and Philistines in Canaan. In S. Deger-Jalkotzy (ed.), *Griechenland, die Ägäis und die Levant während der 'Dark Ages' vom 12. bis zum 9. Jahrhundert v. Chr.*, 99–117. Sitzungberichte der Österreichischen Akademie der Wissenschaften 418. Mykenische Forschungen 10. Vienna: OKW.

García Iglesias, L.

1979   La Península Ibérica y las tradiciones griegas de tipo mítico. *Archivo Español de Arqueología* 52: 131–40.

García y Bellido, A.

1931   Las relaciones entre el arte etrusco y el ibero. *Archivo Español de Arte y Arqueología* 7: 119–48.

1948   *Hispania Graeca*. Barcelona: Instituto Español de Estudios Mediterráneos.

Knapp, A.B.

1992   Bronze Age Mediterranean Island Cultures and the Ancient Near East. *Biblical Archaeologist* 55: 52–72, 112–28

Lo Schiavo, F., E. Macnamara and L. Vagnetti

1985   Late Cypriot Imports to Italy and their Influence on Local Bronzework. *Papers of the British School at Rome* 53: 1–69.

Luzón Nogue, J.M., and L.M. Coín Cuenca

1986   La Navegación Preastronómica en la Antigüedad: Utilización de Pájaros en la Orientacion Nautica. *Lvcentvm* 5: 65–85.

Marazzi, M.

1976   *Egeo e Occidente alla Fine del II Millenio a.C.* Rome: Edizione dell'Ateneo.

Martín de la Cruz, J.C.

1988   Mykenische Keramik aus Bronzezeitlichen Siedlungschichten von Montoro am Guadalquivir. *Madrider Mitteilungen* 29: 77–91.

Montenegro Duque, A.

1970   Los Pueblos del Mar en España y la Nueva Revisión de la Historia de Tartessos. *Boletin del Seminario de Arte y Arqueologia de Valladolid* 36: 237–87.

Pingel, V.

1980   Beziehungen zum westlichen Mittelmeer. In Jürgen Thimme (ed.), *Kunst und Kultur Sardiniens vom Neolithikum bis zum Ende der Nuraghenzeit*, exh. cat. Badisches Landesmuseums Karlsruhe, 162–71. Karslruhe: Müller.

Sandars, N.K.

1985   *The Sea Peoples: Warriors of the Ancient Mediterranean*. London: Thames and Hudson.

Schulten, A.

1922   *Tartessos: ein Beitrag zur ältesten Geschichte des Westens*. Hamburg: L. Friederichsen.

1930   Die Etrusker in Spanien. *Tartessos* 25: 365–432.

Tykot, R.H.

1994   Sea Peoples in Etruria? Italian Contacts with the Eastern Mediterranean in the late Bronze Age. *Etruscan Studies* 1: 59–83.

Vagnetti, L.

1985   I Contatti Precoloniali fra le Genti Indigene e i Paisi Mediterranei. In G. Pugliese Carratelli (ed.), *Magna Grecia: il Mediterraneo, le Metropoleis e la Fondazione delle Colonie*, 127–44. Milan: Electa.

9. The West of Iberia: Meeting Point between the Mediterranean and the Atlantic at the End of the Bronze Age[1]

Marisa Ruíz-Gálvez Priego

Geographical background

According to the 12th century geographer Al Idrisi, the Straits of Gibraltar were formed when Alexander the Great ordered the construction of a canal that would unite the waters of the Atlantic and the Mediterranean, so as to separate the bellicose inhabitants of the North African coast from those of the Iberian peninsula (García Mercadall 1972). This account shows that in the Middle Ages the western frontiers of the Mediterranean were still shrouded with a certain mystery. In this respect, Al Idrisi's story is similar to the those of antiquity, such as those classical accounts which describe the separation of Europe and Africa by Hercules, the tale of the Gorgons or that of the Garden of the Hesperides. Indeed, until the Second Punic War (218–201 BC), when the Roman conquest of Hispania began, Greek and Latin authors had knowledge only of the inhabitants of the east and south of the peninsula, *Iberia*, and they called, indiscriminately and erroneously, all those who dwelled there *Iberoi*.

However, in spite of its being the *finis terrae* for the voyagers of the ancient world, the Iberian peninsula's geostrategic position has made it a melting pot of cultures and peoples. Located in the extreme southwest of Europe, the peninsula is a bridge both between Europe and Africa and between the European western and eastern Mediterranean. Furthermore, apart from the Pyrenees, which joins Iberia to the continent, the rest of its territory is insular, with over half its coastline washed by the Atlantic, and joined to the Mediterranean by the straits of Gibraltar.

The geographic features of Iberia have meant that settlement around the coastline has tended to be denser, longer lasting, and more stable than it has in the interior. This is due to the presence of a very high plateau in the centre of the peninsula, extremely continental in its climate and surrounded by mountain chains that greatly impede communication between the centre and the periphery (Figure 9.1). This explains why the populations of the periphery have traditionally lived facing the sea, with their backs to the interior, even in regions like Cantabria which does not offer good natural conditions for maritime activity (Cabo 1973: 49).

Furthermore, many of the river deltas have changed their configurations over time and were navigable at the time of the first Mediterranean voyages to the peninsula. This is the case for the outlets of the rivers Tinto and Odiel that form the Ría de Huelva. According to ancient authors, the present salt marsh of the Odiel was once open sea and gradually changed into a lagoon, through which vessels could reach fishing villages that now are situated on hills in the interior (Díaz del Olmo 1989: 19; Ruíz Mata 1990: 60). Likewise, the salt marshes of the Guadalquivir were flooded and in the *Ora Maritima* they were called the *lacus licustinus*. This was a wide bay, shallow and open to the Atlantic, around which the principal sites of the Copper Age and the Late Bronze Age/Iron Age were located, among them Seville itself (Caro Bellido 1989: 87–89, fig. 2). The same occurs at the mouth of the river Guadalete and at the port of Cádiz, ancient Gadir (Escacena 1985: 39–42; Aubet 1987: 232–38; Caro Bellido 1989: 89, fig.3) (Figure 9.1).

The west of the peninsula has other attractions, however. First, it is situated in a natural circuit for Atlantic navigation (Figure 9.2). The Gulf stream splits into several currents as it crosses the Atlantic; and, helped by the west winds, one of these currents turns south along the coasts of Galicia and Portugal toward the Canaries and the Mediterranean via Gibraltar. This current divides into two near Ceuta and Algeciras, and one part goes towards the Spanish coast, the other toward the African coast. This permits one to sail with the current as far as Sardinia or Algeria (Gasull 1986: 199). Secondly, the main sources of the ores which were used in antiquity are concentrated in the west of the peninsula (Ruíz-Gálvez Priego 1991: fig. 5a).

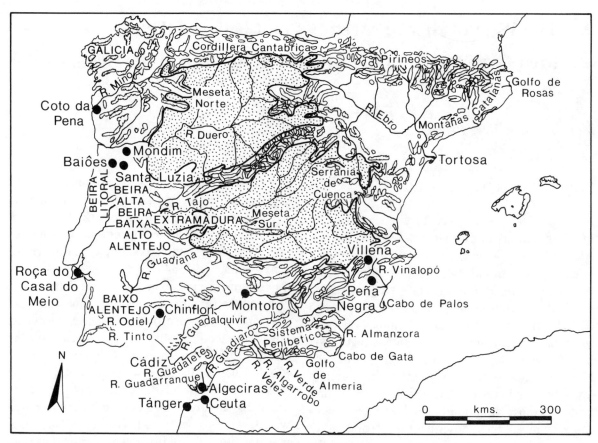

Figure 9.1   Map indicating the location of places mentioned in the text.

If, by contrast, one were to sail through the Mediterranean toward the peninsula, the most logical route with respect to the currents would be from Sicily and Sardinia to the Spanish Levant and Gibraltar (Aubet 1987: 165–68, figs. 28–29). Thus, if one sails from the northeast to the southwest, one comes first to the low, open coastline of the Golfo de Rosas, where the ancient colonies of Emporion and Rhode were located. From there, the coast becomes high and steep until one reaches the Ebro delta. From there to Almería the coast is once again low and open, with many littoral lagoons. This, together with the extended hours of sunshine and scant rainfall, has permitted the exploitation of salt-works since ancient times. From Almería to Gibraltar the coast once again becomes straight, with relatively few points of shelter. Perhaps because of this, the oldest Phoenician trading posts were located at the mouths of rivers (Cabo 1973; Vilá Valentí 1968; Aubet 1987: 256–57). The islands and promontories on which the trading posts were placed would have been politically neutral *terrae nullius* on which ports of trade could be established. Recent geomorphological investigations have demonstrated, however, that changes in the coastline of eastern

Andalusia did not occur before the deforestations that began during the Middle Ages. When Phoenician or Punic-Phoenician trading posts were established at their deltas, rivers like the Guadiaro and Guadarranque in Cádiz, the Vélez or the Algarrobo in Málaga, the Verde or the Seco in Granada, or the Almanzora in Almería were navigable (Arteaga *et al.* 1987). It would be another matter to face the passage through the Straits of Gibralter and encounter the change in winds and currents when leaving the Mediterranean and entering the Atlantic. Gasull (1986) believes that the difficulties of passing through the Straits (which are greater for those who come from the east than for those who come from the west) would explain why the oldest Phoenician establishments were located east of Gibraltar and not west, where the mineral resources are concentrated (Figure 9.2).

Europe during the transition from the Final Bronze Age to the Iron Age: the third agrarian revolution

The transitions from the Copper to the Bronze Age and from the Bronze Age to the Iron Age

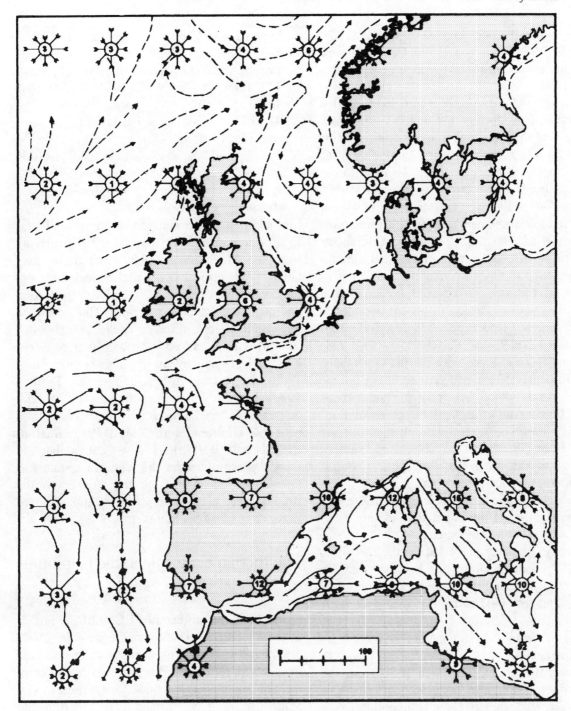

Figure 9.2   Winds and currents in the North Atlantic and the Mediterranean during the month of August, according to the U.S. Defence Mapping Agency, Hydrographic/Topographic Centre, Washington, D.C., 1989. To interpret the compass rose of the winds: the arrows indicate the direction from which the wind blows; the length of the arrow (measured from the exterior of the circle using the given scale) gives the percentage of the total number of observations in which the wind blew from that direction; if the arrow is very long, the percentage is indicated on its shaft; the number of feathers on the arrow indicates the mean force of the wind on the 0–12 Beaufort scale; the number inside the circle indicates the percentage of calm days.

have something in common. Each represents an era of agricultural intensification, and in both cases this manifests itself across Europe with the general presence of common conventions of gold working, warrior's outfits, and communal eating and drinking utensils. All of these indicate the

establishment in both cases of wider social ties that make Europe an open and interconnected continent (Sherratt 1987).

In large parts of central and western Europe these changes are reflected in higher population densities, more permanent use of arable land, and wider long distance contacts. Wells (1983: 147–150; 1984) points out that in Central Europe many more settlement and burial sites are known from 1200 to 800 BC than in the whole of the Early and Middle Bronze Age combined and that the settlements display prolonged occupations for the first time, lasting many generations. This also occurs in parts of Atlantic Europe such as, for example, southern England. There, in areas like Cranborne Chase during the British Middle Bronze Age, walled settlements begin to appear as do field lynchets demarcating cultivated plots (Barrett *et al.* 1991: 222). These developments seem to be associated with changes in agricultural practice that were conducive to the regeneration of the soil. This would favour greater sedentism, with a consequent loss of importance of the funerary landscape. Bradley (1981: 103) and Barrett (1989: 124; Barrett *et al.* 1991: 224) associate these changes with the the appearance of the bilateral inheritance systems characteristic of plough agriculture (Goody 1976). The changes would be the fruit of an 'agricultural revolution' (Bradley 1990: 143), of which legumes like the broad bean (*Vicia faba* L., present in southern England at this time [Bradley, pers. comm.]) would have no doubt been a part.

These changes indicate an increase in the size and the stability of the population and are associated with other features such as:

1. Massive exploitation of salt for the first time. Salt is both important for livestock and for metallurgy, and also for the storage and preservation of foodstuffs for the winter; if 'pecuniary' derives from *pecus*, 'salary' derives from *sal*, and neither etymology is coincidental.
2. The diffusion of the broad bean from the Mediterranean into central and northern Europe. The broad bean is important as a nitrogen fixing agent, has a greater nutritional value (a higher protein and carbohydrate content) than other legumes, and is better adapted to acid soils than the most legumes (Duke 1981: 275–77); the combination of cereals and legumes has a high nutritional value and was traditionally a substitute for meat in poor areas of the Mediterranean (Rivera Núñez and Obón de Castro 1989: 249–53).
3. Other plants that are highly nutritious or resistant to harsh climatic conditions, like lentils, peas, spelt wheat or certain oil seeds, become widespread or increase in importance over

large parts of Europe (Zohary and Hopf 1973: 887, 1989: 83; Hopf 1982: 15; Jäger and Lozeck 1982: 173; Harding 1983: 22, 1984: 173, 1989: 174–76; Wells 1984: 47; Marnival 1988: 55, 129).

4. The use of metal for agricultural instruments (Harding 1976: 513–22).
5. The spread of systems of land division marked by lynchets (co-axial or Celtic field systems) across much of northwest Europe (Harding 1976, 1989).

In addition to the cultigens, new technologies like beaten metalwork and iron were arriving from the Mediterranean, and with them, long before the historical Greek and Phoenician colonies, came new forms of social differentiation and of public displays of wealth. This permitted expansion of long distance exchange networks, in which metal played a fundamental role, not only in the establishment of alliances (Rowlands 1980) and in competition for prestige (Bradley 1990), but also in the accumulation of wealth that can be stored and reconverted within those networks (Halstead and O'Shea 1982; Sherratt and Sherratt 1991: 360). It was then that the Iberian peninsula, after the long hiatus that followed the transition from the Copper to the Bronze Age, became reintegrated into western European exchange circuits.

The Iberian peninsula at the beginning of the Final Bronze Age

From the thirteenth century BC until the arrival of the Phoenicians (Ferrarese Ceruti *et al.* 1987; Matthäus 1989), Cyprus seems to have occupied the vacuum left by the Mycenaeans in the commercial routes to the central Mediterranean (Lo Schiavo *et al.* 1985; Knapp 1990; Sherratt and Sherratt 1991: 375). On those routes, Sardinia occupied an important position. According to Gale and Stos-Gale (1988: 382–383), this was due not so much to the presence of copper on the island as to its privileged location, which allowed it to act as an intermediary on the routes leading to the tin sources on the Iberian peninsula (Penhallurick 1986: 60). Thus, Sardinia would have served as a "gateway community" (Hirth 1978), in the sense that its location enabled it to link two regions with different technologies and social organizations — Cyprus (and more generally the eastern Mediterranean), on the one hand, and the Iberian peninsula, on the other.

In my opinion it cannot be taken for granted that Iberian tin would have been the primary objective of Cypriot interests in Sardinia right during the initial stages of contact. On the contrary, metal analyses show that (except in the northwest of the peninsula, where metallurgical activity had little salience), tin bronzes were rare until the last third of the second millennium BC, and that before the Final Bronze Age metallurgical production was small scale (Ruíz-Gálvez Priego 1987; Montero 1993). That is to say, before the Final Bronze Age tin was not exploited systematically in the peninsula and, thus, could hardly have been the primary goal of Cypriot trade with Sardinia.

It is precisely during the Final Bronze Age that the peninsula undergoes technological, social, and indeed ethnic transformations of great importance:

1. In the northeast, the infiltration of Urnfield peoples across the Pyrenees
2. In the west, the reactivation of Atlantic exchange networks
3. In the south, the first Mediterranean voyages that would culminate in the establishment of Phoenician trading posts from the eighth century BC on.

All the same, the level of socio-economic organization at the beginning of the Final Bronze Age was not the same in all parts of the peninsula. In the southeast and the Levant, from the beginning of the Bronze Age, there were permanent settlements and necropoleis with evidence of hereditary social statuses and bilateral descent systems (Ruíz-Gálvez Priego 1992), like those to which Barrett and Bradley have called attention in southern England for a later time period. In the rest of the peninsula there were discontinuous or, frankly, mobile settlements until the Final Bronze Age or the transition to the Iron Age (Ruíz-Gálvez Priego 1991). The contrast between the southeast and the rest of the peninsula must be explained in terms of differences in agricultural technology. Thus, from the Copper Age, the southeast and the Levant had an efficient agricultural technology that permitted the maintenance of a growing population and the conservation of soil fertility: the plough (Peters and van den Driesch 1990: 75), legumes, animal manure, and possibly also Mediterranean polyculture. Indeed, south-east Spain is a possible centre of broad bean domestication (Rivera Núñez *et al.* 1988: 232). In contrast, the rest of the peninsula provides no

evidence for stable, permanent settlements and demographic growth prior to the Final Bronze Age or the Iron Age (Ruíz-Gálvez Priego 1991).

Case studies

Villena

It is within this context that the first indications of Mycenaean contacts with the Iberian peninsula should be placed. These consist of two Late Helladic IIIA/B (14th–13th century) potsherds from the site of Montoro in the middle basin of the Guadalquivir (Martín de la Cruz 1988, 1992) (Figure 9.1). This find has revived the old question of the Mediterranean connection of the El Argar Culture (Schubart 1976; Martín de la Cruz 1992). In my opinion, however, it would be premature to return to the diffusionist position, since apart from these two sherds the other evidence that has been brought forward to support it is vague and problematical. The issue should be addressed in terms not of parallels and formal similarities, but of the material and social conditions (the infrastructure of technical knowledge and the nature of social networks) that would lead to such similarities. And here, above all, one must take into account the very limited Iberian use of tin prior to the Final Bronze Age.

The best illustration of my point is provided by the example of the discovery of America. Although what Columbus was looking for was the shortest route to Asia and not a new continent, the discovery was by no means a product of chance. It involved, rather, the confluence of a series of technical innovations and of political, ideological, and economic circumstances, some of which, such as the transmission of Greek and Arab science to Europe, had been developing for several centuries (Chaunu 1972: 50–63; Domínguez Ortiz 1973: 54–59; Vernet 1978; Chandeigne 1992). It is fairly probable that other navigators preceded Columbus (Wallace 1991), but the historically effective discovery of America only took place when it was materially and humanly possible, and not before.

Likewise, regular navigation between the opposite ends of the Mediterranean took place when the material means and the social and economic stimuli for it were in place, and not before. Perhaps, then, the Mycenaean sherds from Montoro reflect exploratory voyages in search of new resources and markets or even a one-way journey, and not regular commercial travel. The precise and systematic placement of the Phoenician trading posts in the southern peninsula as of the eighth century BC suggests that such earlier explorations existed and that they provided eastern Mediterranean voyagers with information about itineraries, resources, and locations long before the Phoenicians decided to establish themselves in the west (cf. Aubet 1987: 52–77). Both historical and ethnographic information indicates that the purpose of many long distance voyages is not primarily or exclusively commerce, but the acquisition of knowledge and the collection of information (Helms 1988: 66–80; Kirch 1984: 82). The traveller Al Idrisi himself, to whom we referred at the beginning of this essay, was a 'specialist in knowledge' in the service of the kings of Sicily.

Luzón Nogue and Coín Cuenca (1986: 74) claim that navigation out of sight of land, round-trip journeys from one end of the Mediterranean to the other, regular long-distance trips, and the establishment of commercial routes would have been impossible prior to such great innovations as astronomical navigation and nocturnal piloting. Thus, sea journeys prior to the historically documented ones of the Phoenicians and Greeks would have consitituted 'voyages without return', in which there was no intention of creating commercial routes (Luzón Nogue and Coín Cuenca 1986: 74, 77). This argument is based on classical texts (Pliny's *Natural History* VII, 57 or Strabo's *Geography* I) that attribute the application of astronomy to navigation to the Phoenicians. Nothing proves, however, that such knowledge could not have been acquired prior to the first millennium BC. Furthermore, in spite of fogs and summer hazes (Luzón Nogue and Coín Cuenca 1986: 77), deep sea navigation is possible within the Mediterranean by reference to fixed points on land that are visible from far off shore: even today, this is how fishermen navigate (Schüle 1970; Aubet 1987: 148–50).

Given the increasing frequency of oriental objects found in Italy and the islands of the central Mediterranean (Knapp 1990; Sherratt and Sherratt 1991), one may reasonably suppose that journeys were rather more regular and systematic than the 'pot-luck' voyages posited by Luzón. It is not far fetched to attribute the pre-Phoenician finds of the Late and Final Bronze Age to exploratory voyages seeking new routes to the west. This would have required a supporting infrastructure, such as a network of stopping-points on friendly or neutral territory, which would permit repairs, provisioning or night time anchorages.[2]

This may have been the function of Villena (Alicante), on the coast of the Spanish Levant (Figure 9.1) and may explain the find in that locality of a spectacular treasure of about ten kilograms in weight, consisting of a service of eleven gold bowls, two gold and three silver bottles, 28 cylindrical bracelets, and various smaller pieces and fragments of gold, amber, and iron. The treasure was found in the Rambla del Panadero (Figure 9.3), a dry flood channel about six km north northeast of the city, and has no context, although the area around the location of the find was surveyed and excavated (Soler 1965, 1969; Almagro Gorbea 1974; Schüle 1976). Although the assemblage has been traditionally interpreted as a founder's hoard because of the presence of broken and unfinished pieces (Perea 1991), the uniformity of the bowls and bottles suggests to me that they were part of a single set, and probably the personal property of a single individual (Gaimster 1991: 114), surely male. Luxury services for communal eating and drinking were owned by males all over Late/Final Bronze Age Europe. Perhaps their presence became more common in association with the changes in agriculture and the appearance of patriarchal systems (Ruíz-Gálvez Priego 1992; Goody 1982). Since I have recently analyzed the significance of the Villena treasure in its social and historical context (Ruíz-Gálvez Priego 1992), I will limit my discussion here to three points that suggest the presence of either Cypriot voyagers or Sardinian intermediaries in the Spanish Levant.

1. Villena reflects contacts between Mediterranean traders and indigenous elites and the development of forms of emulation among the latter. Schüle (1976) pointed out that the bracelets and the table service were made locally, and indeed the bracelets have chronological precedents in the local tradition (Ruíz-Gálvez Priego 1992). Although I agree with Schüle that the Villena service has the same vessel forms as the Cogotas I pottery of the post-Argaric Late Bronze Age, it is based on a tradition of gold table services that is foreign and oriental (Sherratt and Sherratt 1991: 360; Ruíz-Gálvez Priego 1992). The amber and the iron also appear to be non-local, although we do not have physical-chemical analyses. The amber from Villena is, significantly, set in gold, a feature whose closest point of reference is Sardinia,

where amber is also imported and of Protovillanovan type (Lo Schiavo and Ridgway 1986: 396–97).

At least one piece of iron is, like the amber, set in gold. This seems to indicate that it was valued for its exotic quality (its exchange value) and not for its practical utility (its use value) (Renfrew 1986). Thus the hoard, must be earlier than the first exploitation of iron in the eighth century, at the Phoenician establishments of Toscanos and Trayamar (Niemeyer 1985; Schubart 1985). Once again Sardinia is the geographical point closest to Villena where iron is documented. There it appears as of the thirteenth century BC

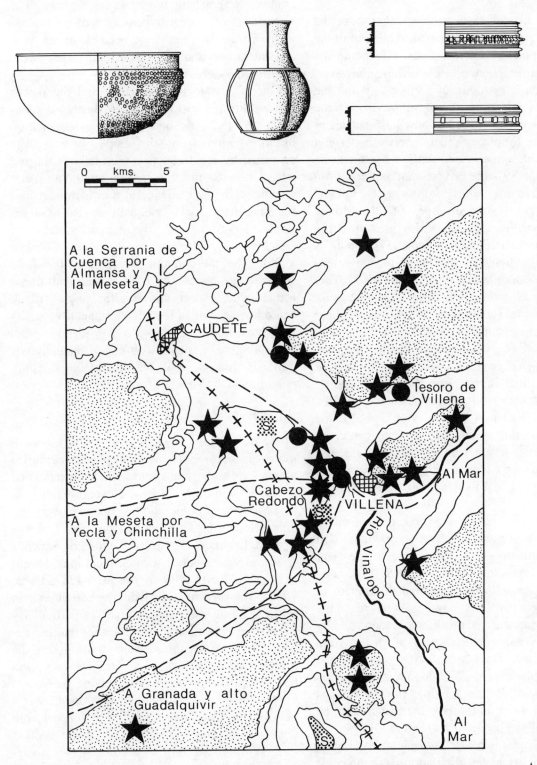

Figure 9.3 The geographic setting of the Villena treasure. Location of Cabezo Redondo, Bronze age sites (★), Saltworks (S), Silver or gold hoards (●), Natural roads (—), Transhumance routes (+).

in contexts with Cypriot imports (Vagnetti 1986: 360; Vagnetti and Lo Schiavo 1989: 227, 232; Muhly and Stech 1990: 210–11). Finally, the system of applique nails that finishes several of the Villena metal pieces has no antecedents in the peninsula, but it is known on Cyprus from at least the thirteenth century on (Catling 1964: 138).

2. Given its lack of archaeological context, the Villena treasure is usually dated in relation to the Phoenician factories in the south of the peninsula and the introduction of iron. Schüle, however, rejected any relation of Villena with the Phoenicians and proposed an approximate date of the tenth century BC. We now have sufficient information to place Villena between *termini post* and *ante quem*. According to Martín de la Cruz (1988: 89), the Mycenaean pottery from Montoro give a *terminus post quem* of 1300 BC for the Late Bronze Age of the lower Guadalquivir. This phase is also present at the site of Cabezo Redondo (Soler 1987), which is the largest settlement (and the only one extensively excavated) near Villena (Figure 9.3). This would give a *terminus post quem* for the treasure, since its table service has the forms of Late Bronze Age Cogotas I pottery. The *terminus ante quem* would be provided by nearby sites like Peña Negra (Figure 9.1), the earliest levels of which are Final Bronze Age, without Cogotas I pottery but with tenth to ninth century imports. Thus, the Villena treasure would be dated between the thirteenth and the tenth centuries, that is to say in an early pre-colonial context.

3. Such a rich find can only be explained in a region which, like Villena, combines exceptional advantages.

i) It is located 60 km from the present coast, two days on horseback or just a few hours if it were possible to go up the course of the river Vinalopó, on whose upper reaches Villena is located. It should be remembered that mouth of the river has changed: today it does not reach the sea, but disappears in the Elche lagoon, a salty marsh (now more or less dry) that formed from the silting up of a marine bay. Four thousand years ago, however, the Vinalopó reached the sea (Cuenca and Walker 1976) in the 'Sinus Illicitanus'. Thus, in the past the distance to the coast must have been shorter (Figure 9.1).

ii) Villena is a hub of communications (Figure 9.3), which articulates circulation from the coast to the mining areas of the upper Guadalquivir, to the pastures of the southern Meseta, and to the

livestock raising area of the Cuenca mountains (where bracelets like those from Villena have been found: Ruíz-Gálvez Priego 1992). Even now transhumant herders come down from the Cuenca mountains to the coast along the Vinalopó valley.

iii) Villena has abundant water resources and controls several salt works in its vicinity. The importance of salt for livestock needs no explanation. These salt works have been exploited since ancient times and in the Middle Ages were controlled by a royal monopoly.

Villena's strategic importance and the power and wealth of its local elites are further demonstrated by the dense and continuous occupation of the region from the Early Bronze Age onwards, by the frequency of smaller gold and silver hoards in this region without metal resources, by the evidence of its funerary record for hereditary social inequalities (Ruíz-Gálvez Priego 1992), and by the use of systems of weights (the gold bracelets: Ruíz-Gálvez Priego 1995). The pre-colonial voyages of the Late Bronze Age would have increased and transformed elite power and wealth, since Villena could have provided the Mediterranean voyagers with meat and its preservatives, with hides and milk products, perhaps with upper Guadalquivir minerals, and above all with a suitable stopping point in which to anchor for the night.

Baiões

These exploratory voyages seem to have been a more or less regular feature of the centuries which followed. This would seem to be indicated by the sporadic presence of eleventh-tenth century Sicilian *ad ochio* and Cypriot *arco serpegiante* fibulae in sites along the coast of the Spanish Levant (Gil-Mascarell and Peña Sánchez 1989), as well as along the coast and inland areas of western Iberia (Blasco Bosqued 1987; Ponte 1989). The presence of Mediterranean objects in hillforts along the Atlantic coast is particularly interesting because it indicates either that indigenous Atlantic peoples were trading in the Mediterranean or that Mediterranean voyagers had solved the problem of traversing the straits of Gibralter and navigating the open sea. I believe that there are arguments to support both possibilities. The more or less sporadic visiting of the Portuguese coast by Mediterranean voyagers is demonstrated by the burial at Roça de Casal do Meio. The Baiões hoard and the site of

Peña Negra are proof of the route to the central Mediterranean taken by Atlantic sailors.

Roça de Casal do Meio is a unique burial site in several respects: first, it is the only known tomb in central Portugal from the Final Bronze Age, a period in which archaeologically recognizable tombs are scarce all over Atlantic Europe; secondly, it is a corbel-vaulted tomb, whose closest parallels are in the Sardinian Late Bronze Age; thirdly, the two individuals buried in the tomb are accompanied by clearly Mediterranean grave goods (a belt buckle, tweezers, an ivory comb, and an *ad ochio* fibula). Spindler and Ferreira (1973) proposed a ninth to eighth

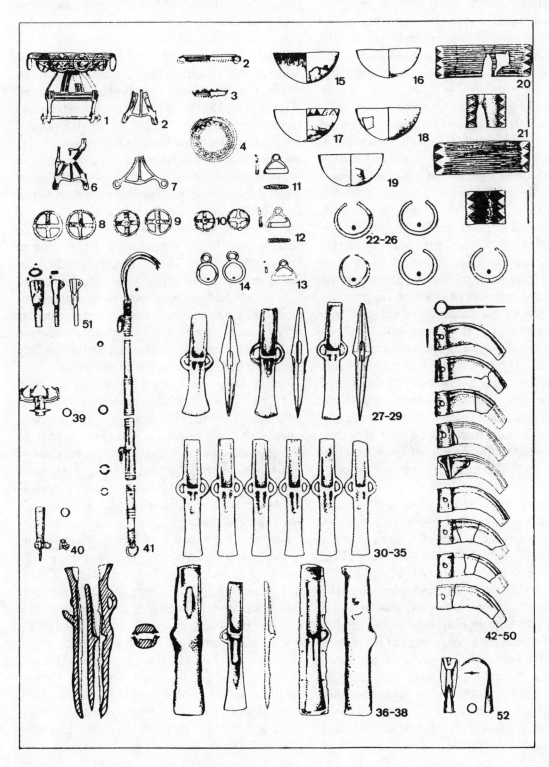

Figure 9.4   The Baiões hoard (after Silva 1986, no scale).

century date for this tomb because this would fit with the colonial setting with which they believed it was connected. For the same reasons, Belén *et al.* (1991) accept this date, although they interpret the site as a burial of Mediterranean traders in a native setting. No one opposes, however, an earlier date of the eleventh to tenth century, which would coincide with that of the fibula and would fit well with the context of the Portuguese hillforts. Several of these hillforts are in the interior, near tin sources, and have yielded these same fibulae (Ponte 1989: fig. 1).

The Baiões hoard comes from one of these hillforts. It consists of a series of objects of mixed origin and differential level of preservation. Among them stand out several pieces of Mediterranean origin: fragments of one or several wheeled vessels, a harness attachment, and a chisel with an iron bit and tubular bronze haft (Figure 9.4, 1–15). Interestingly enough, the iron object (Figure 9.4, 15) is treated very differently to the way it is treated in Villena, and so must have had a different significance. At Baiões iron seems to have been valued as a tool, for practical purposes, but its adaptation to a local tool type — the tubular chisel — suggests only a precarious familiarity with the new metal. This leads me to suggest that the iron was imported and put to use in an indigenous context, hafted into a piece that is clearly of Atlantic type. Tentatively, then, the Baiões hoard could be suggested to be later than Villena but earlier than the Phoenician introduction of iron-working. That is to say, it belonged to a late pre-colonial context.

The wheeled vessel (Figure 9.4, 1–10) is also interesting. It is of Cypriot inspiration, since its decoration is similar to that of Cypriot chariots and tripods (Catling 1964: 210–11, plate 36A, 36N; Matthäus 1985: plates 90, 91, 100, 105, 133/2). The absence of an exact parallel to the Baiões piece suggests, however, that it is an imitation. The Cypriot chariots date to between the thirteenth and tenth centuries, and the tripods are somewhat later (Matthäus 1985: plate 133/2). On Sardinia, Cypriot tripods and local imitations are known as early as the end of the second millennium, and votive chariots appear at the beginning of the first millennium (Lo Schiavo *et al.* 1985: 48–51; Tanda 1987).

The Baiões harness attachment (Figure 9.4, 11–14) also has parallels in Cyprus (Catling 1964: 262, fig. 23/5–6, plate 48/G–I), but its relatively simple form makes it impossible to exclude the possibility that it was made locally.

The axes, sickles, bracelets and rings (Figure 9.4, 20–50) have casting seams (Silva *et al.* 1986: 75) and are surely of local manufacture. They are, furthermore, common types in Final Bronze Age Portuguese hillforts. The spears (Figure 9.4, 51) are also local, since Baiões has also produced the clay moulds from which that type of weapon is made.

Other elements are of more doubtful origin. Some bowls retain casting seams (Silva *et al.* 1986: 75), but others are broken or repaired (Figure 9.4, 18). In any case their metal plate technology has precedents in the Mediterranean, not locally. The 'meat hooks' (Figure 9.4, 39–41) may be local or may have been imported by the Atlantic trade networks. Although these hooks are of Mediterranean origin[3], they are known in Final Bronze Age contexts in central and western Europe, including western Iberia (Hundt 1953; Jockenhövel 1974; Ruíz-Gálvez 1979; Gómez and Pautreau 1988). The Baiões hillfort also produced an articulated roasting spit. The hooks and the spit would both be associated with the communal, ritualized consumption of meat, undoubtedly by men, although the feasts may not have had the same meaning in western Iberia that they had in the Mediterranean (Sherratt 1994).

Unfortunately the hoard was found by accident, and the subsequent excavation provided no information about its context. The various excavation campaigns have also failed to provide a stratigraphy for the site. Finally, the only radiocarbon date[4] for the hillfort has a high standard deviation — the 95% confidence range is 1112–405 BC — and can be rejected (Carballo and Fábregas 1991: 260).

The wheeled vessel is the only object in the hoard that is undoubtedly foreign in its origin, social significance, and cultural setting. That it was found broken and in poor condition indicates that it was present at Baiões as scrap metal and not for its social or ritual significance. This makes arguments like Bradley's (1985) about exchange and social distance applicable. Because of this and because the piece lacks exact Cypriot parallels, I believe that it was not traded from that point of origin. The only other possibilities, then, are that it comes from either Sardinian intermediaries or Atlantic voyagers trading scrap metal in the western and central Mediterranean. Neither possibility can be excluded, but the second is more likely for the following two reasons:

1) there is Iberian metalwork in Sardinia (Ruíz-Gálvez Priego 1986); 2) there is an Atlantic foundry at Peña Negra, half way between the Portuguese coast and Sardinia (Figure 9.1).

Peña Negra

Like Villena, Peña Negra is located near the Vinalopó river, but in its lower reaches, some 20 km from the present coastline (and possibly closer to the sea at the time of its occupation). The Crevillente range, on which the site is situated, today dominates a broad salt marsh (González Prats 1983: pl. 1), which must have formed part of the Sinus Illicitanus. Its location for commerce is, thus, much more favourable than that of Villena, and this would, in my opinion, explain the latter's disappearance. Recent surveys (Navarro 1982: pls. 1, 2) indicate a population shift towards the lower and middle part of the Vinalopó valley at the time of the occupation of Cabezo Redondo or immediately after. Perhaps the inability to retain control over commerce along this important trade route may explain the demise of Cabezo Redondo, the hiding of the Villena treasure, and the loss of power by its owner.

Peña Negra is first occupied in the Final Bronze Age, after Villena, and owes its wealth to a livestock economy emphasizing cattle. Mediterranean commerce is documented from the earliest occupation of Peña Negra onwards. This phase is known as Peña Negra I (González Prats 1983, 1990). The second phase (Peña Negra II) follows without a break and is characterized by the adoption of iron and the potter's wheel. The site eventually grew to a size of thirty hectares, with large urban complexes and possibly with Oriental artisans in residence. Accordingly, the excavator identifies the site with the city of Herna described in the *Ora Maritima* (González Prats 1983: 273, 277; 1990: 104). Peña Negra II would date from the end of the eighth or beginning of the seventh century to the middle of the sixth century, when the city was sacked and destroyed (González Prats 1983: 180, 277).

The earlier phase, Peña Negra I, presents a variety of interesting features. Excavations have revealed a building (Figure 9.5, 1) with evidence of activities that, in my opinion, indicate its use not as a dwelling place, but as a workshop for such craft activities as casting and weaving (González Prats 1990, Ruíz-Gálvez 1990: 337). The 1987 excavation season indicated that metalworking at least was practiced on the site from the very beginning (phase Ia) of its occupation.

The workshop building belongs to the last bronze age level (Peña Negra Ic). It has an oval layout and a stone socle, the usable internal space being 16 m^2. Under the floor a baby was buried at the southern end and a headless sheep/goat at the northern end. Were these simply burials or were they foundation offerings? Inside the building there was a small casting oven consisting of a clay ring of some 60 cm in diameter and an interior cavity of some 20 cm in diameter. Metallurgical activities in the interior of the oven were indicated by signs of thermic alteration to the floor. The casting must have been done outside the building, since it is there that we find the remains of slag, heavy hammers, and moulds. The latter must have been fixed vertically into the ground. According to González Prats (1990: 93–94, 106), the exterior casting made the activity which was carried out in the workshop possible. This was identified during the 1987 season when the cleaning of a clay platform in the western end of the building revealed several loom weights and bone spindles.

The objects cast in the clay moulds and the remains of the casting were analyzed and identified (Ruíz-Gálvez Priego 1990) as belonging to swords, axes, pins, and spears (Figure 9.5, 2–36). These last two elements, at least, clearly belong to the 'Vénat' type of Atlantic metallurgy (Coffyn *et al.* 1981), known from Sardinia to the British Isles (although evidence for its manufacture is only found in the Iberian peninsula). The spears and the mould from the Baiões hillfort and the moulds from Coto da Pena (Silva 1986: plates 88/9–10, 89/9, 14 and p.29, n.128) also belong to the Vénat type. The axes (Figure 9.5, 35–36), cast in sandstone moulds, are of the 'trunnion celt' type and seem to be ingots rather than tools. As far as the sword (Figure 9.5, 2–4) is concerned, it may be assigned, with reservations, to the Vénat type (Ruíz-Gálvez Priego 1990).

The analyses, both of the clay moulds and of the slag and casting remains, suggest a sophisticated metallurgy with high level of technical knowledge. Perhaps the most interesting conclusion, however, is that all the material is recast and is extremely heterogeneous, the product of the recovery and refining of scrap metal (Ruíz-Gálvez Priego 1990). Given the scarcity of metal

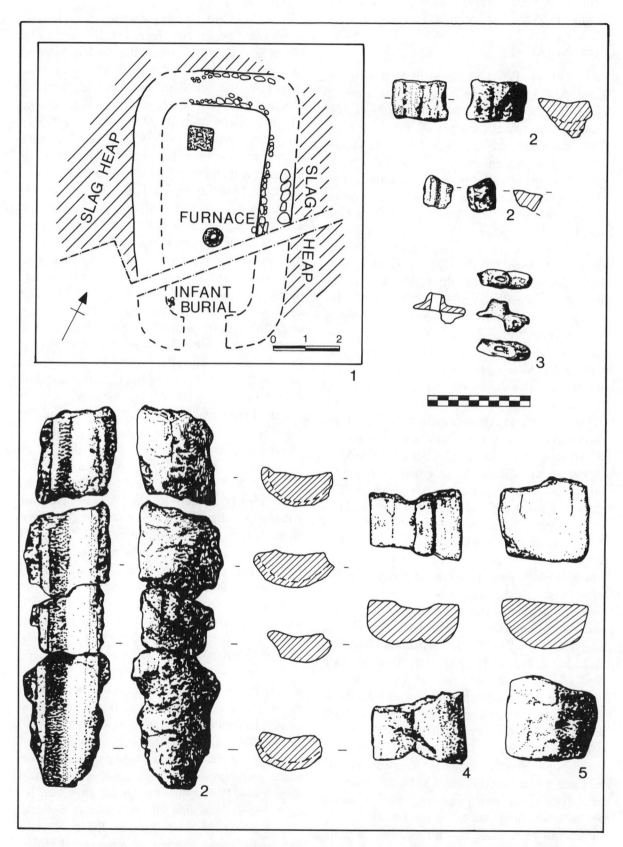

Figure 9.5 a 1: The Peña Negra workshop (after González Prats 1992). **b.** (opposite page) 2–37: Fragments of casting moulds (after Ruíz-Gálvez 1990); nos. 26–27 are plaster casts from molds no. 24 and 25.

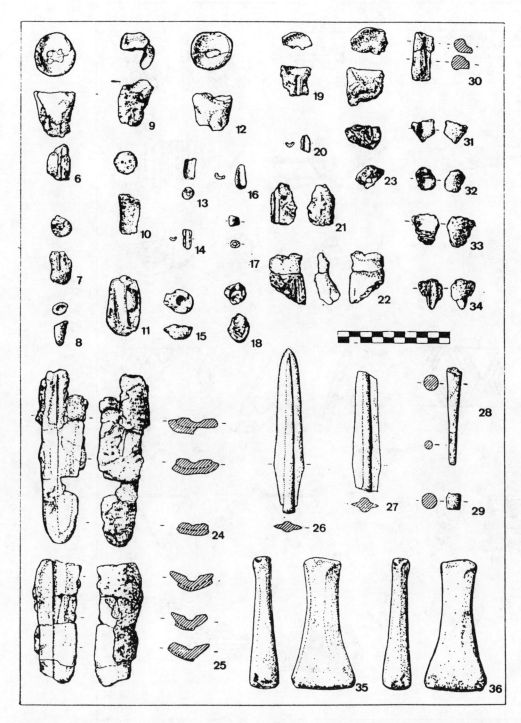

sources in this area, the only explanation for the presence of a metallurgical workshop at Peña Negra, and for the evidence of casting activities from the early stages of occupation of the site onwards is Peña Negra's position as an intermediary on the sea route from the tin sources of Portugal to the central Mediterranean (Figure 9.1).

This raises the question of the origin of the artisans of the Peña Negra workshop. I have three reasons for believing that the metallurgist

at Peña Negra was an itinerant smith. First, it is unthinkable that a local inhabitant of Peña Negra would have produced such work given that the area is unconnected to the Atlantic setting to which all the cast objects belong, except perhaps for the trunnion celts (Almagro Gorbea 1989: 283, 1992: 643). These, however, seemed to have served as copper ingots, a bronze low in copper and tin (González Prats 1985). Second, in spite of the site's size and apparent prosperity, it is difficult to believe that a specialist, even a part-

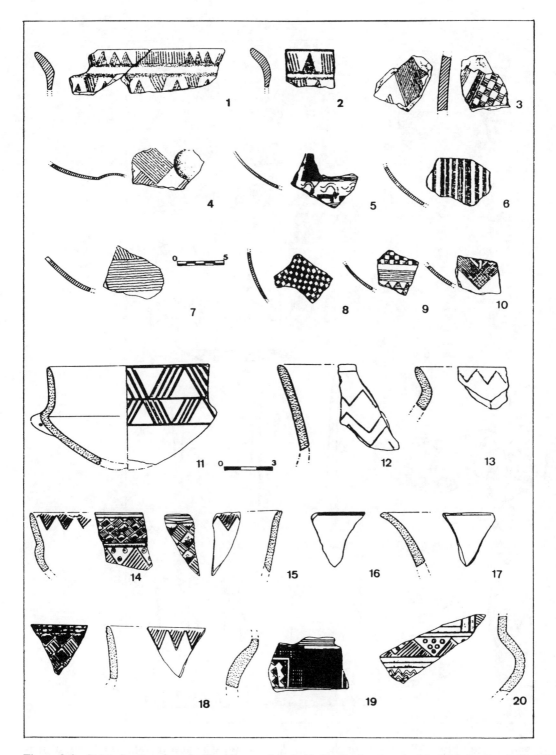

Figure 9.6   Painted pottery from the Final Bronze Age. 1–10: Huelva (western Andalusia) (after Fernández-Miranda 1986). 11–20: Peña Negra (Alicante) (after González Prats 1983).

time one, would produce only for the internal market of Peña Negra, since his/her products do not seem to have penetrated the southeast. Third, in the social context of Europe in the Final Bronze Age only independent specialists, in Brumfiel and Earle's (1987: 5) sense of the term, would have been possible.

Furthermore, the evidence from Mediterranean shipwrecks suggests, in my opinion, that smiths formed part of their crews. Thus, at Gelidonya there is a founder's kit which includes scales, anvils, whetstones, and other tools (Muckelroy 1978: 70–71), and the same can be said of Rochelongue (Hugues 1965; Bouscaras 1971), where the finds included objects which I believe must also be considered to be a founder's kit:

hammers, engraving tools, gouges, axes, ingots of copper and tin. It seems reasonable to suppose that the role of these shipboard metallurgists was to gather and recycle scrap and to sell the products they made. Some of these activities, like casting, may have been carried out seasonally, during the sailing months, but they had to be carried out on land. Therefore if these activities occurred regularly, they would have required a locality for that purpose (cf. Tylecote 1987: 17).

This could explain a specialized building such as that at Peña Negra: there would be the seasonal, but regular arrival of a smith who gathered and recycled scrap and cast it for the native community and also perhaps for Sardinian intermediaries. If I am right, this would explain the presence of weaving in the same workshop. González Prats (1990: 94) has stated that weaving and casting could be compatible activities, but in my view this is unlikely due to the flammable nature of the textiles. Traces of weaving and casting could both be found in the same place, however, if both were occasional activities that did not have to be carried out at the same time.

A seasonal establishment of Atlantic smiths and traders at Peña Negra implies the prior establishment of social alliances that would permit mooring on the southeast coast. This is perhaps what is represented by the Villena type bracelets (Figure 9.3) found in the west of the peninsula from the Final Bronze Age onwards. In the west these bracelets have no earlier precedents, but they are well-known in the southeast from the Early Bronze Age onwards (Almagro Gorbea 1974; Ruíz-Gálvez Priego 1989: 54–55). Their presence along the Atlantic coast reflects the arrival of techniques, and possibly women, from the southeast, as part of alliances that both facilitated the natives' passage from the Atlantic to the Mediterranean and the establishment of bases along the exchange networks.

It is more difficult to determine the identity of the weaver of the Peña Negra workshop, because the final product of his efforts has not been preserved, but I have two reasons to believe that this person had Mediterranean origins: First, the archaeological record shows that the weaving was carried out in a specialized setting and not in a domestic dwelling space. This suggests three possibilities: that the volume of cloth production was greater than that required for the producer's own consumption, that the weaving involved a special facility or technique, or that the weaver did not belong to the Peña Negra community and accordingly worked in an enclosure reserved for foreigners. Secondly, I believe that the red and yellow geometric designs of painted pottery from Peña Negra I may imitate costly textiles. It is significant that these motifs are painted on carefully produced, generally mould-made pottery and that this ware has no local precedent. The painting was applied after firing (González Prats 1983: 71), and therefore is extremely delicate. In my opinion, this shows that the natives were unfamiliar with this technique.

Painted pottery is also known all across southern and southeastern Iberia in the Final Bronze Age and in the Meseta and the northeast during the transition from Bronze/Iron Age to the Early Iron Age (Figure 9.6). The only thing these painted wares have in common is that they are painted, since the decorative motifs and the ceramic fabrics on which the painting was done vary greatly from one area to another. This may explain why they have been interpreted in such different ways (as Mediterranean or native or Urnfield wares) (Martínez Santa Olalla 1935; Almagro Gorbea 1977: 459–61; Fernández-Posse 1981: note 65; Ruíz Zapatero 1985: 759).

Because of this variability, because pottery painted with geometric designs is common to the whole Mediterranean, but above all because there is a specialized weaver's workshop at Peña Negra, I believe that this pottery imitates textiles. The impact of the arrival of rich oriental fabrics would first be felt among the natives of the coast in precolonial times. Subsequently, these ceramics (and perhaps the textiles as well) would reach the interior of the peninsula during the transition to the Iron Age.

That commercial links with the Mediterranean are in evidence in the lowest levels of Peña Negra (phase Ia) (González Prats 1983: 277; 1990: 90–92) indicates that there must have been social links prior to that, as shown by the oriental elements at Villena.

A hero's life

Items like the chariot and the iron from Baiões, the Atlantic roasting spit in the tomb of Amathus on Cyprus (Karageorghis and Lo Schiavo 1989), and the workshop of Peña Negra are evidence of a trade route between the Atlantic and the Mediterranean. These facts indicate to me that the traders were the natives of the west of the Iberian peninsula and the Sardinians (Taramelli 1921: 19–22, 60–63, 79; 1926: 295–298, 36/246, 36/295–298). Their purpose seems to have been the exchange of raw materials and tin from the west Mediterranean, and scrap metal and possibly copper from the east Mediterranean.

Luxury items and new technologies also came to the west of the Iberian peninsula along this route and encountered varying degrees of acceptance and assimilation. The integration was rapid in the case of the Villena type of goldworking (Figure 9.3), and this led rapidly to a merge with Atlantic goldworking (Cardozo 1957), because no profound changes in technology were involved. But the integration was more difficult in the case of iron. As we saw in Baiões, in large parts of the northwest iron only became dominant after the Roman conquest (Ruíz-Gálvez Priego 1991: 290–92). This, together with the absence of painted pottery such as that of the Final Bronze Age in the southern and eastern parts of the peninsula, suggests the existence of clear cultural and technological frontiers. This once again, brings to mind Bradley's (1985) arguments about exchange and social distance.

This route may also explain the presence of the Atlantic spit, an import in the Amathus tomb, according to Karageorghis and Lo Schiavo (1989: 16). It is quite possible that this spit may have come from the west by way of Sardinia as a gift for someone who was not unaware of its use, but who appreciated its exotic manufacture. What is interesting about this find is that may be the proof that western tin was traded to the eastern Mediterranean by way of peninsular and Sardinian intermediaries. In spite of the wide chronological margins within which Karageorghis and Lo Schiavo (1989: 16) place this tomb, I believe it could date to the tenth or ninth century BC. This date corresponds to the dendrochronological date that Gómez (1991) proposes for the metallurgical group to which this spit belongs and to the radiocarbon dates for the Portuguese hillfort of Coto da Pena[5], which relinquished the same kind of material (Silva 1986: 34; Carballo and Fábregas 1991: 257). Once again, we would be dealing with a late precolonial setting.

Within what economic model should this maritime trade route be interpreted? Are the participants heroic adventurers or vulgar traders? Sherratt (1994) has recently commented that although a substantivist model was appropriate to Europe in the Neolithic and Copper Age, most of

the Bronze and Iron Age might be interpreted in terms of both substantivist and formalist models. This would also be true for the Iberian peninsula during the Final Bronze Age, where some regions suggest formalist models, while others are better explained from a substantivist perspective.

Northwest Portugal and Sardinia might correspond to the formalist model. They have in common not their resource wealth but their strategic position, which permits them to act as intermediaries. Northwest Portugal is rich in tin, and hillforts like Baiões and Coto da Pena control it. Even so, the richest tin sources are not there, but in Galicia. While we have evidence for *in situ* casting and there are no spectacular accumulations of metal or weapons found under water recycling, apart from the Baiões hoard. The social and emblematic value of arms and metal displayed in other Atlantic provinces (Bradley 1990) seems to give way in the northwest to the intrinsic value of metal as a commodity (Renfrew 1986; Sherratt 1994).

Sardinia's importance is due more to its position than to its mining resources (Ruíz-Gálvez Priego 1986; Gale and Stos-Gale 1988). The three largest hoards that contain objects of western origin — Monte Sa Idda, Monte Arrubiu, and Forraxi Nioi (Taramelli 1921, 1926; Fiorelli 1882) — seem to have had a practical function. They all contain ingots or tools which are associated with the casting, refining, and finishing of metal pieces. That is to say, the objects they contain were valued for their raw material and not for their social and symbolic worth (Ruíz-Gálvez 1986: 33). Once again, their importance is as commodities. In both cases, it seems that external demand — from the Mediterranean and from the Atlantic world — acted as a catalyst and made it possible for each region to exploit their raw materials and their strategic positions along seafaring routes. In short, the spirit of enterprise and the desire for profit were dominant.

The cases of Villena and Peña Negra are best explained in substantivist terms, although with some qualifications. In both cases their role in the trade network is explained by their location and by the resources which they control. However, the spirit of enterprise that characterizes the previous cases seems to be absent, and from the beginning they appear as the consumers of luxury goods, both Atlantic and Mediterranean. Furthermore, the economic system that Villena and Peña Negra had since Argaric times emphasized the basic means of production rather than the control of long distance exchange (Ruíz-Gálvez Priego 1992).

The southwest of the peninsula and Galicia are also easier to explain from a substantivist perspective. Thus, Ría de Huelva, the largest bronze hoard in the peninsula, has a numbers of features that suggest that it was neither utilitarian nor a hoard of scrap metal. First, except for one small chisel for specialized work, such as jewellery making, the hoard, which contains over 400 pieces, consists of offensive or defensive weapons, items used in clothing or as ornaments, and horse harnesses. This indicates the selective and aristocratic character of the assemblage. Secondly, important metal finds have been made in other parts of the Ría de Huelva (Terrero 1990 [orig. 1944]), a Corinthian helmet (Albelda and Obermaier 1931) among others. Thirdly, in the Final Bronze Age of the southwest metal tools are notably scarce, but weapons and solid gold torques are abundant (Ruíz-Gálvez Priego 1991: fig. 6). Fourthly, the metal alloys of the Ría de Huelva hoard are fairly homogenous (Ruíz-Gálvez Priego 1987)[6], which leads one to conclude that they were all cast in the same area. Finally, there is nothing to indicate that the hoard was the load of a shipwreck. It is impossible to determine the original distribution of the pieces, since they were extracted from the bottom of the river over a period of several weeks by a hydraulic dredge.

In ancient times the southwest of the peninsula was famous for its minerals. A belt of pyrites rich in copper, lead, silver, and gold runs across the region from Sevilla to Portugal. However, large scale exploitation of its mineral wealth, silver in particular, does not occur before the presence of the Phoenicians. During the Final Bronze Age, small mining communities, like Chinflón (Huelva), exploited the copper for brief periods in an area that was barely inhabited (Ruíz Mata 1989: 218–22, 232–39; 1990: 68). Accordingly, the population increase which can be seen throughout the southwest well before the arrival of the Phoenicians (Belén and Escacena 1992; Ruíz Mata 1990: 64–69) could be related not to metal, but to the coastal position of many of the sites and to external demand for resources such as cattle or salt (which is abundant from the estuary of the Guadalquivir to that of the Tagus) (Figure 9.1).

The stelae of the Final Bronze Age of the southwest are related to the control of livestock

droveways and to the important resources that are found along them (Ruíz-Gálvez Priego and Galán Domingo 1991) (Figure 9.7, 4–13). They are concentrated in areas suitable for livestock raising, where the typical 'dehesa' landscape had existed from the fourth millennium BC onwards (Stevenson and Harrison 1992). As precedents they have the anthropomorphic stelae and the 'pebble idols' of the Copper Age and Earlier Bronze Age (Almagro Basch 1966, 1972). Depictions of elements of Atlantic origin on the stelae, such as weapons, are associated at times with pictures of other objects of Mediterranean origin, such as chariots, mirrors, and musical instruments. But while we have evidence that the former were in fact present in the region, there is little evidence for the latter. The few such items that we know of, such as those from the necropolis of La Joya (Huelva) (Garrido Roiz and Orta García 1978: fig.60) are of Iron Age date. Galán Domingo (1993) believes that the representation of Mediterranean elements on the stelae of the southwest represents a phenomenon similar to the representations in Scandinavian rock-art, where the depiction of exotic weapons is more abundant the less frequently they are found in actuality in archaeological contexts (Bradley 1990: 133). It is very likely that, as Galán suggests, few real chariots, mirrors or musical instruments reached the southwest. Their depiction on the stelae must be understood not as reproduction of real objects, but as part of a symbolic and ideological discourse.

Much the same occurred in European iconography during the fourteenth and fifteenth centuries AD at the time of the geographical discoveries and the opening of the trade routes. Thus, news of the marvels of Asia were translated into the appearance of the oriental in art. The third of the Three Magi becomes black as a result of the Portuguese trade for African gold and slaves, and the figure of the 'savage' became common after the discovery of America (Figure 9.7, 1–2) (Azcárate 1948, Reau 1957: 240–242; Sebastián López 1978: 151; Baltrusaitis 1981: 172; Helms 1988: 211–60). In the same way, the Mediterranean elements on the stelae (Figure 9.7, 3–13) might represent the integration into native discourse of the concept of the oriental prince and his attributes, concepts transmitted by the precolonial commerce.

In the southwest the traders of the Atlantic Mediterranean sea route could have obtained harbours, salt, cattle, and perhaps copper, and the

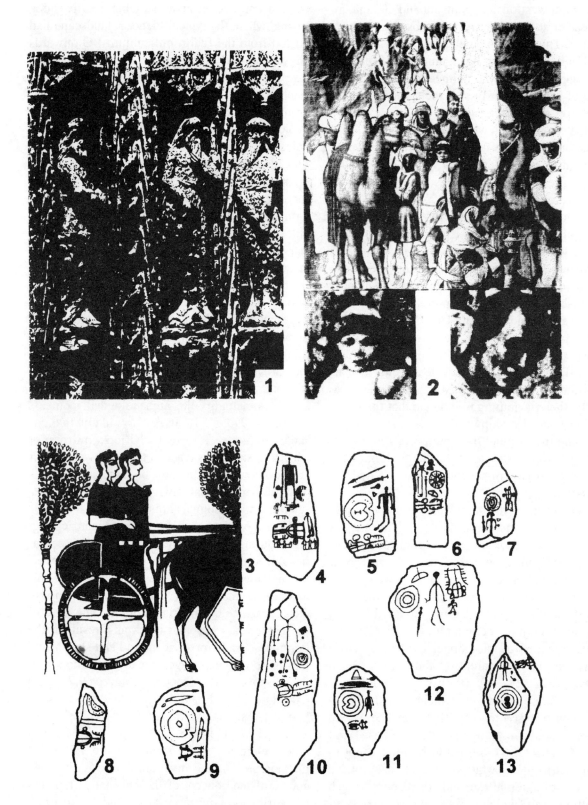

Figure 9.7   1: Representations of savages on the entrance of the Colegio San Gregorio (Valladolid). 2: Detail of the Adoration of the Magi by Andrea Mantegna (Uffizi Gallery, Florence). 3. Representation of chariot from Tiryns (after Fernández-Miranda and Olmos 1986). 4–13: Final Bronze Age stelae from the Southwest (after Almagro Gorbea 1977).

consequent mobilization of the region's potential wealth would have stimulated social competition (Bradley 1982, 1992). This is reflected in the armaments found underwater (Ruíz-Gálvez Priego 1982) and of numerous, heavy, solid gold torques underground (Ruíz-Gálvez Priego 1992). The best example of this, in my opinion, is the Ría de Huelva which, like Flag Fen (Peterborough, England), was a ritual place (Pryor 1989, 1990, 1991, 1992; Pryor *et al.* 1986; Bradley 1990).[7] This consumption of wealth in socially significant public acts corresponds better to the substantivist model of economics than to the formalist model.

Galicia, finally, seems to have been marginal in comparison to northwest Portugal in its integration into the circuit of exchange. The first indications of population growth and of permanent stable settlements do not occur prior to the transition from the Bronze to the Iron Age. There are also no large hoards before this transitional period, and those that exist consist in most cases of heavily amortized axes with a high lead content. Perhaps because of this, arms have only been found in the lower courses of those rivers that were navigable, like the Ulla and the Miño (Balil *et al.* 1991; Ruíz-Gálvez Priego 1982). As in the the case of Ría de Huelva these underwater finds may have had ritual value as a symbolic border between life and death, but also as a territorial border, since both these rivers, like the Ría de Huelva, are the principle routes of access to the interior (Figure 9.1). This conspicuous consumption of symbolically-loaded, prestigious objects is best understood from a substantivist perspective (Bradley 1982).

Death and transfiguration

Although the Atlantic sailors and founders traded scrap metal for a profit, a strictly formalist model does not seem to me to be acceptable prior to the Iron Age and to the establishment of Phoenician trading posts on the Iberian peninsula, and even then it must be applied with caution. Sherratt (1994) is correct when he says that the ideas of the formalist economists only complement those of the subtantivists to a limited extent. Their Mediterranean contacts notwithstanding, the inhabitants of northwest Portugal were essentially Atlantic, socially and ideologically. Their codes, concepts, and conventions concerning

feasts and rituals, funerary and otherwise, are identical to and are expressed in the same manner as those of the rest of the Atlantic world. New cultigens and other agricultural innovations reached them by way of the ocean, and these would be maintained with few changes after the end of the system of Atlantic exchange and until the Roman conquest (Ruíz-Gálvez Priego 1991).

The same could be said of the livestock raisers of the southwest. There, Mediterranean elements, which were surely not strong, were incorporated into the symbolic language of the stelae as reinforcements of the image of the prince, warrior, and lord of the herd. Once again, however, the new elements became associated with conventions, rituals, and practices that were common in the Atlantic west, and they used a medium, the stelae, which clearly had local precedents (Ruíz-Gálvez Priego and Galán Domingo 1991). Here too, some authors (Escacena 1989; Belén and Escacena 1992) maintain that in spite of the profound changes that occurred with the Phoenician colonization, the indigenous population kept their essentially Atlantic character until the arrival of the Romans. According to these authors (see also González Wagner 1983), the transformations which occurred during the Iron Age would have been due to the arrival of authentic Syro-Palestinian agricultural colonists, from whom the local population would have kept their distance. Thus, the Indo-European, Western essence of the native population (Escacena 1989; see also Ruíz Gálvez Priego 1991) would not have died, but become transformed.

In contrast, during the Iron Age Peña Negra intensified its contacts with Mediterranean merchants and its process of 'orientalization'. One reason for this is the site's very location along natural navigation routes (Figure 9.2). Even more, however, this outcome must be attributed to a socio-economic organization that had been more efficient and complex since the beginning of the Bronze Age. This had served to attract Mediterranean visitors by the Late Bronze Age, and it explains Peña Negra's transformation into a city during the Iron Age.

From the beginning to the end

In this article I have defended the following arguments:

1. Maritime relations existed between the Mediterranean and the Iberian peninsula dur-

ing the post-Argaric Late Bronze Age, the thirteenth to tenth centuries BC (Villena, Roça do Casal do Meio).

2. These Atlantic–Mediterranean contacts became more intense during the Final Bronze Age (the tenth to eighth centuries BC) in conjunction with an increase of Atlantic interest in the Iberian peninsula.

3. The object of this commerce seems to have been metal: western tin, scrap metal and copper from the central Mediterranean and perhaps the southwest of the Iberian peninsula. As well as metal, we can detect other, archaeologically less visible commodities: salt and livestock from the southeast and southwest of the peninsula, clothing and ornaments (textiles and fibulae) from the Mediterranean.

The voyages of the Late and Final Bronze Age between the west of the peninsula and the central Mediterranean provided knowledge and experience about routes and resources which undoubtedly facilitated, but which do not explain the subsequent Phoenician colonization. The commercial relations of the Final Bronze Age and of the Iron Age were completely different in kind. Because of this I believe Aubet (1987: 180–90) is right in questioning whether the relations prior to the eighth century BC had the character of a Phoenician precolonization. Innovations in cosmography, cartography and naval construction made the discovery of America possible, but only a conjunction of social and political reasons explains why it was Castile, and not Portugal or Genoa, that made that discovery (Chaunu 1972: 112). Similarly, the causes and the timing of the Phoenician colonization must be sought in the internal dynamics of that society (Aubet 1987: 24–49).[8]

Notes

1 This article was first prepared as part of DGICYT project PBO–90–0262.

2 Perhaps the reason for the late date of regular voyages was not so much ignorance of astronomical navigation as the impossiblity of night sailing prior to the first millennium development of a system of nocturnal navigation (Gasull 1986).

3 At the 'Mycenaean World' exhibit in Madrid in February 1992, a LHIIA meat hook was displayed from the tholos tomb of Myrsinokori (Messenia). The type is very similar to the oldest Central European examples (Hundt 1953).

4 GrN–7484: 2650±130 BP. The sample consists of wood from the shaft of a lance (Kalb 1977: 77).

5 UGRA–200: 2950±100 BP; UGRA–220: 2920±110 BP. Both dates are from seeds and come from the earliest levels, with Vénat metallurgy. Calibrated, the 95% confidence ranges of these determinations are 1415–865 and 1410–826 BC, with intercept dates in the twelfth century.

6 The analyses of metal from the Ría de Huelva will be published by the CICYT project of which I am the principal investigator.

7 I am grateful to Richard Bradley for indicating the importance of a site like Flag Fen to me and for showing it to me, and to the excavator, Francis Pryor, for explaining it to me.

8 I thank E. Galán, A. Gilman, and L. Prados for reading this article, and A. Gilman for translating it.

Bibliography

Albelda, J., and H. Obermaier

1931   El Casco Griego de Huelva. *Boletín de la Academia de la Historia* 98: 442–518.

Almagro Basch, M.

1966   *Las Estelas Decoradas del Suroeste peninsular.* Bibliotheca Praehistorica Hispana 8. Madrid: Consejo Superior de Investigaciones Científicas.

1972   Los Ídolos y la Estela Decorada de Hernán Pérez (Cáceres) y el Ídolo Estela de Tabuyo del Monte (León). *Trabajos de Prehistoria* 29: 83–124.

Almagro Gorbea, M.

1974   Orfebrería del Bronce Final en la Península Ibérica: el Tesoro de Abia de la Obispalía, la Orfebrería Tipo Villena y los Cuencos de Axtroki. *Trabajos de Prehistoria* 31: 39–100.

1977   *El Bronce final y el Período Orientalizante en Extremadura.* Bibliotheca Praehistorica Hispana 14. Madrid: Consejo Superior de Investigaciones Científicas.

1989   Arqueología e Historia Antigua: El Proceso Proto-orientalizante y el Inicio de los Contactos de Tartessos con el Levante Mediterráneo. *Anales de Gerion* 2: 277–88.

1992   Los Intercambios Culturales entre Aragón y el Litoral Mediterráneo durante el Bronce Final. In P. Utrilla Miranda (ed.), *Aragón/Litoral Mediterráneo: Intercambios Culturales durante la Prehistoria*, 633–58. Zaragoza: Institución Fernando el Católico.

Arteaga, O., G. Hoffman, H. Schubart and D. Schulz

1987   Investigaciones Geológicas y Arqueológicas Sobre los Cambios de la Línea Costera de la Andalucía Mediterránea: Informe Preliminar. In *Anuario Arqueológico de Andalucía 1985*, 2: 117–22. Sevilla: Consejería de Cultura, Junta de Andalucía.

Aubet, M.E.

1987 *Tiro y las Colonias Fenicias de Occidente.* Barcelona: Bellaterra.

Azcárate, J.M.

1948 El Tema Iconográfico del Salvaje. *Archivo Español de Arte* 10: 81–92.

Balil, A., G. Pereira and J. Sánchez Palencia (eds)

1991 *Tabula Imperii Romani, Hoja K–29: Porto.* Madrid: Instituto Geográfico Nacional.

Baltrusaitis, J.

1981 *Le Moyen Age fantastique.* Paris: Flammarion.

Barrett, J.

1989 Time and Tradition: The Ritual of Everyday Life. In H.A. Nordström and A. Knaped (eds), *Bronze Age Studies: Transactions of the British Scandinavian Colloquium in Stockholm, May 10–11, 1985*, 113–26. Historiska Museum Studies 5. Stockholm: Historiska Museum.

Barrett, J., R. Bradley and M. Green

1991 *Landscapes, Monuments, and Society: The Prehistory of Cranborne Chase.* Cambridge: Cambridge University Press.

Belén, M., J.L. Escacena and M.L. Bozzino

1991 El Mundo Funerario del Bronce Final en la Fachada Atlántica de la Península Ibérica: I. Análisis de la Documentación. *Trabajos de Prehistoria* 48: 225–56.

Belén, M., and J.L. Escacena

1992 Las Comunidades Prerromanas de la Baja Andalucía. In M. Almagro-Gorbea and G. Ruíz Zapatero (eds), *Paletnología de la Península Ibérica*, 65–87. Complutum 2–3. Madrid: Editorial Complutense.

Blasco Bosqued, C.

1987 Un Ejemplar de Fíbula de Codo 'ad ochio' en el Valle del Manzanares. *Boletín de la Asociación Española de Amigos de la Arqueología* 23: 18–28.

Bouscaras, A.

1971 L'épave des Bronzes de Rochelongue. *Archéologia* 39: 68–73.

Bradley, R.J.

1981 'Various Styles of Urn': Cemeteries and Settlement in Southern England, *c.* 1400–1000 b.c. In R. Chapman, I. Kinnes and K. Randsborg (eds), *The Archaeology of Death*, 93–104. Cambridge: Cambridge University Press.

1982 The Destruction of Wealth in later Prehistory. *Man* 17: 108–22.

1985 Exchange and Social Distance: The Study of Bronze Artefact Distributions. *Man* 20: 692–704.

1990 *The Passage of Arms.* Cambridge: Cambridge University Press.

Brumfiel, E., and T.K. Earle

1987 Specialization, Exchange and Complex Societies: An Introduction. In E.M. Brumfiel and T.K. Earle (eds), *Specialization, Exchange, and Complex Societies*, 1–9. Cambridge: Cambridge University Press.

Cabo, A.

1973 Condicionamientos Geográficos. In M. Artola (ed.), *Historia de España Alfaguara*, 1: 3–183. Madrid: Alianza Universidad.

Carballo, X., and R. Fábregas

1991 Dataciones de Carbono 14 para Castros del Noroeste Peninsular. *Archivo Español de Arqueología* 64: 244–64.

Cardozo, M.

1957 Da Origens e Técnica do Trabalho do Ouro. *Revista de Guimarães* 76: 5–46.

Caro Bellido, A.

1989 Consideraciones Sobre el Bronce Antiguo y Medio en el Bajo Guadalquivir. In M.E. Aubet (ed.), *Tartessos: Arqueología Protohistórico del Bajo Guadalquivir*, 85–120. Sabadell: Ausa.

Catling, J.

1964 *Cypriot Bronzework in the Mediterranean World.* Oxford: Oxford University Press.

Chandeigne, M. (ed.)

1992 *Lisboa Extramuros, 1415–1580: El Descubrimiento del Mundo por los Navegantes Portugueses.* Madrid: Alianza Editorial.

Chaunu, P.

1972 *La Expansión Europea (Siglos XIII–XV).* Barcelona: Labor.

Coffyn, A.

1985 *Le Bronze Final Atlantique.* Paris: Picard.

Coffyn, A., J. Gómez and J.-P. Mohen

1981 *L'Apogée du Bronze Atlantique: Le Dépôt de Vénat.* Paris: Picard.

Cuenca, A., and M.J. Walker

1976 Pleistoceno Final y Holoceno en la Cuenca del Vinalopó (Alicante). *Estudios Geológicos* 32: 95–104.

Díaz del Olmo, F.

1989 Paleografía Tartéssica. In M.E. Aubet (ed.), *Tartessos: Arqueología Protohistórico del Bajo Guadalquivir*, 13–23. Sabadell: Ausa.

Domínguez Ortiz, A.

1973 *El Antiguo Régimen: Los Reyes Católicos y los Austrias.* Madrid: Alianza Universidad.

Duke, J.A.

1981 *Handbook of Legumes of World Economic Importance.* New York: Plenum Press.

Escacena, J.L.

1985 Gadir. *Aula Orientalis* 3: 39–58.

1989   Los Turdetanos o la Recuperación de la Identidad Perdida. In M.E. Aubet (ed.), *Tartessos: Arqueología Protohistórica del Bajo Guadalquivir*, 433–76. Sabadell: Ausa.

Fernández-Miranda, M.

1986   Huelva, Ciudad de los Tartessios. *Aula Orientalis* 4: 227–362.

Fernández-Miranda, M., and R. Olmos

1986   *Las Ruedas de Toya y el Origen del Carro en la Peninsula Ibérica*. Madrid: Ministerio de Cultura.

Fernández-Posse, M.D.

1981   La Cueva de Arevalillo de Cega (Segovia). *Noticiario Arqueológico Hispano* 6: 45–84.

Ferrarese Ceruti, M.L., F. Lo Schiavo and L. Vagnetti

1987   Minoici, Micenei e Ciprioti in Sardegna nella Seconda Metà del II Millennio a.C. In M.S. Balmuth, ed., *Studies in Sardinian Archaeology III: Nuragic Sardinia and the Mycenaean world*, 7–34. British Archaeological Reports International Series 387. Oxford: British Archaeological Reports.

Fiorelli, A.

1882   Forraxi Nioi. *Notizie degli Scavi di Antichità*, 305–309.

Gaimster, M.

1991   Money and Media in Viking Age Scandinavia. In R. Samson (ed.), *Social Approaches to Viking Studies*, 113–22. Glasgow: Cruithne Press.

Galán Domingo, E.

1993   *Estelas, Paisaje y Territorio en el Bronce Final del Suroeste de la Península Ibérica*. Madrid: Editorial Complutense.

Gale, N.H., and Z.A. Stos-Gale

1988   Recent Evidence for a Possible Bronze Age Metal Trade between Sardinia and the Aegean. In E.B. French and K.A. Wardle (eds), *Problems in Greek Prehistory: Papers Presented at the Centenary Conference of the British School of Archaeology at Athens, Manchester, April 1986*, 349–84. Bristol: Bristol Classical Press.

García Mercadall, J.

1972   *Viajes por España*. Madrid: Alianza Editorial.

Garrido Roiz, J.P., and E.M. Orta García

1978   *Excavaciones en la Necrópolis de 'La Joya', Huelva*. Excavaciones Arqueológicas en España 96. Madrid: Ministerio de Educación y Ciencia.

Gasull, P.

1986   Problemática en Torno a la Ubicación de los Asentamientos Fenicios en el sur de la Península. *Aula Orientalis* 4(1–2): 193–201.

Gil-Mascarell, M., and J.L. Peña Sánchez

1989   La Fíbula 'ad ochio' del Yacimiento de la Mola de Agres. *Saguntum* 22: 130–45.

Gómez, J.

1991   Le Fondeur, le trafiquant et les cuisiniers: la broche d'Amathonte de Chypre et la chronologie absolue du Bronze Final Atlantique. In C. Chévillot and A. Coffyn (eds), *L'âge du Bronze Atlantique: Actes du Ier Colloque du Parc Archéologique de Beynac*, 369–73. Beynac-et-Cazenac: Association des Musées du Sarladais.

Gómez, J. and J.P. Patreau

Le crochet protohistorique en Bronze de Thorigné à Coulon (Deux-Sèvres). *Archäologisches Korrespondenz Uatt* 18: 31–42.

González Prats, A.

1983   *Estudio Arqueológico del Poblamiento Antiguo de la Sierra de Crevillente, Alicante*. Alicante: Universidad de Alicante.

1985   Sobre unos Elementos Materiales del Comercio Fenicio en Tierras del Sureste Peninsular. *Lvcentvm* 4: 101–34.

1990   *Nueva Luz sobre la Protohistoria del Sureste*. Alicante: Caja de Ahorros Provincial.

1992   Una Vivienda Metalúrgica en la Peña Negra (Crevillente, Alicante). *Trabajos de Prehistoria* 49: 243–57.

González Wagner, C.

1983   Aproximación al Proceso Histórico de Tartessos. *Archivo Español de Arqueología* 56: 3–35.

Goody, J.

1976   *Production and Reproduction: A Comparative Study of the Domestic Domain*. Cambridge: Cambridge University Press.

1982   *Cooking, Cuisine and Class: A Study in Comparative Sociology*. Cambridge: Cambridge University Press.

Halstead, P., and J. O'Shea

1982   A Friend in a Need is a Friend Indeed: Social Storage and the Origins of Social Ranking. In C. Renfrew and S. Shennan (eds), *Ranking, Resource and Exchange*, 92–99. Cambridge: Cambridge University Press.

Harding, A.

1976   Bronze Age Agricultural Implements in Bronze Age Europe. In G. de G. Sieveking, I.H. Longworth and K.E. Wilson (eds), *Problems in Economic and Social Archaeology*, 513–21. London: Duckworth.

1983   The Bronze Age in Central and Eastern Europe: Advances and Prospects. *Advances in World Archaeology* 2: 1–50.

1984   Aspects of the Social Evolution in the Bronze Age. In J. Bintliff (ed.), *European Social Evolution: Archaeological Perspectives*, 135–46. Bradford: Bradford University Press.

1989   Interpreting the Evidence for Agricultural Change in the Late Bronze Age in Northern Europe. In H.-A. Nordström and A. Knape (eds), *Bronze Age Studies: Transactions of the British-Scandinavian Colloquium in Stockholm, May*

10–11, 1985, 173–81. Historiska Museum Studies 5. Stockholm: Historiska Museum.

Helms, M.

1988 *Ulysses' Sail: An Ethnographic Odyssey of Power, Knowledge and Geographical Distance.* Princeton: Princeton University Press.

Hirth, K.G.

1978 Interregional Trade and the Formation of Prehistoric Gateway Communities. *American Antiquity* 43: 35–45.

Hopf, M.

1982 *Vor- und frühgeschichtliche Kulturpflanzen aus nördlicher Deutschland.* Kataloge vor- und frühgeschichtlicher Altertümer 22. Mainz-am-Rhein: Philipp von Zabern.

Hugues, C.

1965 La découverte sous-marine de Rochelongue, Aude (Hérault). In *Comptes Rendus de l'Académie des Inscriptions et Belles Lettres,* 176–78. Adge: Académie des Inscriptions et Belles Lettres.

Hundt, H.-J.

1953 Über Tüllenhaken und Gabeln. *Germania* 31: 145–55.

Jäger, K.-D., and V. Lozek

1982 Enviromental Conditions and Land Cultivation during the Urnfield Bronze Age in Central Europe. In A. Harding (ed.), *Climatic Change in Later Prehistory,* 162–78. Edinburgh: Edinburgh University Press.

Jockenhövel, A.

1974 Fleischhacken von den Britischen Inseln. *Archäologisches Korrespondenzblatt* 4: 329–38.

Kalb, P.

1977 Uma Data C–14 para o Bronze Atlantico. *O Arqueólogo Português* 17: 141–44.

1978 Senhora da Guia, Baiões: die Ausgrabung 1977 auf einer Höhensiedlung der atlantischer Bronzezeit in Portugal. *Madrider Mitteilungen* 19: 112–38.

Karageorghis, V., and F. Lo Schiavo

1989 A West Mediterranean Obelos from Amathus. *Rivista di Studi Fenici* 17: 15–29.

Kirch, P.V.

1984 *The Evolution of Polynesian Chiefdoms.* Cambridge: Cambridge University Press.

Knapp, A.B.

1990 Ethnicity, Entrepreneurship, and Exchange: Mediterranean Inter-island Relations in the Late Bronze Age. *Annual of the British School at Athens* 85: 115–53.

Lo Schiavo, F., E. Macnamara and L. Vagnetti

1985 Late Cypriot Imports to Italy and their Influence on Local Bronzework. *Papers of the British School at Rome* 53: 1–69.

Lo Schiavo, F., and D. Ridgway

1986 La Sardegna e il Mediterraneo allo Scorcio del II Milenio. In *La Sardegna nel Mediterraneo tra il Secondo e il Primo Millennio a.C.: Atti del II Convegno di Studi "Un Millennio di Relazioni fra la Sardegna e i Paesi del Mediterraneo",* Selargius-Cagliari, 27–30 Novembre 1986, 391–418. Cagliari: Amministrazione Provinciale di Cagliari.

Luzón Nogue, J.M., and L.M. Coín Cuenca

1989 Las Navegacion Pre-astrónomica en la Antigüedad: Utilización de Pájaros en la Orientación Náutica. *Lvcentvm* 5: 65–85.

Marinval, P.

1988 *L'Alimentation Végetale en France du Mésolithique à L'Âge du Fer.* Paris: C.N.R.S.

Martín de la Cruz, J.C.

1988 Mykenische Keramik aus Bronzezeitlichen Siedlungschichten von Montoro am Guadalquivir. *Madrider Mitteilungen* 30: 77–91.

1992 La Península Ibérica y el Mediterráneo en el II° Milenio a.C. In *Catálogo de la Exposición 'El Mundo Micénico: Cinco Siglos de la Primera Civilización Europea, 1600–1100 a.C.',* 110–14. Madrid: Ministerio de Cultura.

Martínez Santa-Olalla, J.

1935 La Cerámica Pintada Céltica de la Península Ibérica. *Actas y Memorias de la Sociedad Española de Arqueología, Etnología y Prehistoria* 14: 263–65.

Matthäus, H.

1985 *Metallgefässe und Gefässuntersäzte der Bronzezeit der geometrischen und archäischen Periode aus Cypern.* Prähistorische Bronzefunde 2. Munich: C.H. Beck'sche.

1989 Cypern und Sardinien im frühen 1. Jahrtausend v. Chr. In E. Peltenburg (ed.), *Early Society in Cyprus,* 244–55. Edinburgh: Edinburgh University Press.

Montero, I.

1993 Bronze Age Metallurgy in Southeast Spain. *Antiquity* 67: 46–57.

Muckelroy, K.

1978 *Maritime Archaeology.* Cambridge: Cambridge University Press.

Muhly, J.D., and B. Stech

1990 Final Observations. In F. Lo Schiavo, R. Maddin, J. Merkel, J.D. Muhly and B. Stech (eds), *Metallographic and Statistical Analyses of Copper Ingots from Sardinia,* 202–21. Sassari: Ministerio per i Beni Culturale e Ambientale.

Navarro Mederos, J.F.

1982 Materiales para el Estudio de la Edad del Bronce en el Valle Medio del Vinalopó. *Lvcentvm* 1: 19–70.

Niemeyer, H.G.

1985   El Yacimiento Fenicio de Toscanos: Urbanística
y Función. *Aula Orientalis* 3: 109–26.

Penhallurick, R.

1986   *Tin in Antiquity.* London: Institute of Metals.

Peña, A. de la

1992   *Castro de Torroso, (Mós, Pontevedra).*
Arqueoloxía/Memorias 11. Santiago de
Compostela: Xunta de Galicia.

Perea, A.

1991   *Orfebrería Prerromana: Arqueología del Oro.*
Madrid: Caja de Madrid.

Peters, J., and A. van den Driesch

1990   Archäologische Untersuchung der Tierreste aus
der kupferzeitlichen Siedlung von Los Millares
(Prov. Almería). *Studien über frühe
Tierknochenfunde von der Iberischen Halbinsel*
12: 51–110

Ponte, S. da

1989   As Fibulas do Bronze Final Atlántico: Iª Idade
do Ferro do Noroeste Peninsular, Abordajem e
Enquadramento Cultural. *Trabalhos de
Anthropologia e Etnologia* 29: 73–79.

Pryor, F.

1989   Look What We've Found: A Case Study in
Public Archaeology. *Antiquity* 63: 51–61.

1990   Flag Fen. *Current Archaeology* 119: 386–90.

1991   *Flag Fen: Prehistoric Fenland Centre.* London:
B. T. Batsford.

1992   Introduction to Current Research at Flag Fen,
Peterborough. *Antiquity* 66: 439–57.

Pryor, F., C. Frech, and M. Taylor

1986   Flag Fen, Fengate, Peterborough I: Discovery,
Reconnaissance and Initial Excavation
(1982–85). *Proceedings of the Prehistoric
Society* 52: 1–24.

Réau, L.

1957   *Iconographie de l'Art Chrétien.* Paris: Presses
Universitaires de France.

Renfrew, C.

1986   Varna and the Emergence of Wealth in
Prehistoric Europe. In A. Apparuddai (ed.), *The
Social Life of Things*, 141–68. Cambridge:
Cambridge University Press.

Rivera Núñez, D., and C. Obón de Castro

1989   La Dieta Cereal Prehistórica y su Supervivencia
en el Área Mediterránea. *Trabajos de
Prehistoria* 46: 247–54.

Rivera Núñez, D., C. Obón de Castro and A. Asensio
Martínez

1988   Arqueobotánica y Paleobotánica en el Sureste de
España: Datos Preliminares. *Trabajos de
Prehistoria* 45: 317–34.

Rowlands, M.

1980   Kinship, Alliance and Exchange in the European
Bronze Age. In J. Barrett and R.J. Bradley (eds),
*Settlement and Society in the British Later
Bronze Age*, 15–55. British Archaeological
Reports British Series 63. Oxford: British
Archaeological Reports.

Ruíz-Gálvez Priego, M.

1979   El Depósito de Hío y el Final de la Edad del
Bronce en la Fachada Atlántica Peninsular. *El
Museo de Pontevedra* 33: 129–50.

1982   Nueva Espada Dragada en el río Ulla: Armas
Arrojadas a las Aguas. *El Museo de Pontevedra*
36: 181–96.

1986   Navegación y Comercio entre el Atlántico y el
Mediterráneo a Fines de la Edad del Bronce.
Trabajos de Prehistoria 43: 9–42.

1987   Bronce Atlántico y 'Cultura' del Bronce
Atlántico en la Península Ibérica. *Trabajos de
Prehistoria* 44: 251–64.

1989   La Orfebrería del Bronce Final: El Poder y su
Ostentación. *Revista de Arqueología*, Suppl. 4:
46–57.

1990   La Metalurgia de Peña Negra I. In A. Gonzalez
Prats, *Nueva Luz sobre la Protohistoria del
Sudeste*, 317–57. Alicante: Caja de Ahorros
Provincial.

1991   Songs of a Wayfaring Lad: Late Bronze Age
Atlantic Exchange and the Building of the
Regional Identity in the West Iberian Peninsula.
Oxford Journal of Archaeology 10: 277–306.

1992   La Novia Vendida: Agricultura, Herencia y
Orfebrería en la Protohistoria de la Península
Ibérica. *Spal* 1: 230–52.

1995   From Gift to Commodity: The Changing
Meaning of Precious Metals in the Later
Prehistory of the Iberian peninsula. In G.
Morteani and J.P. Northover (eds), *Prehistoric
Gold in Europe: Mines, Metallurgy and
Manufacture*, 45–63. ASI NATO Series 280.
Dordrecht: Kluwer Academic Publishers.

Ruíz-Gálvez Priego, M., and E. Galán Domingo

1991   Las Estelas del Suroeste como Hitos de Vías
Ganaderas y Rutas de Comercio. *Trabajos de
Prehistoria* 48: 257–73.

Ruíz Mata, D.

1989   Huelva: Un Foco Temprano de Actividad
Metalúrgica durante el Bronce Final. In Mª.E.
Aubet (ed.), *Tartessos: Arqueología
Protohistórica del Bajo Guadalquivir*, 209–43.
Sabadell: Ausa.

1990   La ría de Huelva: Un Foco Clave de la
Protohistoria Peninsular. In J.Terrero, *Armas y
Objetos de Bronce Extraídos en los Dragados
del Puerto de Huelva*, 57–70. Huelva: Excma.
Diputación Provincial.

Ruíz Zapatero, G.

1985   *Los Campos de Urnas del Noreste de la
Península Ibérica.* Madrid: Universidad
Complutense.

Schubart, H.

1976 Las Relaciones Mediterráneas de la Cultura de El Argar. *Zephyrus* 25–27: 331–42.

1985 El Asentamiento Fenicio del s. VIII en el Morro de Mezquitilla, (Algarrobo, Málaga). *Aula Orientalis* 3: 55–83.

Schüle, W.

1970 Navegación Primitíva y Condiciones de Visibilidad de la Tierra en el Mediterráneo. *Actas, XI Congreso Nacional de Arqueología, Mérida, 1968*, 449–62.

1976 Der bronzezeitliche Schatzfund von Villena, (Alicante). *Madrider Mitteilungen* 17: 142–68.

Sebastián López, S.

1978 *Mensaje del Arte Medieval*. Córdoba: Departamentos de Historia del Arte, Universidades de Córdoba y Valencia.

Sherratt, A.

1987 Cups that Cheered. In W. Waldren and R. Kennard (eds), *Bell Beakers of the Western Mediterranean*, 81–114. British Archaeological Reports International Series 331. Oxford: British Archaeological Reports.

1994 Core, Periphery and Margin: Perspectives in the Bronze Age. In C. Mathers and S. Stoddart, eds., *Development and Decline in the Mediterranean Bronze Age*, 335–45. Sheffield: J.R. Collis.

Sherratt A., and S. Sherratt

1991 From Luxuries to Commodities: The Nature of Mediterranean Bronze Age Trading Systems. In N. H. Gale, ed., *Bronze Age Trade in the Mediterranean*, 351–86. Jensered: Paul Åströms Verlag.

Silva, A.C.F.

1986 *A cultura castreja no noroeste de Portugal*. Paços de Ferreira: Câmara Muncipal de Paços de Ferreira.

Silva, A.C.F., C.T. Silva, and A.B. Lopes

1986 Deposito de Fundidor do Final da Idade do Bronze do Castro de Senhora da Guia, (Baiôes, S. Pedro do Sul, Viseu). *Lucerna* 14: 73–95.

Soler, J. M.

1965 *El Tesoro de Villena*. Excavaciones Arqueológicas en España 36. Madrid: Ministerio de Educación Nacional.

1969 *El Oro de los Tesoros de Villena*. Servicio de Investigación Prehistórica, Serie de Trabajos Varios 36. Valencia: Servicio de Investigación Prehistórica.

1987 *Excavaciones Arqueológicas en el Cabezo Redondo*. Villena: Ayuntamiento de Villena.

Spindler, K., and O. da V. Ferreira

1973 Der spätbronzezeitliche Kuppelbau von der Roça do Casal do Meio in Portugal. *Madrider Mitteilungen* 14: 60–108.

Stevenson, A.C., and R.J. Harrison

1992 Ancient Forests in Spain: A Model for Land-use and Dry Forest Management in Southwest Spain from 4000 B.C. to 1900 A.D. *Proceedings of the Prehistoric Society* 58: 227–47.

Tanda, G.

1987 Il Carro in età Nuragica. In *La Sardegna nel Mediterraneo tra il Secondo e il Primo Millennio a.C.: Atti del II Convegno di Studi 'Un Millennio di Relazioni fra la Sardegna e i Paesi del Mediterraneo', Selargius-Cagliari, 27–30 novembre 1986*, 63–79. Cagliari: Amministrazione Provinciale di Cagliari.

Taramelli, A.

1921 Il Ripostiglio dei Bronzi Nuragici de Monte Sa Idda. *Monumenti Antichi* 27: 373–410.

1926 Scavi nel Nuraghe Sa Donu e S'Orcu. *Monumenti Antichi* 31: 405–55.

Terrero, J.

1990 [orig. 1944] *Armas y útiles de bronce extraídos en los dragados del puerto de Huelva*. Clásicos de la Arqueología de Huelva 3. Huelva: Excma. Diputación Provincial.

Tylecote, R.F.

1987 *The Early History of Metallurgy in Europe*. London: Longman.

Vagnetti, L.

1986 L'Egeo e Cipro. *La Sardegna nel Mediterraneo tra il Secondo e il Primo Millennio a.C.: Atti del II Convegno di Studi "Un Millennio di Relazioni fra la Sardegna e i Paesi del Mediterraneo", Selargius-Cagliari, 27–30 novembre 1986*, 359–67. Cagliari: Amministrazione Provinciale di Cagliari.

Vagnetti, L., and F. Lo Schiavo

1989 Late Bronze Age Long Distance Trade in the Mediterranean: The Role of the Cypriots. In E. Peltenburg (ed.), *Early Society in Cyprus*, 217–43. Edinburgh: Edinburgh University Press.

Vernet, J.

1978 La Navegación en la alta Edad Media. In *Actas, Coloquio della Navegazione Mediterranea nell'Alto Medioevo*, 323–81. Spoleto: Centro Italiano di Studi sull'Alto Medioevo.

Vilá Valentí, J.

1968 *La Península Ibérica*. Barcelona: Ariel.

Wallace, B.L.

1991 The Vikings in North America: Myth and Reality. In R. Samson (ed.), *Social Approaches to Viking Studies*, 221–34. Glasgow: Cruithne Press.

Wells, P.S.

1983 *Rural Economy in the Early Iron Age: Excavations at Hascherkeller, 1978–1981*. Cambridge, MA: Peabody Museum of Archaeology and Ethnology, Harvard University.

1984   *Farms, Villages and Cities: Commerce and Urban Origins in Late Prehistoric Europe.* Ithaca: Cornell University Press.

Zohary, D., and M. Hopf

1973   Domestication of Pulses in the Old World. *Science* 182: 887–94.

1989   *Domestication of Plants in the Old World: The Origins and Spread of Cultivated Plants in West Asia, Europe and the Nile Valley.* Oxford: Clarendon Press.

10. Religious Aspects of Phoenician-Punic Colonization in the Iberian Peninsula: The Stelae from Villaricos, Almería

María Belén Deamos

Introduction

Knowledge of the religion of eastern colonists in the Iberian peninsula is still very limited. This situation is striking when one bears in mind that Phoenician-Punic archaeology has undergone considerable development over the past thirty years. We now have good information about numerous settlements (Schubart 1982: 71–79; Aubet 1987: 228–78), some of them genuinely spectacular, like Castillo de Doña Blanca, currently under excavation, near the bay of Cádiz (Ruíz Mata 1988: 36–48). Strange as it may seem, however, we do not even have adequate information about the funerary customs of the earliest colonists. On top of that, the available facts have not been analyzed adequately. Otherwise one would not be able to understand the changes in interpretation that still occur for some cemeteries which fail to conform to the prevailing normative models of the funerary practices of Phoenician and Punic communities.

All in all, documentation concerning other aspects of religiosity (such as cult places, divinities, etc.) is even scarcer. The few synthesizing works on these subjects that do exist confuse rather than instruct the reader because they do not make a clear distinction between what may be reasonably interpreted as religious elements of the oriental populations in the Iberian peninsula and what may be taken as evidence of the adoption of foreign beliefs by the peninsula's indigenous communities (see also Blázquez 1983: 33–66).

One of the matters which awaits resolution in this area is the absence of *tophets* in the Phoenician-Punic cities of the west. In the opinion of some investigators, this is not a fortuitous circumstance: it is explained historically by the fact that the settlers which reached Iberia came from regions of the Near East in which manifestations of the *moloch* rite also were also rare (Aubet 1987: 287). To date, only Cádiz has pro-vided any evidence for the existence of child sacrifices in the Punic sphere of the peninsula, but unfortunately with a very late date (second half of the first century BC); and other archaeologists working in the city have doubts on the matter. Excavations in 1980 in the necropolis zone of Cádiz uncovered six burials of children whose skulls had apparently been violently smashed. This discovery has been taken as proof that the Punic population practiced certain barbaric customs, abolished by Caesar around the year 61, as Cicero tells us (Pro Balbo 43). Leaving aside the question of the feasibility of this interpretation, it is clear that these children were buried in the same cemetery with adults and with children who died under very different circumstances (Corzo and Ferreiro 1987: 57–61). Children are also buried alongside adults (and not in separate enclosures) in the necropolis of Ibiza (Gómez Bellard 1990: 163).

The current situation is not an encouraging one. It is apparent that the evidence relevant to the religious beliefs of the colonial communities of the Iberian peninsula requires a revision which will involve serious analysis, on the one hand, of data which are already known and, on the other hand, of the abundance of unpublished material from older excavations. Our contribution to this volume constitutes a modest offering to the second line of research.

Some years ago Professor Fernández-Miranda suggested that we study the stelae found in the Punic necropoli of southern Spain. In his view reanalysis of this material would help to clarify the function of the various pieces within the sites at which they had been found and to settle the question (among others) of their ascription to *tophets*. Although I believe that these stone monuments might be of broader interest because of their relation to similar finds in the colonies of the central Mediterranean and of North Africa, such a broad study is not within the limits of this contribution. A smaller sample has therefore

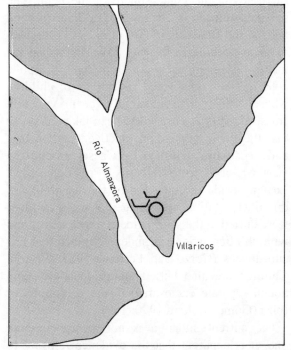

Figure 10.1 Villaricos: the Punic necropolis (open symbol) and settlement (circle) on the river Almanzora (after Schubart 1982).

been selected for analysis, from an assemblage recovered by L. Siret in his excavations at the Punic necropolis of Villaricos (Almería).

Villaricos: the Punic settlement and necropolis

The settlement of Villaricos has the type of location found most frequently among the colonies in southern Iberia. It occupies a place elevated above the mouth of the river Almanzora, facing the Mediterranean (Figure 10.1). The settlement, identified since the 1890s as the ancient Baria, seems to have been established some time in the first half of the sixth century BC. As indicated in Figure 10.2, it is the latest of the Punic colonies known along the Andalusian coast.

Recent studies have confirmed that in the third millennium BC, the mouth of the river was a wide estuary which silted up little by little in later times. These facts lead some researchers to suggest that the first Phoenician-Punic settlement, contemporary to the other coastal foundations, was located further inland, perhaps on one of the hills next to the now silted-up bay. It seems that the principal economic activity of the population was the exploitation of the region's varied mineral resources, as well as fishing and related industries. Villaricos may have had a population of some 1,200 people, comprised of foreigners and natives (González Wagner 1983: 470). Both were buried in the cemetery located west of the settlement (Figure 10.3).

The first excavations in the necropolis were carried out at the end of the 19th century by Louis Siret, who published some of his results within a volume dealing with a variety of subjects. In that study he sorted the burials into six groups based on a classification of the most representative grave goods (Siret 1906: 392 [16]). Siret continued to work for some years after 1906, and in the late 1940s Astruc (1951) published a monograph based on the study of Siret's field notes and of the material from the nearly 2000 tombs which he had excavated. Astruc (1951: 14) classified the burials into ten groups based on the "funerary rite and the shape of the tombs." Of these groups, three (A, E, I) consist of cremations burials, five (B, C, F, G, H) of inhumations, and two (D, J) include tombs that combined the two rites. While this classification is suitable for general purposes, it obscures specific variations in the burial rite. From 1975 to 1978 Almagro-Gorbea resumed archaeological investigations at the site, publishing the results some years later (Mª. J. Almagro Gorbea 1984).

The Villaricos necropolis exhibits a broad range of burial types. The greatest variety occurs within the class of inhumations, but the three essential divisions are the following:

1. Simple trenches dug into the ground.
2. Rectangular pits which open at the bottom of a deep, wide well.
3. Underground chambers, dug into the ground or built of ashlars, with a well or a *dromos* for access.

In all three cases the bodies are frequently placed in wooden coffins. There are some inhumations of children covered with amphoras.

Cremation burials are simpler: the remains were placed directly into pits or ceramic vessels.

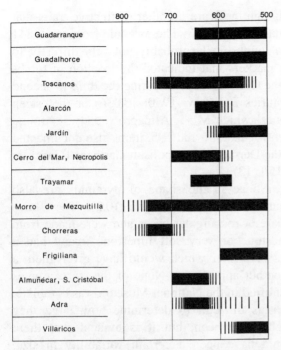

Figure 10.2 The founding of Villaricos in relation to the other Phoenician and Punic establishments along the Mediterranean coast of Andalusia (after Schubart 1982).

Some cremations were placed on the lids covering the inhumation tombs (as in burial 718) or in old underground chambers that had fallen into disuse (Mª. J. Almagro Gorbea 1984: 629–31).

Stelae[1] of the Villaricos necropolis

Many of the stelae we have studied had already been noted in the above-mentioned publications of Siret (1906: 463 [87], pl. XX) and Astruc (1951: pls. L–LII). The information provided by those authors was so general, however, that it was impossible to conclude under what circumstances, or in relation to which tomb, the pieces had been found. Astruc indicates which tombs had stelae, but does not specify which particular piece is associated with which tomb. We consulted the notebooks (deposited in the Spanish National Museum of Archaeology) of Pedro Flores, Siret's foreman and the excavator of most of the necropolis, but found few details on this matter, although the notes were most useful for resolving other problems. Siret had made pencil drawings of some of the stelae, but in only three instances noted the number of the tomb with which they were found.

1. The simplest stelae consist of long, pointed stones with rectangular bases. They must have been the most common, but perhaps many of them were not recognized for what they were by the excavators. In the collections of the National Museum there is a piece which is 57 cm long (the stelae from Villaricos have no inventory numbers, so we cannot give them more explicit references), and Mª. J. Almagro (1984: 85, 117; pls. III, V: 12) found several "of large size" during her excavations in the cremation cemetery of the third to second century BC.

The only stela with a funerary inscription found in the necropolis (Plate 10.1) belongs to this group. It appeared without context among the cremation tombs (Siret 1906: 403 [27], pl. XX, 2) (Astruc 1951: 56, pl. LI). It is 97cm high and has a four line epitaph inscribed on it that has been read as "Tomb of / Ger'as / toret son of / Ba'alpilles" (Solá Solé 1955: 47). The name of the deceased is a *theophorus* which is repeated in various funerary inscriptions at Carthage (Bénichou-Safar 1982: nos. 7, 18, 33; pp. 208, 211, 213 respectively). There is widespread agreement that this stela should be dated to the

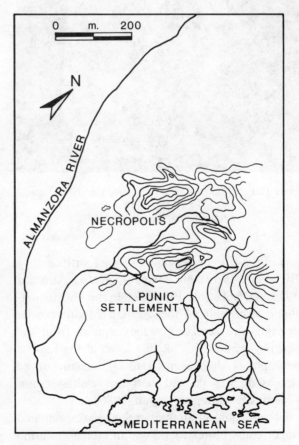

Figure 10.3 Villaricos: the Punic necropolis and settlement (after Siret 1906).

Plate 10.1   Villaricos: stela with epitaph (height: 93 cms.; base: 27 x 22 cms.). (Photograph, Museo Arqueológico Nacional, Madrid).

end of the fifth or beginning of the fourth century BC (Fuentes Estañol 1986: 9; Guzzo Amadasi 1978: 35; Solá Solé 1955: 47). In the Phoenician-Punic necropoli of the western Mediterranean epitaphs are scarce, but they appear from the seventh century BC on: in a tomb at the Laurita necropolis (Almuñécar, Granada) the name of the deceased was painted onto an alabaster urn (Fuentes Estañol pers. comm. 1986).

Other equally simple stelae have rounded upper ends. Flores found one in cremation tomb 309 "arranged as if it were a Saint Anthony". This may be one of the pieces drawn by Siret,

although there are no other distinctive traits that would confirm this. The example from tomb 841 is a rough block, probably not very different to the markers that indicated the location of tombs in the Olbia necropolis during the third to second centuries BC (Levi 1950: 13, 36) or the 'steep stones' which Mª. J. Almagro (1984: 58) found in *hypogaea* 556 and H-5, items also documented in the Dermech necropolis at Carthage (Gauckler 1915/I: 13).

2. Stelae in the shape of pyramids are also common at the site (Plate 10.2). They have square or rectangular bases and were made from sandstone or very soft limestone; many had a coat of plaster which would have given them a smoother appearance. None of the six examples identified in the National Museum was complete, so it is difficult to determine how large they might have been, but it is evident that there would have been a certain variability in size, since some pieces are larger than 50 cm while others are less than 20 cm in length.

Flores's notes indicate that pyramidal stelae were found both in cremation burials (358 and 612[2]) and in inhumation burials (321, 462, 556, 677: 4, and perhaps 460). Interestingly, these tomb markers (Tore 1972b: 262) are also found in burials placed in underground chambers (556 and 677: 4), that is to say, in contexts where they would only be visible to visitors to the interior of the sepulchre. At any rate, the stelae must have always been placed outside the trench or pit burial itself, perhaps at the head, as Flores indicated with respect to tomb 321. The drawings and references are generally imprecise and do not permit us to identify exactly which stela corresponded to which tomb, except in those cases where Siret himself noted the grave number on the drawing of the stelae, as occurs in the specimens from tombs 612 and 677: 4.

It will be possible to determine the chronology of these monuments only once a detailed study of the composition of the grave goods in each burial has been carried out. We have attempted to classify the amphoras from tombs 460 and 462 using Flores's illustrations, and we believe that they may correspond to J. Almagro's type III, in which case they would be dated from the end of the fifth century through the fourth century BC (Mª. J. Almagro Gorbea 1986b: 274, fig. 3). This time span is confirmed by the presence in these same tombs of ostrich eggshells which have been dated from the sixth to fourth centuries BC (San Nicolás 1975: 98). Hypogaeum 556 had a long

Plate 10.2   Villaricos: pyramidal stela (height: 34 cms.;
base: 22 x 22 cms.).

period of use: it yielded materials dating from the fourth to the second centuries BC (Mª. J. Almagro Gorbea 1986a: 633). Finally, tomb 612 confirms that these stelae were still used at Villaricos in Roman times, since the burnt remains were covered by an amphora which definitely belonged to that period.

Pyramidal funerary monuments are well known in the Punic world and exhibit great variability (Cid Priego 1949: 91–126). Pyramidal stelae like those of Villaricos are the simplest and most common type. Similar items have been found in tombs at Ibiza (Gómez Bellard 1990: 111–14, pls. LVII and LX) and Cádiz (Perdigones *et al.* 1990: 37 n. 10, 49; perhaps also Quintero Atauri 1932: pl. IIIB), dating to the sixth and fifth centuries BC respectively. In the central Mediterranean pyramidal stelae are found both in sanctuaries (cf. for Tharros: Moscati and Uberti [1985: pls. IV:13 and V:16]; for Motya: Moscati and Uberti [1981/II: pls. VII:56, VIII:57]; for Sulcis: Bartoloni [1986: pl. I:6–7]) and in funerary contexts. A piece identical to those at Villaricos comes from Tharros (Tore 1972b: fig. 3:11), and Tamburello (1967: 362 n. 2) found *cippi* in the form of single and multiple truncated pyramids inside some Palermo tombs dated to

the third century BC. Finds from the Sétif necropolis (Février and Gaspary 1967: 46), dating to the second and third centuries AD, and from Tipasa prove that pyramid-shaped stelae lasted into Roman times.

Lancel (1970: 187, figs. 33–35 and 39–40) suggests that the pyramids would have crowned a pillar-shaped monument, which he reconstructs as shown in Figure 10.4 (Lancel 1970: fig. 38). In describing two of the Villaricos stelae, Siret (1906: 463[87], 3 and 4) also indicated that they "probably were placed on top of another stone." A *cippus* from the Tharros necropolis shows that Siret was not mistaken and that this type of emplacement must have been common (Tore 1972b: fig. 2: 1), but Lancel's reconstruction, in the style of pillar stelae, seems to us to be plausible as well, when one takes into account that the inhabitants of Villaricos had a tradition of that kind of monument. The sphinx found at this site (Chapa 1985: 58, 218) also possibly crowned a pillar erected over the tomb of an important personage. This sculpture, which has stylistic affinities to the Phoenician world, has been dated to the end of the seventh or beginning of the sixth century BC, and the tomb to which it supposedly belonged (cf. Chapa 1985: 221) is considered a prototype for similar native Iberian monuments (M. Almagro-Gorbea 1983: 17). Lancel's suggestion becomes even more acceptable when one takes into account the formal and

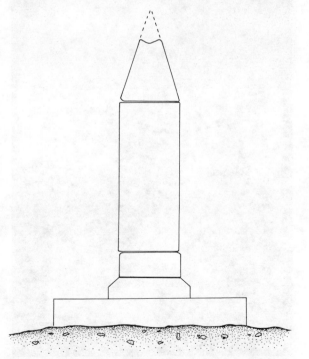

Figure 10.4 Reconstruction of a funerary monument from Tipasa, after a photograph by Lancel 1970.

symbolic similarities which exist between simple pyramids and those other monolithic monuments composed of a tubular pedestal with a pyramidal crest (Tore 1972b: 249–267), known from Cyprus (Tore 1972b: fig. 4: 1–2), the *tophet* of Carthage with a date in the fifth to sixth centuries BC (Picard 1957: 130, Cb 357 and pl. XLIX), Motya (Tore 1972b: fig. 4: 4), and Tharros (Tore 1972a: pl. XXVI; 1972b: pl. V: 2). Similar monuments are also found in the necropolis of Les Andalouses dating to the second to first centuries BC (Vuillemot 1965: 290, fig. 124).

Undoubtedly, however, the most unusual piece known within the style of the pyramidal stela variant is found in the necropolis of Villaricos itself. It is about 50 cm high, and its peculiarity is the carving, on one side of the limestone pillar, of the head of a man with an Egyptian hairstyle and, on the opposite side, of an Aeolian capital (Plate 10.3). Unfortunately, the piece was reused

as part of the lid of tomb 521 (Astruc 1951: 175), and thus has no original context. Authorities have stressed that this stela was inspired by Cypriot art of the period of Egypt's greatest influence on the island (Astruc 1951: 175; Bisi 1966: 43–45) (on the subject of Egyptian influence on Phoenician religious architecture, see Bisi [1967: 191, 202] and Wagner [1980]). The date attributed to the piece, the sixth century BC (Bisi 1966: 44), would make it the oldest funerary monument in Villaricos, together with the above-mentioned sphinx.

3. Altars. This group includes items of very different morphology but of supposedly identical function; they range from simply dressed blocks to examples with separately carved tops and feet. The largest group is made up of pieces which have in common a truncated pyramidal shape in common, with moulding and *gula* on the front

Plate 10.3   Villaricos: stela with human protome, frontal (left) and posterior views (right). Actual height: 50 cms.; pillar base: 18 x 23 cms.; pyramid base: 15.5 x 18 cms.

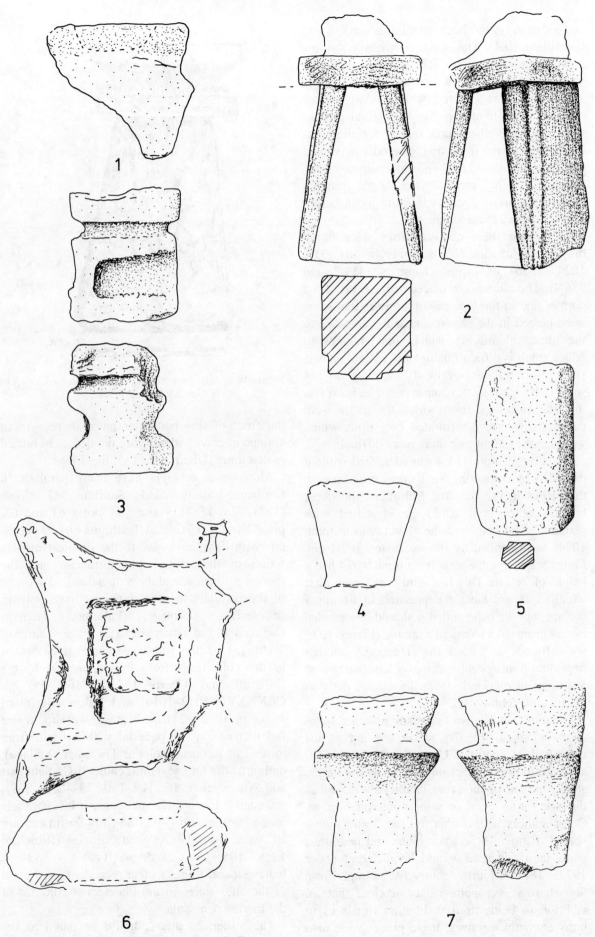

Figure 10.5 Altars from Villaricos, drawn by L. Siret.

and sides only, the back remaining vertical and flat (Plate 10.4). The upper part has a shallow rectangular depression. The altars are made of sandstone, except for a few carved from limestone, and were covered with a white plaster coating. Even though it has the formal characteristics of the other altars, one of the altars has the corners of the front side lowered and painted red like the moulding. The dimensions of the altars are quite variable, the height ranging between 20 and 65 cm, while the mean height falls between 25 and 35 cm.

Items with these characteristics were found only in inhumation tombs; either in pits (718, 1024, 1626) or inside chambers (411.2 and 986.4). The altars were placed at the head of the corpse, and in the *hypogaea* it appears that some were placed in the passage, near the entrance to the tomb. Identifying which altar belongs to which tomb is difficult using only Flores's notes, since even the measurements he cites do not seem to be accurate. It is quite possible, however, that the soft rock from which the altars were carved may have deteriorated over time, which would make identifying them more difficult.

The altar of tomb 411.4 was identified without difficulty by comparing Siret's drawing of it with the pieces in the National Museum collections, but no other item could be identified with certainty. The height of the altar found in tomb 1024, as illustrated by the excavator, is 64 cm. Flores states that the stela from tomb 986.4 had a height of 36 cm. This last item is the only altar which does not have a depression in its upper surface, but we believe that it should be included in this group. An identical example (Figure 10.6) was found in Riotinto (Huelva), another important mining centre that may have harboured a settlement of people from the east as early as the seventh century BC.

The *tophet* at Tharros had many so-called base-altars identical to the stelae we have just described. Moscati and Uberti (1985: 25, 32–33) attribute the same function to them as the throne stelae: in their opinion they would have served as the base for an iconic or anthropomorphic image. Other authors believe that, on the contrary, one should distinguish between altars and pedestals, since their functions would be different (Tore 1972a: 188). A fourth century BC example from the Tharros necropolis makes it clear that, in addition to being used in libation rituals or to burn aromatic essences, these pieces were also conceived as authentic funerary stelae, since on

0   50 cms.

Figure 10.6 Altar from Riotinto, Huelva (after a drawing by A. García y Bellido 1952).

the front of this particular piece there was an epitaph engraved identifying the deceased buried in that tomb (Uberti n.d.: 115, fig. 156).

Altar stelae or *cippi* have many parallels in Carthage, Sicily, and Sardinia. G. Tore (1971–72a: 118–119 and 188, notes 61 and 63, pls. XIX–XXIV) related the throne-*cippus* pedestals with Egyptian *gulae* to the simplest models found in the central Mediterranean and the Iberian peninsula, and drew up a detailed account of the parallels these monuments have both in cemeteries (Carthage, Palermo, Tharros, Cagliari) and in sanctuaries (Carthage, Tharros). To his list we may add the examples documented in the collections from the *tophets* at Motya (Moscati and Uberti 1981/II: fig. 65, pl. CLXXXVI: 1012–1014) and Sulcis (Bartoloni 1986: pl.III: 21–24). In closing, we should not fail to mention the pedestal with a basin from tomb 2 of the necropolis at Trayamar (Málaga), dating to the late seventh century BC (Schubart and Niemeyer 1976: 129–130, 231–232, 237); although it has a different shape, it has parallels in the Punic world — cf. the fifth–fourth century BC piece from the *tophet* at Carthage (Ribichini 1988: 105, 614, catalogue 179) — and we believe it constitutes a clear precedent for the use of the altar stelae in the Phoenician colonies of the Iberian peninsula.

The Villaricos altars should be dated to the fifth and fourth centuries BC. Tombs 718, 1024,

Observations

Stone monuments, stelae or *cippi* have been found on top of tombs in most of the Punic necropoli of the central and western Mediterranean. Research has concentrated, however, on the votive stelae, which are much more numerous and have an incomparably richer iconographic repertoire. But in one context or another, these monuments appear to be rare before the sixth century BC (Bénichou-Safar 1982: 71; Bisi 1967: 228; Moscati and Uberti 1981: 57; Moscati and Uberti 1985: 51). In Phoenician-Punic necropoli further west, funerary stelae are also effectively unknown in earlier contexts. The simple non-iconic examples from the Ibiza necropolis date to the sixth century BC (Gómez Bellard 1990: 95, 97, 113, pls. 28–29, 34, 57, 60). In Villaricos stelae are not found in tombs of groups A and B, which Astruc dated to that same century, but the stela with the human figures and the sphinx (which we mentioned earlier) indicate that about that time the custom of placing monuments above tombs was already known. The special character of these monuments may indicate that the custom of marking tombs with something more elaborate than a simple standing stone was uncommon.

Most of the stelae we have discussed here belong to the phase at the height of the settlement's development, dating to the fifth and fourth centuries BC. The simple pyramidal monuments, which probably also had a *baetylic* character (Tore 1972b), were associated more frequently with inhumations, but were also found in some cremation burials. The latter might be later in time generally speaking, and in some cases can be securely dated to the Roman period.

Altars were found only in inhumation burials, both in pits and in underground chambers.

None of the documented stelae is associated with child burials. (We have already indicated that tomb 612, which Astruc classified as an infant inhumation, is described clearly by Flores as "remains of a burnt corpse in a place like a small cave and covered with half a jar"[3]). This eliminates the possibility that some of the pieces had a votive function and were related with some act of sacrifice. In our opinion, the interpretation of the stelae from Cádiz (Marín Ceballos 1984: 38) and Ibiza (Mª. J. Almagro Gorbea 1967: 11) as proof of the existence of child sacrifice will also have to be revised, since they may well be

Plate 10.4   Villaricos: altar (height: 30,5 cms.; base: 14 x 10 cms.).

and 1626 had amphoras that we believe could be assigned to this time period because of their similarity to amphora types I and III of Mª. J. Almagro (1986b: 270–74, figs. 2–3). Tombs 1626 and 411.2 also had ostrich eggshells, not found on the site after the fourth century BC (San Nicolás 1975: 98).

4. Siret (1906: fig.18, pl. XX: 5) found other stone monuments in the Villaricos necropolis, but in closing we only wish to mention the piece that Astruc (1951: 81–82, pl. L: 5) describes as a "large pyriform cippus", made of limestone with a mortice at the base and another on its upper portion. Its shape is reminiscent of *baetyls* that preside over the throne altars at Carthage (Lézine 1960: 37, figs. 18 and 20) or Tharros (Moscati and Uberti 1985, II: pls. LVIII: 147, LXI: 149, LXII: 149–150). That altars with oval *baetyls* lasted until Roman times is demonstrated in the necropolis of Tipasa. Lancel (1970: 187, fig. 40) relates this monument to the obelisk topped by an oval element that was found in the Roman necropolis of Baelo (Cádiz) (París and Bonsor 1925: fig. 21). The piece from Villaricos was probably also placed on a pedestal, outside an underground chamber (Astruc 1951: 81).

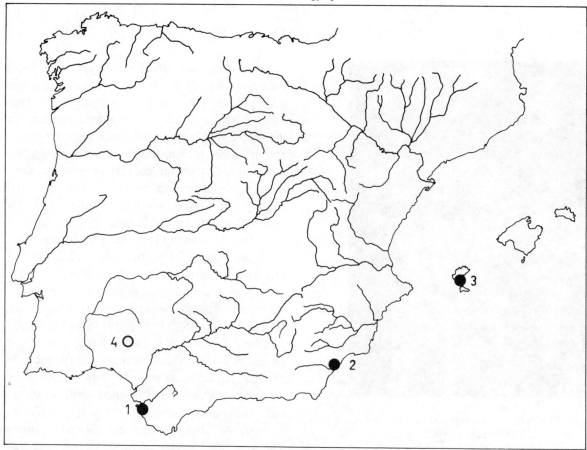

Figure 10.7 Places in the Iberian peninsula where stelae have been found. Necropoleis: 1: Cádiz; 2: Villaricos; 3:Ibiza. Isolated finds: 4: Riotinto.

funerary stelae, as might be expected from the contexts in which they were found (Quintero Atauri 1932: 7–8; Mª. J. Almagro Gorbea 1967: 5; Gómez Bellard 1990: 147). We wish to suggest, not that there were no *tophets* in the colonies in the west, only that to date there is no evidence for them. In contrast, there is evidence from many of the towns of the Spanish Mediterranean coast for the cult of a female goddess that protected these sanctuaries (Marín Ceballos 1987: 43–79). Tanit was venerated in caves in Ibiza (Aubet 1986: 622–23), Villaricos, and Cádiz (Marín Ceballos 1984: 15–16), the three cities which we have mentioned as having funerary stelae. (Astruc [1951: 79] indicates that at Villaricos Siret found a cave sanctuary, related perhaps to the *favissa* in which numerous perfume holders shaped like female heads were found [J. Almagro-Gorbea 1983]. A poorly preserved sculpture [Siret 1906: fig. 18] from the necropolis depicts a female figure seated on a throne. These figures have sometimes been interpreted as representations of the goddess Tanit [Marín Ceballos and Corzo 1991: 1031–34]). At Cádiz, furthermore, there was a temple dedicated to Baal-Hammon (Marín

Ceballos 1984: 30). There is, however, no archaeological evidence of the practice of blood sacrifices, apart from the supposedly murdered children in first century AD contexts from Cádiz.

The use of stone monuments placed above tombs by the Punic population at Villaricos was surely brought about by the introduction of religious ideas involving important changes in funerary rituals. Such changes affected the entire Punic world beginning in the sixth century BC (Aubet 1986: 612–20), and resulted in a surprising degree of uniformity in rituals involving the treatment of corpses, in funerary architecture, and in the types of monuments found in all the Punic establishments of north Africa and the central and western Mediterranean. Some authors (Aubet 1986: 523) interpret this unification of religious beliefs as the result of the ideological and political domination of Carthage.

In all these regions the Punic substrate continued to manifest itself well into Roman times. This is evident in burial practices, as well as in many other aspects of the archaeological record which lie beyond the scope of this article. In Sardinia (cf. Moscati 1988; Uberti 1986: 127, text figs. 181–182), north Africa (Gauckler 1915,

II: 334–43; Lancel 1970: 206), and in Andalusia cemeteries prove that some traditions were maintained for many years. We have already referred in this article to the survival of Punic customs in tombs of the Roman period at Villaricos and Cádiz. The signs of Punic identity are equally powerful in the necropoli of Baelo (Paris and Bonsor 1926: 110; Remesal 1979: 49) and Carmona (Bendala 1976: 38–43; Belén 1983: 217), an important centre of Carthaginian interests in the Guadalquivir valley.

Acknowledgments

We are grateful for the generous assistance of Professor M. Fernández-Miranda, who provided us with some of the data and with the photographs included in this chapter, and of Dr. A. Rodero, Curator of the Spanish National Museum of Archaeology, who cordially and diligently attended to our numerous requests for information. We thank our colleague, Professor Oswaldo Arteaga, for information on the coastal geomorphology of the Almanzora river mouth.

Notes

1. The specialized literature uses both the terms *cippus* and *stela*. We use the latter in the sense recorded by the Dictionary of the Royal Spanish Academy: "Commemorative monument which is erected above ground in the form of a slab, pedestal or *cippus*."

2. This tomb is listed, perhaps by mistake, among the inhumations of Group G by Astruc (1951: 52).

3. Translation of field notes kept in the Spanish National Museum of Archaeology: notebook 587–624, sheet 27 paragraph 28.

Bibliography

Almagro Gorbea, M.J.

    1967   *Excavaciones Arqueológicas en Ibiza*. Excavaciones Arqueológicas en España 56. Madrid: Ministerio de Educación y Ciencia.

    1983   Un Depósito Votivo de Terracotas de Villaricos. In *Homenaje al Prof. Martín Almagro Basch*, 2: 291–307. Madrid: Ministerio de Cultura.

    1984   *La Necrópolis de Baria*. Excavaciones Arqueológicas en España 129. Madrid: Ministerio de Cultura.

    1986a Excavaciones en la Necrópolis Púnica de Villaricos. In *Homenaje a Luis Siret*, 625–37.

    Sevilla: Consejería de Cultura, Junta de Andalucía.

    1986b Las Ánforas de la Antigua Baria (Villaricos). In G. del Olmo and M.E. Aubet (eds), *Los Fenicios en la Península Ibérica*, 1: 265–83. Sabadell: Ausa.

Almagro Gorbea, M.

    1983   Pilares-estela Ibéricos. In *Homenaje al Prof. Martín Almagro Basch*, 3: 7–20. Madrid: Ministerio de Cultura.

Astruc, M.

    1951   *La Necrópolis de Villaricos*. Informes y Memorias 25. Madrid: Comisaría General de Excavaciones Arqueológicas, Ministerio de Educación Nacional.

Aubet, M.E.

    1986   La Necrópolis de Villaricos en el Ámbito del Mundo Púnico Peninsular. In *Homenaje a Luis Siret*, 612–23. Sevilla: Consejería de Cultura, Junta de Andalucía.

    1987   *Tiro y las Colonias Fenicias de Occidente*. Barcelona: Bellaterra.

Bartoloni, P.

    1986   *Le Stele di Sulcis, Catalogo*. Collezione di Studi Fenici, 24. Rome: Consiglio Nazionale delle Ricerche.

Belén, M.

    1983   Aportaciones al Conocimiento de los Rituales Funerarios en la Necrópolis Romana de Carmona. In *Homenaje al Prof. Martín Almagro Basch*, 3: 209–26. Madrid: Ministerio de Cultura.

Bendala, M.

    1976   *La Necrópolis Romana de Carmona (Sevilla)*. Sevilla: Excma. Diputación Provincial.

Bénichou-Safar, H.

    1982   *Les Tombes Puniques de Carthage: Topographie, Structures, Inscriptions et Rites Funéraires*. Paris: Études d'Antiquité Africaine, CNRS.

Bisi, A.M.

    1966   *Kipriaka: Contributi allo Studio della Componente Cipriota della Civiltá Punica*. Roma: Gherardo Casini.

    1967   *Le Stele Puniche*. Studi Semitici 27. Rome: Istituto di Studi del Vicino Oriente, Università di Roma.

Blázquez, J.M.

    1983   *Religiones Prerromanas*. Primitivas Religiones Ibéricas 2. Madrid: Editorial Cristiandad.

Chapa, T.

    1985   *La Escultura Ibérica Zoomorfa*. Madrid: Ministerio de Cultura.

Cid Priego, C.

    1949   El Sepulcro de Torre Mediterráneo y sus Relaciones con la Tipología Monumental.

Ampurias 11: 91–126.

Corzo, R., and M. Ferreiro

1987   Sacrificios Humanos en el Cádiz Antiguo. In *Actas del II Congreso Andaluz de Estudios Clásicos, Antequera-Málaga, 1984*, 2: 57–61. Málaga: Universidad de Málaga.

Février, P.A., and A. Gaspary

1967   La Nécropole Orientale de Sétif: Rapport Préliminaire sur les Fouilles Effectuées de 1959 à 1964. *Bulletin d'Archéologie Algérienne* 2: 11–93.

Fuentes Estañol, M.J.

1986   *Corpus de las Inscripciones Fenicias, Púnicas y Neopúnicas de España*. Barcelona: Author.

García y Bellido, A.

1952   El Mundo de las Colonizaciones. In R. Menéndez Pidal (ed.), *Historia de España*, 1: 311–647. Madrid: Espasa Calpe.

Gauckler, P.

1915   *Nécropoles Puniques de Carthage*. Paris: Picard.

Gómez Bellard, C.

1990   *La Colonización Fenicia de la Isla de Ibiza*. Excavaciones Arqueológicas en España 157. Madrid: Ministerio de Cultura.

González Wagner, E.C.

1983   *Fenicios y Cartagineses en la Península Ibérica: Ensayo de Interpretación Fundamentado en un Análisis de los Factores Internos*. Tesis doctorales de la Universidad Complutense 30/83. Madrid: Universidad Complutense.

Guzzo Amadasi, M.G.

1978   Remarques sur la présence Phénico-Punique en Espagne d'après la documentation épigraphique. In *Actes, II Congrès International d'Étude des Cultures de la Méditerranée Occidentale*, 33–42. Algiers: Société Nationale d'Édition et de Diffusion.

Lancel, S.

1970   Tipasitana IV, la Nécropole Romaine occidentale de la porte de Césarée: rapport préliminaire. *Bulletin d'Archéologie Algérienne* 4: 149–266.

Levi, D.

1950   La Necropoli Puniche di Olbia. *Studi Sardi* 9: 5–120.

Lézine, A.

1960   *Architecture Punique: Recueil de Documents*. Publications de l'Université de Tunis, Faculté des Lettres, 1ére Série: Archéologie, Histoire 5. Paris: Presses Universitaires de France.

Marín Ceballos, M.C.

1984   La Religión Fenicia en Cádiz. In *Cádiz en su historia: II jornadas de historia de Cádiz, abril de 1983*, 5–41. Cádiz: Caja de Ahorros de Cádiz.

1987   ¿Tanit en España? *Lvcentvm* 6: 43–79.

Marín Ceballos, M.C., and R. Corzo

1991   Escultura Femenina Entronizada de la Necrópolis de Cádiz. In *Atti, II Congresso Internazionale di Studi Fenici e Punici*, 3: 1025–38. Rome: Consiglio Nazionale delle Ricerche.

Moscati, S.

1988   Le stele. In S. Moscati (ed.), *I Fenici*, 304–327. Milan: Bompiani.

Moscati, S., and M.L. Uberti

1981   *Scavi a Mozia: Le Stele*. Rome: Consiglio Nazionale delle Ricerche.

1985   *Scavi al Tofet di Tharros: I Monumenti Lapidei*. Rome: Consiglio Nazionale delle Ricerche.

Paris, P., and G. Bonsor

1926   *Fouilles de Belo (Bolonia, Province de Cádix, 1917–1921)*. II. *La Nécropole*. Bordeaux: Bibliothèque de l'École des Hautes Études Hispaniques.

Perdigones, L., A. Muñoz and G. Pisano

1990   *La Necrópolis Fenicio-Púnica de Cádiz: Siglos VI–IV a.C.*. Studia Punica 7. Rome: Università degli Studi di Roma.

Picard, C.G.

1957   *Catalogue du Musée Alaoui, Nouvelle Série*. Collections Puniques 1. Tunis: Institut des Hautes Études de Tunis.

Quintero Atauri, P.

1932   Excavaciones en Cádiz: Memoria de las Excavaciones Practicadas en 1929–1931. *Memorias de la Junta Superior de Excavaciones y Antigüedades* 117: 4–28.

Remesal, J.

1979   *La Necrópolis Sureste de Baelo*. Excavaciones Arqueológicas en España 104. Madrid: Ministerio de Educación y Ciencia.

Ribichini, S.

1988   Le Credenze e la Vita Religiosa. In S. Moscati (ed.), *I Fenici*, 104–25. Milan: Bompiani.

Ruíz Mata, D.

1988   El Castillo de Doña Blanca: Yacimiento Clave de la Protohistoria Peninsular. *Revista de Arqueología* 85: 36–48.

San Nicolás, M.P.

1975   Las Cáscaras de Huevo de Avestruz Fénico-Púnico en la Península Ibérica y Baleares. *Cuadernos de Prehistoria y Arqueología de la Universidad Autónoma de Madrid* 2: 75–100.

Schubart, H.

1982   Asentamientos Fenicios en la Costa Meridional de la Península Ibérica. *Huelva Arqueológica* 6: 71–99.

Schubart, H., and H.G. Niemeyer

1976   *Trayamar: los hipogeos fenicios y el asen-
        tamiento en la desembocadura del río
        Algarrobo.* Excavaciones Arqueológicas en
        España 90. Madrid: Ministerio de Educación y
        Ciencia.

Siret, L.

1906   *Villaricos y Herrerías: Antigüedades Púnicas,
        Romanas, Visigóticas y Árabes.* Madrid: Jaime
        Rates.

Sola Solé, J.M.

1955   Inscripciones fenicias de la Península Ibérica.
        Sefarad 15: 41–53.

Tamburello, I.

1967   Palermo. Necropoli: l'esplorazione 1953–54.
        Notizie degli Scavi di Antichità 21: 354–378.

Tore, G.

1972a   Due Cippi-Trono del Tophet di Tharros. *Studi
        Sardi* 22: 99–248.

1972b   Su Alcuni Amuleti di Tharros. *Studi Sardi* 22:
        249–68.

Uberti, M.L.

1986   Fenici e Punici in Sardegna. In: A. Antona *et al.*,
        (eds), *Il Museo Sanna in Sassari*, pp. 111–28.
        Sassari: Banco di Sardegna.

Vuillemot, G.

1965   *Reconnaissances aux Échelles Puniques
        d'Oranie.* Autun: Musée Rolin.

Wagner, P.

1980   *Der ägyptische Einfluss auf die phönizische
        Architektur.* Bonn: Rudolf Habelt.

11. Phoenician Gold in the Western Mediterranean: Cádiz, Tharros and Carthage

Alicia Perea Caveda

The overall picture of research into the production of goldwork in the Phoenician colonies of the western Mediterranean has undergone a substantial change in the last five years. This is due both to new papers published on the subject and to recent archaeological discoveries. This chapter is based, therefore, on an analysis of the new situation, new perspectives and the future direction of research.

The Carthaginian necropoli, which have generated so much scientific and descriptive literature, have for along time lacked a complete published list of the items made of gold. In 1987 Quillard published a second volume, completing her analysis of the material from the Bardo National Museum and the Carthage National Museum which had begun in 1979.

In the case of Sardinia, recent years have seen a real deluge of publications related to the 'genres' of Phoenician craftsmanship, as Moscati (1973, 1976, 1987, 1989, 1990) likes to define production in the various materials. The new series *Studia Punica*, edited by the Department of History of the Università degli Studi di Roma, uses the methodological approach adopted by this author, which is more commonly associated with the history of art than with archaeology. With regard to Tharros, the study of the gold material preserved in the Sardinian Museums (Quattrocchi Pisano 1974; Pisano 1985; Moscati and Uberti 1987; Moscati 1988) and the British Museum in London (Barnett and Mendleson, 1987) has now been completed.

Cádiz has been one of the sites less favoured by research. In 1985 I published a study of Phoenician gold, in which I dealt with the pieces from the city museum and those preserved in Spain's National Museum of Archaeology (Perea 1985a, 1985b). Later I began research on gold metallurgical technology, and the results of this study have been published recently (Perea 1990, 1991a). Although there have been constant references to the wealth of Phoenician and Punic

Cádiz in the research, there had been no previous monographic study of this material (see for example Nicolini 1990).

Between 1985 and 1988 the rescue excavations which were carried out in the modern city centre brought to light a series of burials with grave goods that included many gold items (Perdigones *et al.* 1990). A large part of this material belongs to the ancient seventh–sixth century BC necropolis and this substantially changes the previous picture, which was based mainly on the material from the fourth century BC necropolis excavated at the beginning of this century.

This state of affairs makes it necessary to revise previously held ideas and suggest future approaches to fill the gaps in our knowledge. In doing this I shall look at the particular features of each of the three sites separately — Carthage, Tharros and Cádiz — and then make a comparative analysis.

Carthage

Some 350 gold objects were retrieved from the early excavations at Carthage and Utica. To date no piece which could be dated earlier than the second half of the seventh century BC has been documented. From that date until the end of the fourth century BC the production is characterized by a strong influence of eastern Mediterranean techniques, types and iconography. This influence came from Cyprus, Egypt and the Near East. It did not, however, prevent a certain originality in the creation of new types, and the re-creation of others that do not have exact parallels with the industry of the eastern Mediterranean. The problem is that there are very few surviving pieces originating in the east which can be used to make genuinely valid comparisons.

Although an exhaustive technical study has not been carried out, in relative terms it could be said that the quality and variety of the jewellery

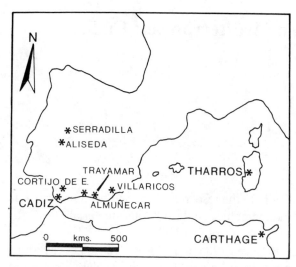

Figure 11.1 Location of the sites mentioned in the text.

during this first stage is high. The idea that these pieces were the result of systematic imports no longer seems defensible, but rather the existence of local workshops which obviously flourished at this time is implied.

From the fifth century BC the grave goods became impoverished. Archaeologists are not fully in agreement about the causes of this. This apparent economic recession seems to have been overcome in the fourth century BC when gold is once again found in the tombs. However, the metalworking techniques used demonstrate that the price of the raw material had increased: gold plating on a silver or bronze core becomes standard practice, and decorations in granulation are reduced in favor of filigree. Although there is typological continuity of some shapes, the general tendency is towards hoop earrings and rings to the detriment of the wide variety of pendants and amulets of the earlier period. Such characteristic types as amulet boxes with lids in the shape of an animal's head are still found. Finally, another characteristic of this second stage is contact with the Hellenistic communities, which is manifested in the form of the selective assimilation of a series of types and iconographies.

Tharros

Taking into account the gold pieces from both the Cagliari and Sassari museums, and the British Museum in London, there are over a thousand examples. This makes Sardinia the most important centre for the study of Phoenician goldworking in the entire Mediterranean.

However, even though Sardinia has produced a vast quantity of gold, there are a number of factors which make it enormously difficult to study Sardinian gold production. First, the archaeological contexts of discoveries, which come mostly from ancient hoards, is almost completely lacking. Secondly, the Tharros production seems to be characterized by conservatism, partly due to the prevalence of hoarding. All this makes it impossible to establish a chronology that is reliable. As a result, Carthaginian gold production becomes the inevitable point of reference for Tharros, with all the inherent problems of stylistic comparison within typological parameters that do not always coincide. A final problem is the absence of gold deposits in Sardinia: the raw material must have been imported, and although there are no analytical studies of the gold used, it is assumed to have come from the Iberian peninsula. This assumption is based on evidence from the classical sources.

Many authors seem to be in agreement about dating the height of the goldworking industry on Tharros to the seventh and greater part of the sixth centuries BC, but this is not provable on the basis of evidence of local workshops. While Pisano and Uberti consider that the highest quality pieces, if not all of them, would have been imported from the east, Moscati suggests that the vast majority of the jewellery must have been made locally. Paradoxically, neither argument, for or against, prevents them referring to the 'autonomy' and 'radiating function' of Tharros, on the grounds of its comparative technical excellence. It is even suggested that Carthaginian craftsmen were affiliated with Tharros (Pisano 1985: 208).

Characteristics of this archaic phase are the baroque ornamentation, and the originality of shapes and motifs. From the end of the sixth century until the third century BC production deteriorated progressively and we can observe the same phenomenon that is seen in Carthage: standardization, a reduction in technical quality (probably due to a scarcity of the raw material); and the assimilation of Hellenistic forms. The frequent use of silver in the Sardinian workshops is another peculiarity, and this is explained by the rich sources of silver on the island. It is at this time that the conservatism becomes most obvious, and therefore pieces from this long Punic period are generally dated *en bloc*.

Cádiz

The quantity of Cádiz jewellery recovered to date has increased by fifty or so pieces in recent years (Corzo 1983; Perdigones *et al.* 1990), bringing it to 235 pieces in total. The mythical wealth of the city does not appear to be confirmed archaeologically, although it must be remembered that the conditions of the site have not helped preservation: the erosion by the sea, constant and uncontrolled rebuilding of the city, and pillage of tombs have all had their effect. The archaeological investigations at the beginning of the century were very active in terms of recovery work but were also destructive due to the absence of scientific method. There are, however, some strong associations and contextualized grave goods of incalculable value for establishing a chronology, coupled with the recent rescue excavations, which is the only kind of archaeology possible in the city itself.

The oldest documented examples of colonial gold work based on eastern Phoenician traditions is in the south of the Iberian peninsula. Two of these examples come from Cádiz and lack an archaeological context although their exact provenience is known. The first is a gold swivel ring with a scarab that has a Phoenician inscription dated to the first half of the seventh century BC. It is a real name seal, carrying the name of the deity Na'am'el (the favoured of the god El) (Solá-Solé 1957: 26). It appeared in 1873 in the area know as Puerta de Tierra, where the old necropolis was situated, so it can be deduced that it came from an assemblage of grave goods (Perea 1991a: 164, 208). The second piece is the well-known statuette of the god Ptah with a gold mask, known as the 'priest of Cádiz'. It was found in the area where the Phoenician settlement was situated, so it is probably an offering to a temple or sacred place. The chronology of the statuette has been much debated, but it can be dated without too much risk to an archaic period between the end of the eighth and the beginning of the seventh century BC.

Various pieces with an archaeological context can also be dated in the first half of the 7th century BC. These are grave goods in tomb 1 of the Cerro de San Cristóbal necropolis in Almuñécar (Granada), which included a swivel ring and two hoop earrings. In Tomb 14 there was a cylindrical silver box for carrying amulets that is the earliest example of its kind recorded to date

(Perea 1991a: 159, 208; Pellicer 1963).

Two stages can be clearly distinguished for Cádiz gold production: an archaic phase, during the seventh and sixth centuries BC, and a Punic phase from the fourth century BC. As in Carthage, a recession throughout the fifth century can be observed, the reasons for which I do not propose to analyze here.

The fourth century Cádiz workshop is well known because of the large number of pieces preserved (Perea 1985a, 1985b, 1989, 1990, 1991a, 1991b). They all have very homogeneous typological and technical characteristics: gold plating and gilding with gold on a core of bronze and silver, substitution of granulation by filigree of exceptional quality and variety, and the use of enamel or faience. It is an industrialized production in which, however, various levels of complexity and quality can be distinguished, probably determined by the demands of the clientele. A factor which must be borne in mind is that this production is limited to the domestic consumption of the city. The fourth century workshop continued throughout the third, with the occasional example of exceptional quality, and then disappeared as a result of the assimilation of Roman forms and techniques.

The archaic phase used to be represented by three pieces only; two of them, a ring with a truncated cone-shaped mounting and a semi-circular pendant earring made in openwork filigree, are creations exclusive to the Cádiz workshop since there is nothing like them anywhere else in the Mediterranean, although they demonstrate influence from the Cypriot and Etruscan production industries respectively (Perea 1985: pls.1b, 5b). However, pieces from the classical Phoenician repertoire such as the Trayamar medal with Egyptian-style decoration, to cite a well-known example, had already been recorded in other colonial settlements. Recent discoveries fill this gap with a series of types which had previously only been recorded only in Tharros and Carthage, plus other original types:

1. Signet rings with a cartouche bezel. These had already been documented in collections such as that of Aliseda, as belonging to the 'orientalizing' or Tartessian tradition, and in settlements such as Villaricos (Almería), where there was a mixed indigenous and colonial population. A particular feature of the Cádiz examples is that they have no decoration on the seal.

2. Boat-shaped earrings with the heads of falcons at each end, and chain pendants, masks, palmettes and cubes with a pyramid of granules. The boat-shaped type of earring had already been found in Tharros, and the pendant in the shape of a cube both in Tharros and in Carthage. The variation which appears in Cádiz combines existing features in an original way.

3. Medals with triangular engraving at the bottom and a central stud. Throughout the Mediterranean there are a number of variations, since to this form the astral iconography of the crescent and disc may be added, or an Egyptian-style scene with a *sacrum* framed by a *ureus*.

4. Cylindrical rings decorated with palmettes or with a simple line of filigree. These have only been found in Cádiz.

5. Spherical pendant decorated with granulation. Already known from Trayamar and Aliseda, this is a simple and relatively commonplace shape in Carthage and Tharros.

6. Cartouches or prismatic necklace beads decorated with granulation. The type is found in Tharros and Carthage although there is wide technical and decorative variation between the three workshops.

Discussion

Looking at the production of the three colonies as a whole, what is immediately noticeable is the high degree of overall typological and iconographic homogeneity that stands out above the obvious local variations. This homogeneity continues to be confirmed as archaeological research advances and can be quantified in a more or less objective way by counting the different types of pieces which appear in each colony. If we take the production at Carthage as a point of reference and use the typology established by Quillard (1979: table II: 1987: tables IV, VI, VIII, X, XII) sixty-eight types have been distinguished. Forty-four of them appear in Sardinia and thirty-two in Cádiz. There are eight types in Sardinia not represented in the Carthage production, and eleven in Cádiz. In percentage terms, we could say that the homogeneity, as we have defined it, between Sardinia and Carthage is 84.6%, whilst between Cádiz and Carthage it is 74.4%. These figures can neither be interpreted as proof of centralized

production for all the Phoenician settlements in the Mediterranean, nor as confirmation of the hypothesis on systematic imports from the east.

The existence of workshops in Cádiz, Carthage and Tharros is supported by the following considerations:

1. The appearance of features exclusive to each centre. In Cádiz the examples are numerous. I have already mentioned the most significant ones, to which circular pendant earrings, pendants in the shape of a Hercules knot, and the multiple pendant, amongst others (Perea 1985: pls. 6b, 9ab) can also be added. The hinged cylindrical hoops must be emphasized as a type that defines the Cádiz workshop of the fourth century BC (Perea 1985: pl. 2b, 3ab). In Tharros there is a type of jointed bracelet, a pendant formed by two hoops of different sizes joined by a rectangular panel, the earrings which have been termed *globo mammellato*, (i.e. consisting of pendants with the image of a female deity with hands holding her breasts), to mention the most significant (Quattrocchi Pisano 1974: pls. X: 127, XI: 133, XIX: 273–75, XXIV: 417). The case of Carthage is more difficult to evaluate since types were created there which were later assimilated by other centres; this is the case of the amulet box with a zoomorphic lid (Quillard 1973). Another original and exclusively Carthaginian type is the triple-tongued pendant (Quillard 1979: pl. I: 1).

2. The creation of variations by the juxtaposition of existing features and the addition of new ones. This is the case of the boat-shaped earrings; a very ancient eastern shape, they reappear in Tharros with the ends finished off as the heads of falcons and have a smooth or granulated body in the shape of a palmette. On the lower part of the earring there is a pear-shaped pendant, or a pendant in the shape of a cube with a pyramid of granules; between the body of the earring and the pendant there is always the figure of a falcon as an intermediate feature (Quattrocchi Pisano 1974: pls. I, II). In Cádiz the pendant features are loop-in-loop chains with cubes at the end and the intermediate feature is a mask which could be interpreted as a Hathoric head, or a palmette (Perdigones, Muñoz and Pisano 1990: pls.

IX, XII; Perea 1991a: 180).

3. The same features are different in appearance and use different forms of ornamentation. The Tharros production can be defined as comparatively ostentatious. A tendency to excessive ornamentation can be observed in traditional features such as the medals with lower triangular engraving and a central stud, and the amulet box. In contrast, the Carthaginian style is more austere, although it demonstrates a preference for colour in the use of hard stones and enamels. In the case of Cádiz, it seems premature to make a comparative analysis of this kind because fewer pieces have been preserved; it must be remembered that here examples are being compared, whereas before comparisons were being made between types.

These three points require confirmation in a comprehensive technological study. Until now technological investigation has gone no further than recording the use of particular techniques of a generic nature: gold plating, gilding, filigree, granulation, engraving, inlaying, stamping, etc. (Quattrocchi Pisano 1974: 16–18; Quillard 1979: 33–44). All of these are common to the three workshops. A specific definition of each technique needs to be made: the different types of filigree threads used, the size and configuration of the granulation, the methods of soldering, the qualities of the finishes, the methods of cutting sheets, how worn the pieces are, the technical defects observed, etc. In short, a study is needed which would give us models for the archaeological and technological definition of each workshop. Furthermore, this study is essential for dealing with the problem of chronology.

The Cádiz workshop is the only one for which a technological study of this kind has been carried out (Perea 1990, 1991a, 1991b). However, since it does not share homogeneous comparative elements with other Mediterranean workshops, the conclusions obtained cannot be other than partial and incomplete. It has served, however, to identify and define an industry which was influenced by eastern techniques and styles and which had been confused for a long time with colonial production. Traditionally the idea that collections such as those of Aliseda, Cortijo de Ebora, Serradilla, and all those pieces which defined Tartessian goldwork came from the Cádiz workshop had been defended. Both an analysis of the solders and the study of the pieces using a scan-

ning electron microscope has made it possible to identify their origins as being from indigenous eastern-style workshops. These workshops obviously owed a debt to Phoenician craftsmen, but developed in an independent and personal way. Gold production acquired its own characteristics which distanced it from the strictly colonial style: these indigenous characteristics included complex design and technique, ornamental Baroque, and a prediliction towards ostentation.

The existence of a geographically widespread eastern-style metallurgical production is perhaps the characteristic which most distinguishes the development of the goldwork of the Iberian peninsula from that of the Mediterranean colonies considered here. The case of the Iberian peninsula is comparable only to the period of eastern influence in Etruria.

On the other hand, they have many factors in common. Both in Cádiz, and in Carthage and Tharros, two very distinct phases can be identified: an archaic one that developed in the seventh and sixth centuries BC and a more recent one from fifth to fourth centuries. The fifth century BC recession affected the three colonies equally and typological development before and after it does not alter the pattern of homogeneity observed. We can conclude that Cádiz, Tharros and Carthage remained in contact with one another throughout their history. This contact would not appear to have taken the form of exporting and importing ready-made pieces, but rather the interchange of craftsmen who enjoyed a large measure of mobility, both within their area of influence, as in the case of the Iberian peninsula, and throughout the central and western Mediterranean.

Bibliography

Barnett, R.D., and C. Mendleson (eds)

1987   *Tharros: A Catalogue of Material in the British Museum from Phoenician and Other Tombs at Tharros, Sardinia.* London: British Museum.

Corzo, R.

1983   Cádiz y la Arqueología Fenicia. *Anales de la Real Academia de Bellas Artes* 1: 5–29.

Moscati, S.

1973   Centri Artigianali Fenici in Italia. *Rivista di Studi Fenici* 1: 37–52.

1976   L'arte Fenicia Rivisitata. *Rivista di Studi Fenici* 4: 4–10.

1987   *Le Officine de Tharros.* Studia Punica 2. Rome:
        Università degli Studi di Roma.

1988   *I Gioielli di Tharros: Origini, Caratteri,
        Confronti.* Rome: Consiglio Nazionale delle
        Ricerche.

1989   *Tra Tiro e Cadice: Temi e Problemi degli Studi
        Fenici.* Studia Punica 5. Rome: Università degli
        Studi di Roma.

1990   *Techne: Studi sull'Artigianato Fenicio.* Studia
        Punica 6. Rome: Università degli Studi di Roma.

Moscati, S., and M.L. Uberti

1987   *Iocalia Punica: La Collezione del Museo
        Nazionale G.A. Sanna di Sassari.* Rome:
        Accadema Nazionale dei Lincei.

Nicolini, G.

1990   *Techniques des Ors Antiques: La Bijouterie
        Ibérique de VIIe au IVe Siècle.* Paris: Picard.

Pellicer, M.

1963   *Excavaciones en la Necrópolis Púnica
        'Laurita', del Cerro de San Cristobal
        (Almuñécar, Granada).* Excavaciones
        Arqueológicas en España 17. Madrid: Ministerio
        de Educación Nacional.

Perdigones, L., A. Muñoz and G. Pisano

1990   *La Necrópolis Fenicio-Púnica de Cádiz, Siglos
        VI–IV a.C..* Studia Punica 7. Rome: Università
        degli Studi di Roma.

Perea, A.

1985a   La Orfebrería Púnica de Cádiz. *Aula Orientalis*
        3: 295–322.

1985b   Piezas Singulares de Orfebrería Gaditana en el
        M.A.N. *Boletín del Museo Arqueológico
        Nacional* 3: 37–42.

1989   Cádiz: orfebrería fenicia. In *El Oro en la España
        Prerromana*, 58–67. Madrid: Monografías de la

        Revista de Arqueología.

1990   Estudio Microscópico y Microanalítico de las
        Soldaduras y Otros Procesos Técnicos en la
        Orfebrería Prehistórica del sur de la Península
        Ibérica. *Trabajos de Prehistoria* 47: 103–60.

1991a   *Orfebreria Prerromana: Arqueología del Oro.*
        Madrid: Caja de Madrid.

1991b   Metodología y Técnicas Actuales Para el
        Estudio de la Orfebrería Antigua: El Taller de
        Cádiz. In *Atti del II Congresso Internazionale di
        Studi Fenici e Punici, Rome 1987*, 3: 1133–42.
        Rome: Consiglio Nazionale delle Ricerche.

Pisano, G.

1985   Nuovi Studi Sull'oreficeria Tharrense. *Studi
        Fenici* 13(2): 189–210.

Quatrrocchi Pisano, G.

1974   *I Gioielli Fenici di Tharros nel Museo
        Nazionale di Cagliari.* Rome: Consiglio
        Nazionale delle Ricerche.

Quillard, B.

1973   Les étuis port-amulettes Carthaginois. *Karthago*
        16: 5–32.

1979   *Bijoux Carthaginois I: Les Colliers.* Aurifex 2.
        Louvaine-la-Neuve: Publications de l'Institut
        Supérieure d'Archéologie et d'Histoire de l'Art
        de l'Université Catholique de Louvain.

1987   *Bijoux Carthaginois II: Porte-Amulettes,
        Sceaux-Pendentifs, Pendents, Boucles, Anneaux
        et Bagues.* Aurifex 3. Louvain-la-Neuve:
        Publications de l'Institut Supérieure
        d'Archéologie et d'Histoire de l'Art de
        l'Université Catholique de Louvain.

Solá-Solé, J.

1957   Miscelánea Púbico Hispana II. *Sefarad* 17:
        18–35.

12. Models of Interaction between Punic Colonies and Native Iberians: The Funerary Evidence

Teresa Chapa Brunet

Introduction

One of the most interesting aspects of the archaeology of the western Mediterranean during the first millennium BC is the Phoenician and Punic colonization and settlement. By a study of this process we can observe the phenomena of adaptation and interaction within a pattern of continuous change. The foreign people inhabiting the coastal sites often maintained their own identity and many of their cultural traditions were clearly different from those of the indigenous population. This situation is reflected in the world of contemporary research, where it is common to find scholars who are interested only in the colonial phenomenon, while others study indigenous process without paying enough attention to its connection with the wider world. The case of the Iberian peninsula clearly exemplifies the contradictions of this situation. In the past, scholars interested in the colonial side of interaction have always considered that Iberian Culture was simply the result of Phoenician and Greek influence on the local population, but at the same time such theories have not fully explored how the forces of acculturation might have operated. Each part of the Mediterranean had its particular history, and the cases of, for example, Sardinia and the Iberian peninsula are not the same, but nevertheless contact between different peoples took place in both territories. By making a comparison we can search for models that can help us understand the processes of culture change that both areas experienced in common.

In this paper, I suggest that, from the sixth century to the end of the third century BC, Punic colonization did not seek territorial domination, but rather was organized to profit from the economic potential of distribution systems left in the hands of the local Iberian aristocracy. Punic colonies controlled the export and import of goods to the rest of the Mediterranean. This (obviously simplified) argument has been advanced before (González Wagner 1989), but it has not been tested against the archaeological record, which provides a much more complete record than the few written documents that we possess. I will present briefly the evolution of the colonial phenomenon in the Iberian peninsula, paying particular attention to the interaction between the southeast coast and the indigenous territory in the uplands of the provinces of Granada and Jaén (the eastern portion of 'alta Andalucía').

The colonial presence

The Phoenician colonies were established on the south coast of the Iberian peninsula from at least the beginning of the eighth century BC, although navigation and commerce in the area must certainly have begun earlier. Nevertheless, from about 800 BC onwards there are permanent settlements from Gadir on the Atlantic coast to the Mediterranean provinces of Málaga, Granada, and Almería (Figure 12.1: 12–15). The Phoenician presence is stronger towards the end of the eighth century BC and during the seventh century BC, when its influence extends towards the southeast. The effect on the indigenous population was rapid and far-reaching. The introduction of new rituals can be observed, including cremation burials in large tombs with rich grave goods, new manufacturing techniques (such as the potter's fast wheel), and novel ceramic shapes and decorations which characterise assemblages for a long time thereafter. The presence of a number of foreigners can be discerned who seek not only to settle in places with a territory that could be economically self-sufficient, but also to establish positive contacts with the local inhabitants who seem to receive and accept them. Changes occurred in both ritual, economic and technological spheres, and included the development of some kinds of craft specialization. The introduction of the fast

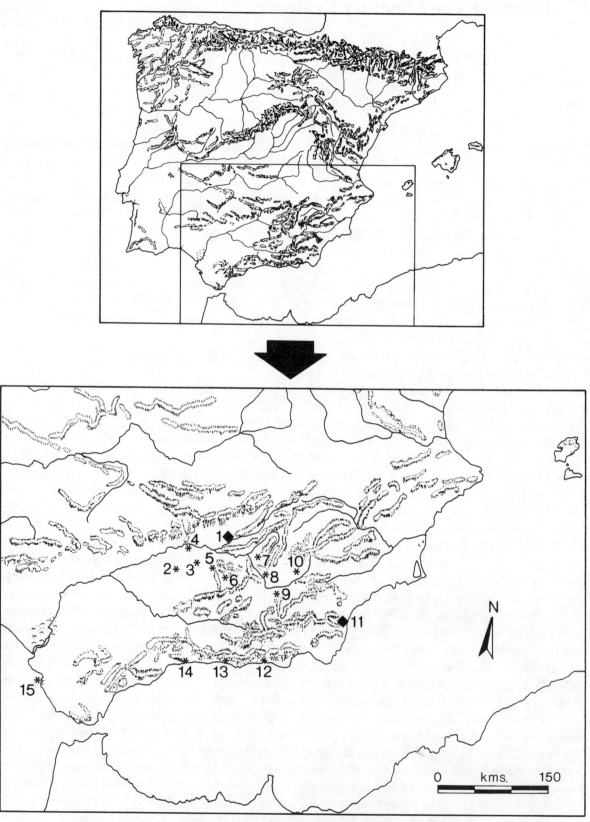

Figure 12.1 Location of sites mentioned in the text: 1. Cástulo. 2. Porcuna (Ipolca/Obulco). 3. Cerro Villargordo. 4. Los Villares de Andújar. 5. Puente Tablas. 6. La Guardia. 7. Toya. 8. Los Castellones de Ceal. 9. Baza. 10. Galera. 11. Villaricos. 12. Adra. 13. Almuñécar. 14. Toscanos. 15. Cádiz.

potter's wheel heralded changes in the organization of ceramic manufacture, but it need not be assumed that similar specialization occurred in intensified mining, agricultural, and pastoral activity.

In the sixth century, however, there were clear changes in these spheres. Eastern Andalusia developed strong centres of economic and political control, with large settlements that were generally located in the middle of highly productive land. The landscape was divided into territories with political frontiers marked by the construction of towers (Ruíz and Molinos 1989). This part of Andalusia had a very strong economic potential, based (in general terms) on dry farming in the western area, mining in the northern area, and pastoralism and irrigation agriculture in the eastern area. The whole region underwent a rapid process of development, which can be seen not only in the settlements, but also in the development of elaborate funerary architecture and monuments at the cemeteries, and the manufacture, for the first time, of luxury pottery with a remarkable variety of shapes and decorations (Pereira 1988, 1989) (Figure 12.2). Iron objects are present, although very infrequently until the fifth and fourth centuries BC. From the sixth century BC onwards there is a continuous process of change that leads to the organization of an Iberian society that exhibits a strongly hierarchical political system and that maintains a dynamic relationship with the new Punic order.

If the colonial side of the equation is examined, it can be seen that the old Phoenician foundations are in crisis during the sixth century BC, as Iberian commerce with Greece increases (it is precisely in the Ionian cities of Asia Minor that the models can be found for some of the earlier Iberian funerary sculptures). At the same time, the Carthaginians sought to exert greater influence in all parts of the western Mediterranean, and this is indicated in many of the early Phoenician colonies, where funerary rites involving inhumations in chambered tombs can be found with grave goods including undecorated ceramics, amphoras, razor blades, ostrich eggshells, and masks. The Carthaginian presence, characterized by large settlements with special characteristics which are clearly different from those of indigenous sites, is best exemplified at Villaricos and Ibiza. This situation seems to continue during the following centuries (particularly the third and fourth), when a strong commercial relationship between Punic and indigenous territories can be detected, but without any real mixing taking place between them. This argument is supported by the archaeological evidence, mainly of funerary origin, that is now being obtained from several necropoli in eastern Andalusia.

One example of interaction: the Iberian cemeteries of eastern Jaén province and the province of Granada

In this area, the northeast of Andalusia, my colleague Juan Pereira and I have studied the assemblages recovered from previous excavations of Iberian cemeteries at Galera and Baza in Granada, and Toya and Castellones de Ceal in Jaén. We augmented this information with the results of our own excavations at the latter site, where the remains of the Iberian settlement and necropolis were reasonably well preserved. All these sites lie along the course of the river Guadiana Menor, which flows first in an east–west direction through the northeast of the province of Granada, then in a north–south direction after reaching the province of Jaén, eventually joining the Guadalquivir river. This course along with that of the river Almanzora, is one of the easiest routes from the coast, where the Punic settlement of Villaricos is situated, to the mining area on the southern slopes of the Sierra Morena, where the most important settlement was Cástulo in the basin of the river Guadalimar. All these indigenous villages have a number of characteristics in common, many of which can be considered the result of continuous contact with the Punic colony of Villaricos. As a result of this, we believe that this region is a good place to study the interaction between Punic and Iberian worlds.

The settlements of Galera, Baza, Toya, and Castellones de Ceal are located on hills that dominate areas of high agricultural productivity which are irrigated by the rivers, areas that stand in strong contrast with the very poor soils and sparse vegetation of the surrounding mountains and hills (Figure 12.3). At these sites, the earliest important tombs date to the sixth century BC, but it is in contexts dating to the fifth century BC and later that most of the evidence that shows the increasing activity along this route can be found. The site of Castellones de Ceal is founded in this period, and from the earliest level a well-organ

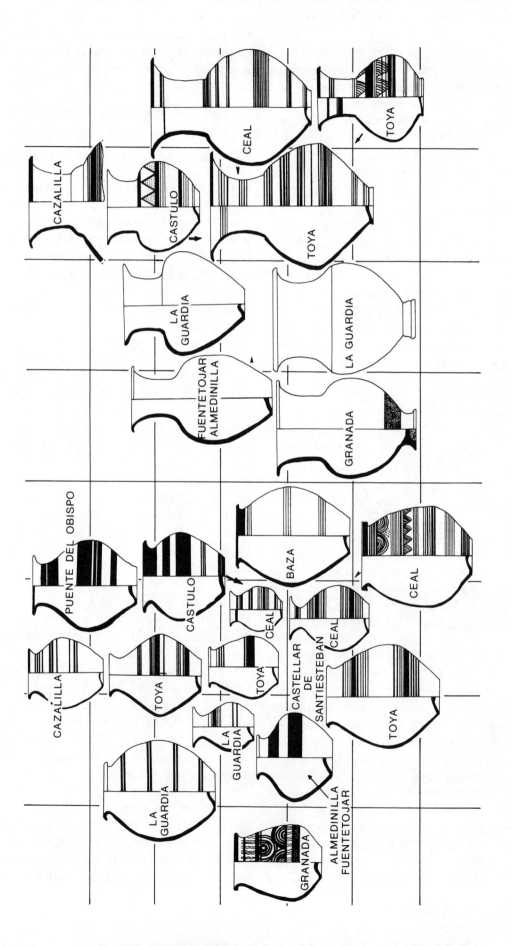

Figure 12.2 Some forms of Iberian pottery (after Pereira 1989).

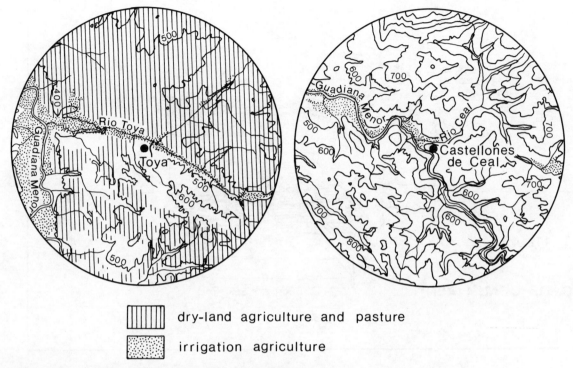

dry-land agriculture and pasture

irrigation agriculture

Figure 12.3 Land use at the sites of Toya and Castellones de Ceal.

ized settlement is indicated, with large grinding stones, iron cart wheels, and high quality pottery, including a considerable quantity of Greek imports. There are also chamber tombs, with and without entrances, which are accompanied by other types of funerary monuments, such as small tumuli or simple holes covered with mud bricks. The wide variety of funerary practices reflects the marked hierarchy of this Iberian society.

Examination of this funerary evidence permits us to recognize some relationships between these tombs along the Guadiana Menor and burials at the Punic colony of Villaricos. The following two sections detail some of the similarities.

Funerary chambers

Funerary chambers consists of a room with walls built or covered by wood, mud bricks or masonry. Funerary chambers can have a door for access and a corridor. Plaster is usually used to cover the walls, and in some cases, the floor. Such tombs are very common at the Punic colony of Villaricos (Almería), where more than 50 of them have been recorded (Siret 1907). Because these tombs were used for collective burials, they must have contained a large number of individuals. At any rate, these are typical Punic tombs, being common not only in Carthage, but also on the western Mediterranean islands and along the south coast of Spain (Molina *et al.* 1982).

Within Iberian territory, there are more than 25 funerary chambers at the necropolis of Galera (Granada). Many of these are also 'collective' or family tombs in the opinion of the excavator (Cabré 1920: 15), and they were also covered with wood and plaster. Some were even painted with geometric or figurative motifs, which were, unfortunately, destroyed at the time of their discovery. Chambers of this sort are also present at Toya (Jaén) (Figure 12.5: 1), where one of the most complex structures was discovered. It was made of stone and its interior was divided into three different rooms with shelves on the walls designed to hold some of the funerary vases (Cabré 1925). At least two, smaller chamber tombs have been found at Castellones de Ceal (Chapa Brunet *et al.* 1991). These are also collective tombs covered with wood and plaster and decorated with paintings (Figure 12.5: 2). Points in common between Villaricos (Figure 12.5: 5) and Ceal (Figure 12.5: 3, 6) also include the use of wood inside the graves and the excavation of trenches along the periphery of the chambers.

Grave goods

Some of the objects inside Iberian tombs could have been obtained through commerce with the Punic colony of Villaricos. Substantial amounts of Attic pottery reached the Iberian settlements and were placed in graves as cremation urns or

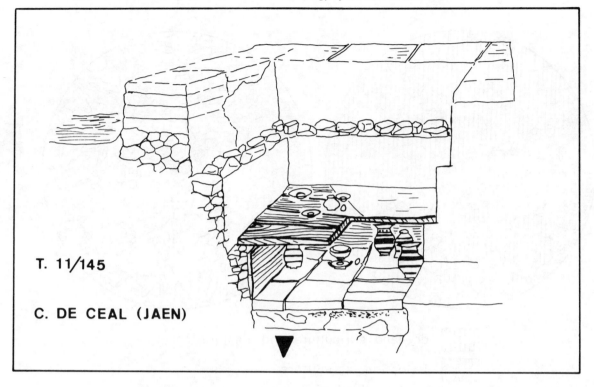

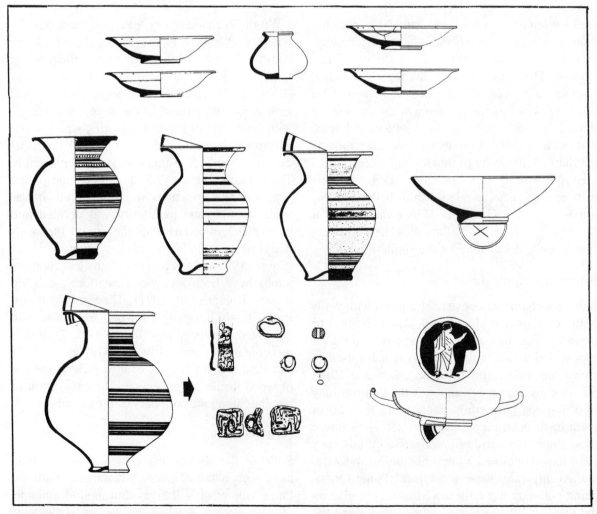

Figure 12.4 Reconstruction of tomb 11/145 at Castellones de Ceal, and its grave goods.

funerary offerings. These vases were often brought to the Iberian peninsula in Punic ships. The 'El Sec' shipwreck (Calviá, Mallorca) is a good example of this type of trade. At the time it was wrecked (between 375 and 350 BC) the ship carried a large quantity of amphoras, pottery, bronze vessels, bronze ingots, grinding stones, and several types of nuts and grapes. The goods came from all over the Mediterranean, and the authors of the report on the discovery (Arribas *et al.* 1987: 651–52) suggest that the ship began its voyage in Samos, continued to Athens (the Piraeus), Carthage, perhaps Sicily, and Ibiza, but failed to get beyond the bay of Palma. The types of Attic pottery that were due to be sold upon arrival fit in perfectly with those we find in Iberian graves and settlements in eastern Andalusia, and it seems perfectly feasible that the cargo would have been put ashore in Villaricos, to be transported inland to supply the indigenous market.

The Iberian sites also contain imports from Near Eastern or Carthaginian workshops. An alabaster figurine representing a woman seated on a throne flanked by sphinxes was found long ago at the necropolis of Galera. The head and the upper part of the body are hollowed out in order to receive a liquid (milk?) that would flow out through the breasts into a bowl held in the figure's hands. Technical and morphological features point to the Near East — perhaps Syria — as the source of this small sculpture. The date of its manufacture could be the seventh century BC, but it had a long use-life and was finally deposited in a chamber tomb with other grave goods dating to the middle or the end of the fifth century BC. Morphologically it has all the features of eastern-style sphinxes (Chapa 1980a: 313). The same stylistic interpretation can be put forward for another sphinx that had somewhat different characteristics. This sculpture was made of limestone and was found in a particular area of the necropolis ('Cabezo N') of Villaricos, where it was probably associated with a funerary monument. Buildings with sculptures were quite common in Iberian necropoli, particularly at the end of the sixth through the fifth centuries BC (Chapa 1980b). In this instance the sphinx was broken up and removed in Iberian times, the stone being used in new buildings. Thus it is not possible to relate this sculpture to a particular grave with any degree of certainty.

Other, more common objects in Iberian necropoli also have a foreign, probably Punic, origin. Some are small vessels made of coloured glass; others are amulets depicting male human heads, with the hair, eyes, beard, and mouth painted on or inlaid. These had been noted during the first excavation at Castellones de Ceal (Fernández Chicarro 1956: 107) and were dated to the fourth century BC, according to the catagorisation of Cintas (1946). Finally, there is a special kind of funerary urn consisting of a stone box. These are common in Iberian burials along the Guadiana Menor and are also found at Villaricos. The use of stone urns, together with the use of funerary chambers have been used to define a cultural territory that would have belonged to the 'Bastetani' (Almagro Gorbea 1982). It is important to note that the stone urns are found in both cultural zones, although at Villaricos they may have been placed in the graves of individuals of Iberian origin (Madrigal, in press).

The above are only some of the features that clearly demonstrate the contact and similarities between the Iberian settlements and the Punic colony of Villaricos. For the sake of my argument, however, it is equally important to underline the important differences between Iberian and Punic burials. These differences show that Villaricos did not exert any direct control, but rather used the local aristocracy as intermediaries. Up to now no typically Punic funerary assemblages have been identified inside the Iberian zone. We can see this clearly when we analyze the funerary ritual in detail. One of the most important normative features of funerary ritual is the treatment of the body after death, since this is based on a complex set of ideas about how the dead will better reach their new world. In the Iberian Culture the only treatment of the dead is cremation. Every cemetery is strictly limited to this one ritual formula without any known exceptions. At Villaricos, however, inhumation predominates, at least from the fifth to the third century BC. Corpses are generally put into wooden coffins and placed inside collective burial chambers or individual trench graves. The grave goods that accompany the dead are also different from the Iberian custom. At Villaricos two kinds of objects, Punic amphoras and ostrich eggs with plain or decorated surfaces, are particularly frequent. In Iberian burial assemblages amphoras are quite unusual and, when present, are always of local manufacture. No ostrich eggs have been found in indigenous burials, which instead feature pottery,

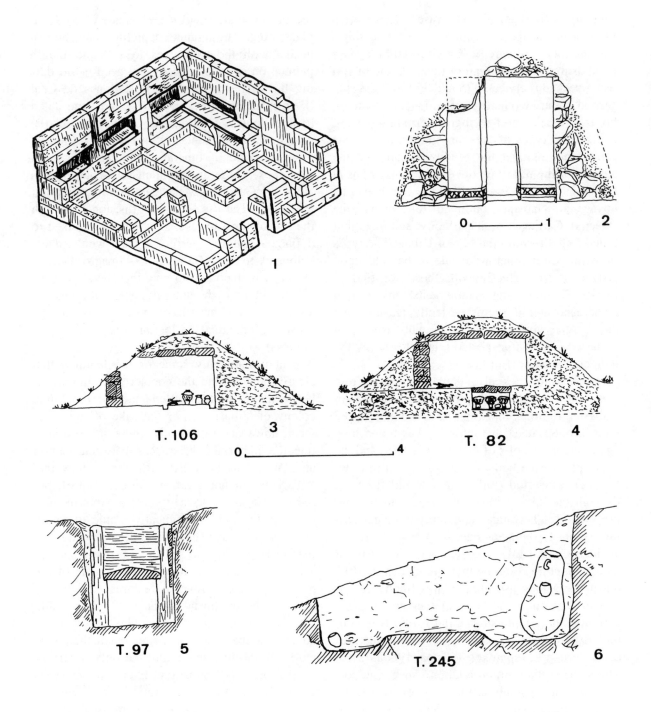

Figure 12.5 1–4: Iberian chambered tombs: Toya (1), Ceal (2), Galera (3, 4). 5 and 6: Punic tombs at Villaricos.

weapons, and loom weights as standard assemblage components.

Villaricos shows, then, quite a different ensemble of funerary features, that clearly relates the colony with the rest of the Punic world. Some Iberian tombs have been identified at this site, which indicates that an indigenous group lived there together with the colonists. However, the same situation cannot be found in the inland territory: no purely Punic funerary contexts have been identified. Some formal elements can be observed that indicate a degree of contact between the two areas, but we cannot say that Punic colonization reached the interior with the intention of dominating and forcibly changing Iberian society. The latter continued to practice their own rituals and maintained their own distinctive structure. There were obviously territorial conflicts: it can be seen that the Iberian aristocracy possessed special weaponry and chose to be buried with it. But, as far as is known, those conflicts were internal, as is clearly indicated by the funerary sculptures at Porcuna (Jaén) which depict two groups of Iberian warriors fighting to the death (Negueruela 1990).

Conclusion

Having studied the archaeological evidence for the funerary practices of a native Iberian society and a colonial Punic society, we suggest that the Iberian aristocracy based an important part of its power on the organization of the production and transport of raw materials and other goods from the lands they dominated to the port from which the goods were to be exported. Direct Punic representation is not in evidence inland (through, for example, different funerary rites such as inhumations, or characteristic grave good assemblages). What can be seen is that the Iberian upper class, without making any basic change in their customs, adopted some colonial funerary fashions. Moreover, an Iberian presence is recognizable at Villaricos in the form of typical cremation burials accompanied by weapons and indigenous pottery.

Here we have a situation, then, where a model of colonization based on conquest maintained by military force cannot be supported. There is evidence of neither resistance nor defence on the part of the indigenous population. It could be suggested that a population of Punic origin lived

on the coast, sponsored an open market for a variety of commodities, and maintained a different cultural personality from the natives of the interior. The natives, in turn, took advantage of this foreign presence and developed control over the production and transport of those commodities. If problems arose, they arose both between and within the indigenous groups as they jostled for control of a system more complicated than anything that had previously been seen in the prehistory of the Iberian peninsula.

Bibliography

Almagro Gorbea, M.

1982   Tumbas de Cámara y Cajas Funerarias Ibéricas: su Interpretación Sociocultural y la Delimitación del Área Cultural Ibérica de los Bastetanos. In *Homenaje a Conchita Fernández Chicarro*, 249–58. Madrid: Ministerio de Cultura.

Arribas, A., G. Trías, D. Cerdá and J. de Hoz

1987   *El Barco de El Sec (Calviá, Mallorca): Estudio de Materiales*. Palma de Mallorca: Universitat de les Illes Baleares.

Cabré, J.

1920   La Necrópoli de Tútugi: Objetos Exóticos o de Influencia Oriental en las Necrópolis Turdetanas. *Boletín de la Sociedad Española de Excursiones* 28: 1–44.

1925   Arquitectura Hispánica: El Sepulcro de Toya. *Archivo Español de Arte y Arqueología* 1: 73–101.

Cabré, J., and F. Motos

1920   *La Necrópolis Ibérica de Tútugi (Galera, Provincia de Granada)*. Madrid: Junta Superior de Excavaciones y Antigüedades.

Chapa, T.

1980a   Las Esfinges en la Plástica Ibérica. *Trabajos de Prehistoria* 37: 309–44.

1980b   *La Escultura Zoomorfa Ibérica en Piedra*. Madrid: Universidad Complutense.

Chapa Brunet, T., J. Pereira Sieso, A. Madrigal Belinchón and M.T. López Trapero

1991   La sepultura 11/145 de Los Castellones de Ceal (Hinojares, Jaén). *Trabajos de Prehistoria* 48: 333–48

Cintas, P.

1946   *Amulettes Puniques*. Tunis: Publications de l'Institut des Hautes Études.

Fernández Chicarro, C.

1956   Prospección Arqueológica en los Términos de Hinojares y La Guardia (Jaén), II. *Boletín del Instituto de Estudios Gienenses* 3: 101–27.

González Wagner, C.

1989   The Carthaginians in Ancient Spain: from
Administrative Trade to Territorial Annexation.
In *Studia Phoenicia*. X. *Punic Wars*, 145–52.
Leuven: Peeters.

Madrigal, A.

1994   Cajas Funerarias Ibéricas de Piedra de Villaricos
(Almería). In *Actas, II Congreso de Historia de
Andalucía (Córdoba 1991), Historia Antigua*,
113–120. Córdoba: Obra Social y Cultural
Cajasur.

Molina, F., A. Ruíz and C. Huertas

1982   *Almuñécar en la Antigüedad: La Necrópolis
Fenicio-Púnica de Puente de Noy.* Granada:
Caja Provincial de Ahorros de Granada.

Negueruela, I.

1990   *Los Monumentos Escultóricos Ibéricos del*

Cerrillo Blanco de Porcuna (Jaén). Madrid:
Ministerio de Cultura.

Pereira, J.

1988   La Cerámica Ibérica de la Cuenca del
Guadalquivir, I: propuesta de clasificación.
Trabajos de Prehistoria 45: 143–74.

1989   La Cerámica Ibérica de la Cuenca del
Guadalquivir, II: Propuesta de Clasificación.
Trabajos de Prehistoria 46: 149–60.

Ruiz, A., and M. Molinos

1989   Fronteras: Un Caso del Siglo VI a.n.e.
Arqueología Espacial 13: 121–35.

Siret, L.

1907   *Villaricos y Herrerías: Antigüedades Púnicas,
Romanas, Visigóticas y Árabes.* Madrid: Jaime
Rates.

13. Sanctuaries of the Iberian Peninsula: Sixth to First Centuries BC

Lourdes Prados-Torreira

During the last decade the study of Iberian Culture from the sixth to first centuries BC has undergone a transformation. The new approach has been particularly influential in the study both of settlement patterns and of the relations between settlements and their necropoleis. These changing views invite a new look at Iberian religion, and particularly at its religious sanctuaries.

First, the field of indigenous religion needs to be approached from a theoretical point of view. The New Archaeology included among its goals the possibility that religion could be investigated like any other area of culture (Binford 1968: 21). Research on this subject, however, usually adopts one of the two traditional positions that Renfrew refers to in his book on the sanctuary of Philakopi: either an outright rejection that religion can be studied by any methodology, since this would entail transcending the boundaries of archaeological inference, or an argument that any kind of theory is valid (Renfrew 1985: 1).

These same attitudes are often reflected in the study of ritual and religiosity during the Iberian period. Despite the existence of an extensive bibliography, what knowledge there is about this subject is one-sided and fragmentary. This is because, unlike other regions with similar geographic and cultural characteristics, there is no clear overview of the Iberian sanctuaries.

When studying the sanctuaries of the Iberian period it is important to stress the fact that we are dealing, in most cases, with sites that were excavated many years ago and which lack basic information about the archaeological context in which they were situated. Furthermore, many of the excavated deposits have provided many esoteric objects (such as the bronze, stone or terracotta votive figurines) which offer only partial insights because the rest of the material culture was disregarded. Additionally, in most cases there is very limited data of their architectonic remains. Finally, the relationships between the settlements and the sanctuaries are not very clearly established. This, in turn, makes it difficult to study proto-urban or rural characteristics of the places of worship, their areas of influence, the reasons why a place would be selected as a sacred site, and whether the siting of the sanctuary was articulated through the religious character of the site or, on the contrary, was determined as part of the territorial organization of these communities. I will try to analyze some of the specific characteristics of the most prominent Iberian sanctuaries, highlighting both their geographic and territorial location. This is not an exhaustive classification or inventory of all the sanctuaries of the Iberian periods (Lucas 1981; Ruano 1988), but instead, an overview of the most important sites of worship classified by geographic region (see Figure 13.1 for the location of some of the principal sites discussed below).

Murcia

Sanctuaries

Coimbra del Barranco Ancho (Jumilla)

The Iberian site of Coimbra del Barranco Ancho consists of a settlement, a sanctuary and three necropoli. The establishment dates from the end of the fifth century BC to the beginning of the second century BC. In the sanctuary, which was discovered by chance in 1979, only superficial excavations have been conducted. These resulted in the identification of a large series of terracotta votive figurines made in the shape of human heads (Page *et al.* 1987: 12, 54).

Recuesto (Cehegín)

The site is located on a small rocky mountain. The remains of the structure have almost disappeared, and the material found seems to indicate a centre of worship. Attic ceramics found at the site indicate that it was in use at the end of the

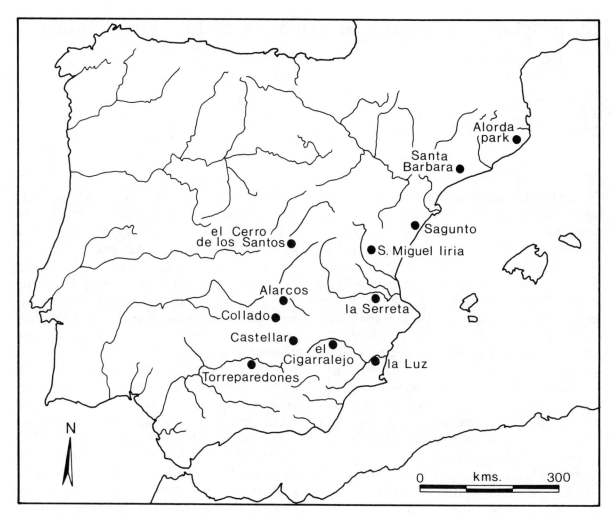

Figure 13.1 Location of the principal sites mentioned in the text.

fourth century BC (Lillo Carpio 1981: 25–26).

El Cigarralejo (Mula)

Excavated by Cuadrado in the 1940s, this sanctuary is located near the village of Mula. The site is on top of a hill that dominates both the settlement and a necropolis of more than 400 excavated graves. A Roman villa with several rooms was built on top of the sanctuary. The stone pavement of a small patio covered the remains of a wall and of a small cellar or *favissa*, which contained the *exvotos* (consisting almost entirely of horse figurines). The sanctuary is dated to between the fourth and second centuries BC and must have been destroyed in the second half of the third century BC. It was reconstructed, and was again destroyed in around the second century BC (Cuadrado Díaz 1950; Blázquez 1983).

La Luz

The sanctuary of La Luz is located in the lower foothills of the Sierra of Carrascoy. The original layout of the sanctuary is poorly preserved. The *exvotos* were found on the platform where the centre of worship is supposed to have been located. Ruíz Bremón argues for the existence of a spring that once flowed a few metres away from the present-day hermitage at the site, and which today has been channeled to the interior of a nearby convent. This site's heyday must have been between the third and first centuries BC (Mergelina 1924-25; Ruíz Bremón 1988).

Votive deposits

La Encarnación

The shrine of La Encarnación is located on a hill, and a number of *exvotos* were found nearby. Stratigraphic test pits have shown the site was first used for an Iberian cult which took place at some time between the fourth and first centuries BC, and then for a cult of the Roman period (Ruano and San Nicolás 1990; Ramallo 1993).

Caves

There are several caves located in Murcia, especially to the north, including Cueva del Calor in Cehegín, Las Canteras in Calasparra, Peliciego in Jumilla, Peña Rubia in Cehegin, and La Nariz in Umbria de Salchite, Moratella. This last one has been the object of careful study by Lillo. Among the material found in this cave, the urn known as 'la diosa de los lobos' (the goddess of the wolves) is of particular importance. This site was occupied between the second and first centuries BC (Lillo Carpio 1981: 37–43).

Andalusia

Sanctuaries

The two main sanctuaries in the province of Jaen are Collado de los Jardines and Castellar de Santisteban. They are well known for having provided a large number of bronze *exvotos*. Both sanctuaries were discovered and excavated at the beginning of this century. Calvo and Cabré excavated the sanctuary of Collado de los Jardines (Calvo and Cabré 1917, 1918, 1919) and Lantier the site at Castellar de Santisteban (1917). These two sanctuaries are located in caves in rugged terrain, close to natural springs.

Collado de los Jardines

This site is located in the canyon of Despeñaperros, hidden among imposing cliffs. The cave of the sanctuary is found on the slope of a mountain and there is a natural spring in its vicinity. The limited notes of Calvo and Cabré's three excavation campaigns are the only observations there are to provide clues in a study of these deposits. The settlement was located on top of the hill and was linked to the sanctuary by means of several paths. The excavations produced abundant metal slag, as well as many bronze figurines. This settlement was surrounded by a wall and, at the time of occupation, the sanctuary would have been outside the wall. The most interesting discovery in the houses was the residue of hearths and remains of the material for casting the metal that was used to make the bronzes. There is no precise date for the site, though in my opinion the production of votive figurines here took place earlier than at Castellar (Prados Torreira 1992).

Castellar de Santisteban

This site has been excavated in the last few years by a team directed by Nicolini. It consists of a natural cave that probably had, at some point, a spring running from it. The only human alteration to the cave is in the form of a system of stairs and ramps cut into the rock to allow access to the interior. The sanctuary raises interesting questions about its origin. According to Nicolini's interpretation of the style of certain *exvotos*, this site dates from the end of the seventh century BC. But according to my own research, it represents a technological tradition and metallurgical production that is more evolved than that of Collado and would not predate the fifth century BC (Nicolini 1969; Prados Torreira 1988, 1992). The stratigraphic sequences obtained in recent excavations seem to indicate a period corresponding to the end of the fourth and, definitely, the third century BC (Nicolini *et al.* 1990).

Cástulo

The ritual site consists of a building in the settlement of Muela, near Cástulo. The structure has been interpreted as a site of ritual feasts because of the design of its construction (a magnificent mosaic of black and white pebbles of the late seventh and early sixth centuries BC) and because of its location on the banks of the Guadalimar river. Residues from feasts were deposited in a pit dug specially for this purpose (Blázquez and Valiente 1981: 202).

Torreparedones

The sanctuary is located outside the southern wall of a settlement in an elevated spot with springs close by. The area was densely populated and well situated, since it is located near the Via Obulco-Ulia. A survey of the terrain revealed the presence of a building of small dimensions, but of undoubted importance, considering the associated architectural fragments that were found. On the surface of this promontory *exvotos* have been found, all of them made of stone. The sanctuary dates to the second century BC (Morena López 1989).

Other finds

The presence of *exvotos* in other places should be stressed, such as the series of bas-reliefs and carvings of horses from Mesa de Luque in Córdoba. This find raises the question of the possible existence of an Iberian sanctuary close to this site (Cuadrado y Ruano 1989). Likewise, we consider the following sites to be votive deposits or sanctuaries yet to be discovered: Pinos Puente (Cerro de los Infantes, Granada) which is known only from the discovery of a large number of stone horse *exvotos* that lack any stratigraphic context (Rodríguez Oliva *et al.* 1983) and Torre de Benzala (Torredonjimeno) where *exvotos* were also found (Ruano 1987). Other possible sites in the province of Jaén are indicated by *exvotos* of uncertain origin held at the Museum of Jaén (Marín Ceballos and Belén 1987).

Caves

Finally, the surface find of Iberian materials (including a small head carved from limestone) in the cave of La Murcielaguina in Priego de Córdoba raises the possibility that there were sanctuary caves in Andalusia similar to those found in the Spanish Levant (Vaquerizo 1985).

Spanish Levant

Caves

Caves used for religious purposes are both numerous and characteristic of this region (the provinces of Castellón, Valencia and Alicante). Particularly interesting are La Cova de les Dones, Les Maravelles and Villagordo del Cabriel all of which are in the province of Valencia. The ritual character of these sites, located far from any settlement, is clear. Many of these caves seem to have been used for religious purposes throughout an extensive period, from the Bronze Age to the Middle Ages. Among the material from the Iberian period, the small calyciform cups are especially interesting. Spindle whorls and animal bones can also be found. On the other hand, imported metal and ceramics are found only sporadically. In many of the caves, the underground water may have been used for its health-giving properties. Burnt ceramic cups and bones are also common finds. These caves tend to be found in concentrations, and it is possible that different caves served different functions depending on the presence of water or of stalactites and stalagmites (Aparicio Pérez 1976-77; Gil-Mascarell 1975).

Sanctuaries

La Serreta (Alcoy, Alicante)

This settlement is on top of the Sierra de Alcoy,

and the sanctuary was built on a steep peak. The village dates from the fourth century BC to before Roman times. The sanctuary, however, seems to have had an extremely long life being used until the time of the late Roman Empire, even though the village itself had ceased to exist centuries before. Most of the materials from the sanctuary are terracotta *exvotos*, many of which represent female figures. The sanctuary dates from between the second and first centuries BC with its heyday during the second and third centuries AD (Juan i Molto 1987).

Santa Barbara (Vilavell, Castellon) and Muntanya Frontera (Sagunto, Valencia)

Located on elevations, both sites appear to have been founded in the pre-Augustan period and lasted throughout the life of the Roman Empire. It is interesting to note the apparently votive character of the coins of the Roman period, which are very common in both deposits. These must have substituted for other offerings of a more typically indigenous character. Censers are also common. Furthermore, it is possible that a sanctuary existed in the Castillo de Guardamar del Segura, due to the abundance of censers and absence of other materials more characteristic of necropoli or villages.

Temples

Illeta dels Banyets (Campello, Alicante)

This ritual centre consists of a group of buildings located inside a village. One of the buildings is rectangular with a columned portico that gives access to three chambers, behind which are the remains of two other chambers. Amphoras and part of a sculpture of a man's head were found inside. Opposite this building, on the other side of the street, there is a rectangular building, divided into four aisles which each have small spaces at the far end which are holders of amphoras and casks. This is believed to have been a temple storeroom. Across another narrow street to the west, there is another building of worship with a square plan, where an altar of perfumes was found, built in the eastern style (Llobregat 1985).

San Miguel de Lliria (Valencia)

Recent publications concerning this village propose that areas 12, 13 and 14 of this settlement are actually a sacred site. We would not then be dealing with a common house but a temple. This interpretation is supported by the presence of a *baetyl* in area 14 and a votive deposit in area 12. Accordingly, the well-known ceramic cups decorated with dancing human shapes, war scenes, etc., would have had a ritual character (Bonet *et al.* 1990).

La Escuera (Alicante)

We are dealing here with what Nördstrom (1967) suggests is a centre of worship, based on the spectacular architectural remains and the existence of bones and ashes. Abad (1986) dates this deposit to between the fourth and second centuries BC.

Domestic chapels

Some scholars suggest the possibility of identifying a series of cult spaces located in the interior of the settlements that served functions clearly different from those of sanctuaries or temples. Examples of these could be areas 1 and 14 of Puntal dels Llops, with their concentrations of heads, *exvotos*, lanterns, etc., or area 2 of Castellet de Bernabé, with a round ritual hearth (Bonet *et al.* 1990), or Alcudia de Elche itself (Lucas 1981).

Catalonia

Caves

Several caves located in Catalonia could have been used for ritual purposes. They differ from those in Valencia in that they usually have only one room into which the exterior light entered easily. The material culture is also different, including typically indigenous vases such as the 'kalathos', a few small calyciform vases, and a scarcity of imported ceramics (Vega 1987; Ruano 1988).

Temples

These important buildings are always inside oppida. They have been classified by their excavators as temples. We should mention, for instance, the so-called temples at Ullastret, one of which has two columns in front of the portico, and 'Molí d'Espigol' in Tornabous (Maluquer 1986b). A building has been found in Alorda Park (Calafell, Barcelona) that dates from the end of the fifth and the fourth centuries BC. It does not appear to be a domestic structure, since it contained both ritual offerings deposited on the floor and a hearth (Sanmartí and Santacana

1987). Finally, La Moleta del Remei in Tarragona should be mentioned, where two important buildings have been located in the area of the village that dates from the end of the fifth century BC (Gracia *et al.* 1988).

The Castilian Plateau

Sanctuaries

El Cerro de los Santos (Montealegre del Castillo, Albacete)

This is the grandest sanctuary in the interior of the region. Situated on the via Heraclea, it is isolated and located on a small elevation. Little remains of the sanctuary. The site has been known since the 19th century, and it is here that the famous stone statues representing male and female figures making offerings were found. They have been extensively studied. Hardly any portion of the sanctuary remains, other than a few slabs of stone, cornices and the remains of a capital. The archaeological stratigraphy of the site is unknown, as a result of both natural erosion and human activity. The chronology of this site is therefore imprecise, although there seems to have been a period of destruction around the first century BC (Ruíz Bremón 1989; Ruano Ruíz 1987; Chapa 1983).

An attempt at systematization

Caves

As we have suggested, cave sanctuaries are characteristic of the Levant region in eastern Spain, and it is becoming obvious that they were also present in Andalusia. Caves can be included under the term 'sacred sites of nature', that is to say, their intrinsic natural characteristics make them sacred. This is common to many religions, and includes places such as mountains, caves, woods, rivers, creeks, etc. In their natural state, caves have been used as places of shelter, burial or refuge. The presence of votive objects, therefore, identifies them as sacred sites, as do other characteristics, such as their proximity to a spring or creek, which provides topographic context. Due to their multiple functions, the caves have usually been in continuous use, and for that reason it is difficult in most cases to be precise about their chronology. Their religious function would be geared towards small communities, usually rural, that are not generally too near to the cave. It is possible that in areas with a cluster of caves, each might have served a specific function.

Rural sanctuaries

These would have their origin in places of nature, like those mentioned above. They are usually found in rugged spots, close to natural water sources, or may have originated from one or more caves. These were the places where sanctuaries developed that were frequented by the inhabitants of rural communities, particularly at an early stage of their development. Later on, the sanctuaries may have evolved due to characteristics such as their proximity to important roads, or their location in an area of natural resources.

With the passing of time and the further development of these sanctuaries, an artisan population became associated with them. This population was able to make a living, at least partially and temporarily, i.e. when the agricultural cycle allowed it, by manufacturing votive figurines that they sold to the pilgrims (either from nearby villages or on their way to other places) who used these sanctuaries. There is evidence of this, for instance, in the remains of crucibles found in the village of Collado de los Jardines. This would enrich both the development of the village, and possible commercial trade between the sanctuaries.

As the prototype of this kind of rural sanctuary, there are the examples of Collado de los Jardines and Castellar in Jaén. It is possible that, as time went by, some sanctuaries of rural origin, due to a variety of circumstances (including the existence of important economic resources, and their connection with crossroads), became increasingly dependent on a political centre. In the specific case of sanctuaries in Jaen, I believe they could also have acted as 'frontier sanctuaries' that controlled the canyon of Despeñaperros, which provides access both to the Castilian plateau and the mining region of Sierra Morena.

Proto-urban sancturies

The birth and consolidation of sanctuaries in the Iberian proto-cities (El Cigarralejo, Verdolay, etc.) that flourished between the fourth to third centuries BC is a well known phenomenon. These were sanctuaries directly connected to settlements. They were usually located outside the settlement wall, but with easy access from the inhabited area. That they were generally connected to a stream or a small forest, which would explain the selection of their location, but they were always a part of the development of the proto-urban system itself. That is to say, sanctuaries of this kind would develop from the ideological needs of the proto-urban structure itself. The presence of water would not be as important as in the case of the rural sanctuaries. The presence of water may be related to the purification rites that were needed when entering and leaving the oppidum, though it is possible that in certain moments, their main function of the water were therapeutic.

From Andalusia the sanctuary of Torreparedones could be included in this group; it dates from the second century BC, and is located outside the walls of the settlement. In Murcia the principal sanctuaries were established as part of a proto-urban settlement plan involving three related areas; the sanctuaries, the town itself and the necropolis. These sanctuaries would, then, be at the service of the oppidum, and may have been dedicated to its tutelary deity. At Cigarralejo, for example, most of the *exvotos* are horses (as opposed to the usual anthropomorphic or healing items), so the town's divinity may have protected that animal, in a manner found in other Mediterranean societies in the Iron Age. The fact that the sanctuaries are located outside the town walls also indicates their protective and purifying character. Extra-urban sanctuaries, those further away from human settlement, could serve a purpose as protectors of the roadway. The possible funerary function of some sanctuaries should be taken into consideration, especially for those close to the necropoli.

Ethno-political sanctuaries

An example of this is the sanctuary of Cerro de los Santos. It is located at an important crossroads, at an equal distance from several population centres, and at a site that is possibly related to a territorial supra-organization. The sanctuary could have functioned as a meeting point to sanctify ties between several communities (Ruano 1988) or it could have even played the role of a 'frontier sanctuary' that would indicate the boundary of one or more communities' area of influence. In this case, offerings would be made to a divinity that protected the roads or, in other words, that protected the political *status quo*.

Temples

Traditionally the existence of temples in the Iberian Culture has been denied. But this assumption changed with the discovery of large buildings inside oppida (Campelló and Alorda Park). These are considered temples by their excavators. The function of these buildings is again being reinterpreted, however. The new controversy originates from the excavation of what was first interpreted to be a grand sanctuary, Cancho Roano in Extremadura, an area that is not properly Iberian, and which today is interpreted as possibly a palace marked by eastern influences (Almagro-Gorbea *et al.*1990). In other words, this is a similar problem to the Etruscan palace of Pogio Civitate in Murlo (Siena, Italy), which was also once interpreted as an orientalizing sanctuary.

Domestic chapels

Finally, I want to refer to the small sacred rooms. Their existence indicates a function clearly differentiated from the sanctuaries or temples that represented the official religion. Their function would be linked to the practice of ceremonies of a domestic or familiar character.

Conclusions

I wish to conclude by outlining some of the general issues suggested by the evidence of Iberian sanctuaries. It is logical to suppose that the Iberians developed collective cults so as to justify their world views, their relationship to nature, their desires, hopes, and anxieties. It is very difficult, however, to define *when* the earliest traces of a celebration of the sacred occurred in the Iberian world. A few cult sites may perhaps belong to the sixth century BC. Sanctuaries related to nature (caves, groves, springs, and so on) may have originated before the development of the Iberian Culture itself. The bronze age rock art near Collado de los Jardines, or the remains of earlier periods found in Valencian cave sites may be examples of this. The greatest development of sanctuaries belongs to a later phase of the Iberian Culture, however. It is difficult, almost impossible, to give them a precise chronology given the lack of reliably

excavated contexts, so only a hypothetical sequence for their development can be presented.

Some sacred places related to nature may, under a variety of circumstances, have developed into rural or proto-urban sanctuaries, near a sizeable population nucleus that would, in part, have lived off the wealth generated by the sanctuary itself. This would be the case for the Andalusian sanctuary of Collado de los Jardines. It is possible that from the fifth century BC this location developed under aristocratic patronage, as is demonstrated by the iconography of many of its *exvotos* (horsemen, fully armed warriors, great ladies, etc.) and by other offerings (belt buckles, fibulae, etc.) which were deposited there. Over time the sanctuary would have been used by a wider segment of the population. This may be reflected by the presence of 'schematic' *exvotos* (small bronze bars with heads or other anthropomorphic signs) and 'anatomical' ones (human body parts, such as arms or legs, that suggest a specific malady), which were probably not manufactured by craft specialists. The anatomical *exvotos* would be tied to the development of healing sanctuaries possibly from the third or second century BC. Other sanctuaries, such as the one near Castellar, developed in later times, from the third century onwards. From the beginning they have a less aristocratic social character, indicated by a much reduced typological spectrum of *exvotos*: half of these are schematic and none of them represent horsemen. The new excavations at the site by Nicolini *et al.* (1990) confirms both this scenario and the site's chronology. The other more securely dated sites indicate that sanctuaries began to develop in the fourth century BC (Cigarralejo, La Encarnación, La Escuera), and particularly in the third (Castellar, La Luz) and second (Torreparedones, La Serreta) centuries BC. The large edifices sometimes thought to be temples (and which, as mentioned before, may in fact be aristocratic residences) and the cave sanctuaries present less precise chronologies. Furthermore, many of these cult sites continue into Roman times. It can be seen, therefore, that the development of cult sites takes place largely during the main phase of the Iberian Iron Age (the fifth and fourth centuries BC) and, above all, during the late phase (the third to first centuries BC).

What functions can be attributed to these sanctuaries? First, some of these sites, in addition to their religious significance, were real *economic* centres. It is possible the certain sanctuaries played an important role both in wealth exchange, and as a stage for the public recognition of individual prestige: as in other Mediterranean cultures, donors would have made public offerings of wealth (instead of funerary deposits), only a small part of which was incorporated in the archaeological record. An economic function would also be involved if these cult centres acted as centres of commerce and related activities by attracting merchants and even, perhaps, sponsoring great fairs and markets. Secondly, the *political* functions of these sanctuaries must not be underestimated; this was mentioned in the discussion of Cerro de los Santos. Under the protection of the sanctuaries, differing communities, or their representatives, could meet to conduct negotiations requiring divine sponsorship (as we know occurred at Fanum Voltumnae in Italy). Finally, the purely *religious* functions of the sanctuaries must be underlined. It has been shown that the presence of water is a regular feature: the existence of a fountain or spring would have represented one of the reasons for establishing a cult locality at a particular spot. Many sanctuaries would have originated as, or developed into, fountains with votive deposits. Water would also be critical in healing sanctuaries, of course, and a concern with fertility is reflected in the iconography of many of the *exvotos* deposited in them. The placement of sanctuaries at or near the gates of oppida would have a protective function.

The study of religious locales offers many insights into the culture of the Iberian Iron Age. In spite of the difficulties that the study and interpretation of sanctuaries present, we hope that current research will soon bear fruit.

Bibliography

Abad, L.
  1986   Castillo de Guardamar. In *Arqueologia en Alicante, 1976–86*, 151–52. Alicante: Instituto de Estudios 'Juan Gil-Albert'.

Almagro Gorbea, M., A. Domínguez de la Concha and F. López-Ambite
  1990   Cancho Ruano: Un Palacio Orientalizante en la Península Ibérica. *Madrider Mitteilungen* 31: 251–308.

Aparicio Pérez, J.
  1976–77 El Culto en Cuevas el la Región Valenciana. *Revista de la Universidad Complutense* 25: 9–30.

Binford, L.R.
  1968   Archaeological Perspectives. In L.R. Binford and S.R. Binford (eds), *New Perspectives in Archaeology*, 5–32. Chicago: Aldine.

Blázquez, J.M.
  1983   *Religiones Prerromanas*. Primitivas Religiones Ibéricas 2. Madrid: Editorial Cristiandad.

Blázquez, J.M., and J. Valiente
  1981   *Castulo III*. Excavaciones Arqueológicas en España 117. Madrid: Ministerio de Cultura.

Bonet, H., C. Mata, and P. Guérin
  1990   Cabezas Votivas y Lugares de Culto Edetanos. *Verdolay* 2: 185–99.

Calvo, I., and J. Cabré
  1917   *Excavaciones en la Cueva y Collado de los Jardines (Sta. Elena, Jaén): Memoria de los Trabajos Realizados en la Campaña de 1916*. Madrid: Junta Superior de Excavaciones y Antigüedades.
  1918   *Excavaciones en la Cueva y Collado de los Jardines (Sta. Elena, Jaén): Memoria de los Trabajos Realizados en la Campaña de 1917*. Madrid: Junta Superior de Excavaciones y Antigüedades.
  1919   *Excavaciones en la Cueva y Collado de los Jardines (Sta. Elena, Jaén): Memoria de los Trabajos Realizados en la Campaña de 1918*. Madrid: Junta Superior de Excavaciones y Antigüedades.

Chapa, T.
  1983   Primeros resultados de las excavaciones en el Cerro de los Santos (Montealegre del Castillo, Albacete): campaña de 1977–81. *Actas, XVI. Congreso Nacional de Arqueología, Murcia-Cartagena 1982*, 643–54.

Cuadrado Díaz, E.
  1950   *Excavaciones en el Santuario Ibérico del Cigarralejo (Mula, Murcia)*. Madrid: Comisaría General de Excavaciones Arqueológicas.

Cuadrado, E., and E. Ruano
  1989   Esculturas de Équidos de la Colección Alhonoz, Puente Genil (Córdoba). *Trabajos de Prehistoria* 46: 203–28.

Gil-Mascarell, M.
  1975   Sobre las Cuevas Ibéricas del País Valenciano: Material y Problemas. *Papeles del Laboratorio de Arqueología de Valencia* 11: 281–332.

Gracia, F., G. Munilla and R. Pallarés
  1988   *La Moleta del Remei (Alcanar, Montsiá), Campañas 1981–86*. Tarragona: Diputació de Tarragona.

Juan i Molto, J.
  1987   El Conjunt de Terracotas Votivas del Santuari de la Serreta. *Saguntum* 2: 295–329.

Lantier, R.
  1917   *El Santuario Ibérico de Castellar de*

Santisteban. Madrid: Comisión de Investigaciones Paleontológicas y Prehistóricas.

Lillo Carpio, Pedro A.

1981   *El Poblamiento Ibérico en Murcia*. Murcia: Universidad de Murcia.

Llobregat, E.

1985   Dos Temples Ibèrics a l'Interior del Poblat de l'Illeta dels Bayets. *Fonaments* 5: 103–12.

Lucas, R.

1981   Santuarios y Dioses en la Baja Época Ibérica. In *La Baja Época de la Cultura Ibérica*, 232–96. Madrid: Asociación Española de Amigos de la Arqueología.

Maluquer de Motes, J.

1986a   *El Santuario Protohistórico de Zalamea de la Serena, Badajoz*, 3. Barcelona: Departamento de Prehistoria y Arqueología, Universidad de Barcelona.

1986b   *Molí d'Espigol, Tornabous: Poblat Ibèric*. Barcelona: Generalitat de Catalunya.

Marín Ceballos, M.C., and M. Belén

1987   Nuevos Exvotos Ibéricos de la Provincia de Jaén. *Anales de la Universidad de Cádiz* 3–4: 79–106.

Mergelina, C. de

1924–25   *Memoria de las Excavaciones en el Eremitorio de Nuestra Señora de la Luz, en Murcia*. Madrid: Junta Superior de Excavaciones y Antigüedaes.

Morena López, J.A.

1989   *El Santuario Ibérico de Torreparedones (Castro del Río-Baena, Córdoba*. Córdoba: Excma. Diputación Provincial de Córdoba.

Nicolini, G.

1969   *Les Bronze Figurés des Sanctuaires Ibériques*. Paris: Presses Universitaires de France.

1983   La campaigne de fouilles 1981 à Castellar. *Mélanges de la Casa de Velázquez* 19: 443–86.

Nicolini, G., N. Zafra and A. Ruíz Rodríguez

1990   Informe Sobre la Campaña de Excavaciones de 1987 en 'Los Altos del Sotillo' (Castellar de Santisteban, Jaén). In: *Anuario Arqueológico de Andalucía, 1987* 2: 216–20. Sevilla: Consejería de Cultura, Junta de Andalucía.

Nördstrom, S.

1967   *Excavaciones en el Poblado Ibérico de La Escuera (San Fulgencio, Alicante*. Valencia: Servicio de Investigación Prehistórica.

Page, V. and J.M. García Cano

1987   *Diez Años de Excavaciones en Coimbra del Barranco Ancho (Jumilla)*. Murcia: Consejería de Educación y Turismo.

Prados-Torreira, L.

1988   Exvotos Ibéricos de Bronce: Aspectos Tipológicos y Tecnológicos. *Trabajos de Prehistoria* 45: 175–99.

1992   *Exvotos Ibéricos de Bronce del Museo Arqueológico Nacional*. Madrid: Ministerio de Cultura.

Ramallo, S.

1993   La Monumentalización de los Santuarios Ibéricos en Época Tardo-Republicana. *Ostraka* 2: 117–44.

Renfrew, C.

1985   *The Archaeology of Cult: The Sanctuary at Philakopi*. London: British School of Archaeology at Athens.

Rodríguez Oliva, P., F. Peregrín Pardo and J.R. Anderica Frías

1983   Exvotos Ibéricos con Relieves de Équidos en la Vega Granadina. *Actas, XVI. Congreso Nacional de Arqueología, Murcia-Cartagena, 1982*, 751–68.

Ruano, E.

1987   *La Escultura Humana de Piedra en el Mundo Ibérico*. Madrid: Author.

1988   El Cerro de los Santos (Montealege del Castillo, Albacete): Una Nueva Interpretación del Santuario. *Cuadernos de Prehistoria de la Universidad Autónoma de Madrid* 15: 253–73.

Ruano, E., and M. San Nicolás

1990   Exvotos Ibéricos Procedentes de 'La Encarnación' (Caravaca, Murcia). *Verdolay* 2: 101–07

Ruíz Bremón, M.

1988   Aproximación al Estudio del Santuario Ibérico de La Luz. *Archivo Español de Arqueología* 61: 230–244.

1989   *Los Exvotos del Santuario Ibérico del Cerro de los Santos*. Albacete: Instituto de Estudios Albacetenses.

Sanmartí, J., and J. Santacana

1987   Un Recinte Cultual al Poblat Ibèric d'Alorda Park (Calafell, Baix Penedès). *Fonaments* 6: 157–67.

Vaquerizo, D.

1985   La Cueva de la Murcielaguina en Priego, Córdoba: Una Posible Cueva Santuario Ibérica. *Lvcentvm* 4: 115–24.

Vega, J. de la

1987   Contribució Catalana a l'Inventari de les Probables Coves Santuari Ibèriques. *Fonaments* 6: 171–90.

14. The Iberians in Sardinia: A Review and Update

Juan A. Santos Velasco

In 1935 García y Bellido published an article in the journal *Emerita* under the title which has been given to this chapter. García y Bellido addressed a subject of research that would catch his full attention in the 1940s and 1950s: the Iberian presence in different parts of the Mediterranean. García y Bellido's article is an example of the approach that characterized mid-twentieth century Spanish historiography (see also García y Bellido 1954): it assumes that the statements made by the historians and geographers of antiquity were completely accurate, and that there is, therefore, a connection between archaeological evidence and literary sources. In particular, García y Bellido sought to prove the accuracy of the sources recounting two episodes. One, in the remoter past, was the mythical emigration of the Tartessian people in connection with the founding of Nora. The other was the arrival of the 'Balaroi' in Sardinia during the period of Carthaginian occupation.

The first colonization

The Greek text of Pausanias is the source for this first event:

> The Iberians came to Sardinia after Aristaeus, under the leadership of Norax, and founded the city of Nora. It will be remembered that this was the first city on the island. It is said that Norax was the son of Erytheia, daughter of Geryon. (Pausanias X, 17, 5)

The archaeological evidence for this event is sought in typological similarities between certain elements of material culture in the Argaric horizons (in the southeast of the Iberian peninsula) and those of the Late Balearic and Sardinian Bronze Age, with special reference to the island of Menorca (García y Bellido 1935: 243–45).

Today it is difficult to support such close links between the Argaric, Balearic and Sardinian Late Bronze Age, but for various reasons, the central problem posed by this line of argument is the use of the term 'Iberian'. Iberian Culture tends to be defined as the culture typical of the Mediterranean coast of Spain in the second half of the first millennium BC. Taking the term Iberian in its broadest sense, however, it could be identified with everything from the Iberian peninsula, at any point in history. However, when this term is used to refer to the peoples and cultures of Balearic prehistory, it goes beyond current geographical and cultural boundaries and has the ultimate effect of creating or suggesting, a political unity with the islands in the more remote past. Thus, calling the Talayotic Culture 'Iberian' clearly reflects the apogee of nationalism in Europe during the first half of the twentieth century.

García y Bellido, who was well acquainted with the sources, draws attention to the connection between the passage quoted above and another, that of Iolaus, a surviving hero of the Trojan War, who arrived in Sardinia after Norax. Common to both myths — that of Norax, grandson of Geryon, and that of Iolaus — is the figure of Heracles, whose well-known struggle with Geryon is recounted as one of his famous labours (García y Bellido 1935: 235). This is a subject which brings us to the problem of real and mythical Greek geography, and the question of the first Hellenic navigation to the west. For scholars such as Caro Baroja myth is no more than the synthesis of real events: thus, the Geryon myth would not be not Tartessian, but Greek, although set in the west. The foundation of colonies by kings and their descendants is widespread in the Greek myths, and this occurs at a secondary level in the Tartessian case with Nora (Bermejo 1978: 221).

This line of argument permits us to relate Sardinia with the Iberian peninsula at some point in the heroic past, but I myself do not propose to approach the subject from the point of view of the literature, and prefer instead to move on, from mythology to archaeological evidence. In this respect there is, without a doubt, abundant

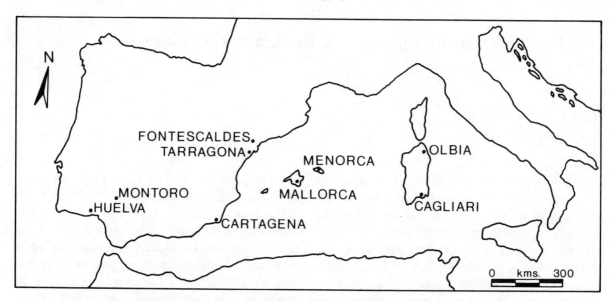

Figure 14.1 Map showing the location of the places and sites referred to in the text.

evidence of the links between the Tartessian cultural horizon and Sardinia between the ninth and seventh centuries BC in the periods corresponding to the Late Tartessian Bronze Age and Phoenician colonization in the west.

From the ninth century BC in Sardinia there are data which provide evidence of this link:

1. Two-handled palstaves of the Padilla de Abajo type, at Sa Idda and Monte Arrubiu.
2. Huelva-type swords, at the Siniscola site (Ruíz Gálvez 1986: 11).

From the eighth century BC items typical of southwest France and the Portuguese Atlantic area are also present:

1. Palstaves with one or two-handles (Figure 14.2: 7, 8)
2. Peninsular socketed axes (Figure 14.2: 9).
3. Rocanes sickles (Figure 14.2: 10).

I shall not belabour these points, which have recently been examined by Ruíz-Gálvez. According to this writer, at an early date (ninth and early eighth centuries BC) maritime traffic must have been in the control of the indigenous population. The Norax myth may be referring precisely to this fact. However, relations between the Iberian peninsula and Sardinia were changing, and throughout practically the whole of the eighth and seventh centuries commercial shipping appears to have been wholly or partially in Phoenician control (Ruíz Gálvez 1986: 34).

One of the questions posed is whether the Tartessians were capable of controlling maritime traffic at this time. Some authors think they were. The Tartessian peoples would have acted as intermediaries between the areas where metals

were obtained on the Atlantic coast of the Iberian peninsula and certain areas of the central Mediterranean, after the Mycenaeans had disappeared from these lands and before the arrival of the Phoenicians (Fernández-Miranda 1987: 487).

The objection must be raised that parallels exist not between the archaic Sard artefacts and those in the Tartessian area of southwest Iberia, but rather links exist with what is now the Portuguese Atlantic seaboard. These evident relations with Tartessian centres occurred in the second half of the eighth century and the beginning of the seventh century BC, when Sardo-Iberian relations should probably be seen in the context of Phoenician colonization and commercial activity in the west.

This circumstance, however, does not necessarily invalidate the myth of the Tartessian origin of Norax, since in the opinion of Pallotino (1952: 149) the legends relating to this apparent Iberian colonization by Norax belong to a period after the Phoenicians landed in Sardinia, and probably occurred in a Sardo-Punic context. Neither does this mythical Phoenician event necessarily contradict the above-mentioned myths relating Heracles to the far west, since Melqart, the Phoenician Heracles, had an important place of worship in Cádiz, built, according to Mela, by the Tyrians (Ruíz Mata 1987: 42).

Finally, returning to the remote past of Greek myth in the west and to the archaeological evidence, the recent discovery of two fragments of Mycenaean pottery in Montoro, Córdoba (Martín de la Cruz 1986–87: 198), dated as Late

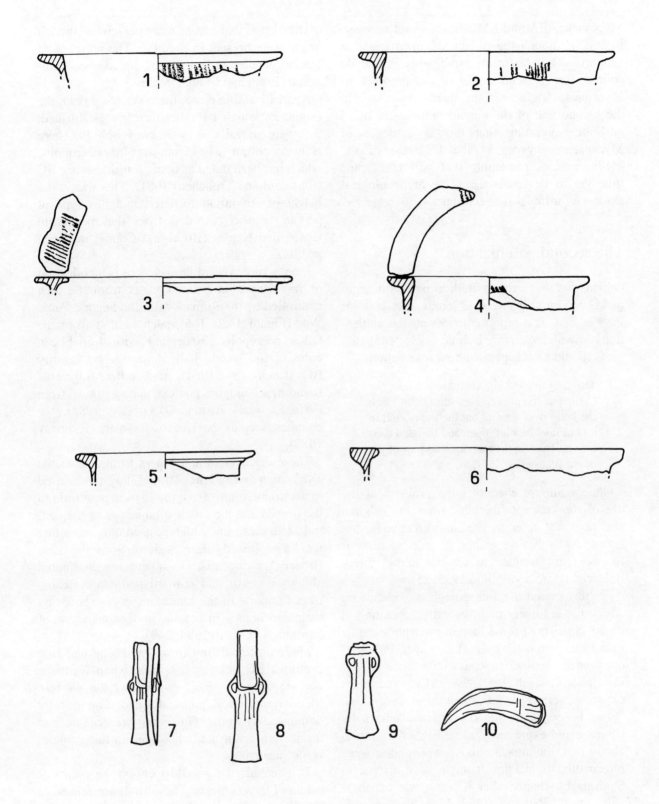

Figure 14.2 1 to 6: fragments of Iberian painted pottery found in Sardinia (according to D'Oriano 1984). 7: Palstave. 8: Two-handled palstave. 9: Socketed axe. 10: Rocanes-type sickle (according to Ruíz-Gálvez 1987).

Mycenaean IIIA and LMIIIB, must not be over-looked. Although these data are insufficient to support solid historical arguments, they do counter the repeated denial of the presence of Mycenaean artefacts in the Iberian peninsula in the second half of the second millennium BC. I am not suggesting that this is evidence of Mycenaean voyages to the far west of the Mediterranean, something that will take some time yet to be resolved, as the archaeological evidence for this period continues to increase.

The second colonization

On this matter García y Bellido bases his argument on another passage from the text of Pausanias. It is a report of an event the authenticity of which García y Bellido (1935: 245) suggests should be accepted without reservations:

> The Libyans and the Iberians amongst the Carthaginian mercenaries disagreed with the latter over sharing out the booty, and in a fit of rage they left them and founded their own colonies in the mountainous part of the island (Pausanias X, 17, 5).

Once again we encounter the problem of the use of the concept 'Iberian', since the original text does not refer to Iberian mercenaries, but Balearics, so that the author, in order to make it fit, does not hesitate to use the term 'Ibero-Balearic' (García y Bellido 1935: 25).

For this period the archaeological evidence on which the argument of a second colonization is based, consists of some Iberian inscriptions, now in the Museum of Cagliari. Years later, Pallotino questioned the Iberian character of one of the inscriptions (Hübner 1899: 513) and also expressed serious doubts about the stela of Nora. When he considers the copyist of Cagliari, he cannot avoid expressing "some slight reservation about that monument, about whose discovery information is lacking. It might have arrived in Sardinia by chance after it was made or originally used" (Pallotino 1952: 154). This inscription has recently been included in the Lexicon of Iberian inscriptions (Siles 1985), as follows:

 – serdum or serton
 – sorsear (probable personal name)
 – seltar (probable personal name)

If its original archaeological context could be ascertained, this would be a particularly important piece of evidence, since we should have to acknowledge that one or more persons of Iberian origin were present in Sardinia. The presence of Iberian peoples in Etruria has already been proposed (Bruni and Conde, in press).

Apart from this piece, there are other data, the origins of which have been clearly established, that were unavailable to García y Bellido. There is an Ampurian vessel from the Nora necropolis, which has been dated as being fourth century BC (Bartoloni and Tronchetti 1981). This was at the height of Ampurian fortunes, and this type of pottery is also recorded from that period in Genoa and Naples (Bruni and Conde, in press) and Ibiza.

From a more recent period there is a collection of fragments and painted vases from the area controlled by the Romans after the Second Punic War (Figure 14.2: 1–6), such as that from the Olbia necropolis, associated with Republican coins of the second half of the second century BC (Lamboglia 1954), and other fragments found in a Nuraghic context, such as those from Perfugas and Austis (D'Oriano 1984), or colonies, such as the Tharros fragment (Ridgway 1989).

These discoveries and others from around the Tyrrhenian Sea and the south of Italy can be used to determine routes from the Iberian peninsula to the islands and the continental coasts of the central Mediterranean, which re-used old routes that we know linked these regions from the Late Bronze Age onwards. The objects are distributed along the coasts and redistributed, on occasion, from the ports to the hinterland, as is shown by their appearance in certain indigenous areas of Sardinia (D'Oriano 1984: 249).

These pieces, dating from the second and first centuries BC, appear at a time when Carthage was no longer a great power and the western Mediterranean was politically and economically dominated by Rome. Thus, their presence outside the Iberian peninsula, when seen in this context, is not surprising.

To conclude, we should mention the points of origin of these objects. These finds are related to articles produced in Fontescaldes (Tarragona), linking the extra-peninsular distribution of the vases produced by potters of that site with the growing importance of Tarraco from the beginning of the Roman presence in Hispania (Santos Velasco 1982–83). Now, however, there are new data of the greatest interest, because articles produced in or around Ensérune have been recognized as being imitations of those made in

Fontescaldes, and are dated from the mid-second century to the beginning of the first century BC. These data pose new questions on the subject of the diffusion of Iberian artefacts in the Mediterranean basin, a subject always open to further research.

Discussion

Sixty years after García y Bellido's first publications concerning a possible Iberian presence in Sardinia, there has been little progress in our knowledge, historical or archaeological. This level of stagnation is interesting from an historiographical point of view and deserves some comment. It is clear that there is absolutely no connection between the ancient texts (Pausanias) and the archaeological record. This is a recurrent problem: on all too many occasions the archaeology of protohistoric Europe does not in any way confirm the information we can obtain from the ancient historians. In the 1940s and 1950s the consensus view in Spain was to give greater credibility to literary than to archaeological sources, but the case we have examined here reminds us that it is essential to be critical of the ancient texts, in which there are often ambiguities, contradictions, and mythical elaborations far removed from historical reality.

From the point of view of Spanish historiography, it is interesting that discussions of an Iberian presence in Sardinia conflates a number of distinct cultural, geographical, and chronological entities under the term 'Iberian': the earlier Bronze Age of the southeast of the peninsula, the Balearic Bronze Age, the Tartessian later Bronze Age of the southwest of the Peninsula, and the properly 'Iberian' Second Iron Age of the Mediterranean littoral. It can now be seen that this is a genuinely explosive historicist mixture (as I am sure a scholar of the stature of García y Bellido was aware), but one which was typical of the nationalist positions that were dominant in Spain during the post-Civil War, post-World War II period. In the final analysis, what was involved during that period was an attempt to legitimise the contemporary political and national unity of Spain using the most remote antiquity. The origins of Spanish ethnic and cultural unity could be traced to before the Roman conquest, thereby underlining the common signs of Spanish identity and giving them a pedigree of 25 centuries' standing.

The evidence we have reviewed here indicates that the only tangible evidence of an 'Iberian' presence in Sardinia consists of some isolated finds of elements belonging to the later Bronze Age (the bronzes of Sa Idda, Monte Arribiu, and Siniscola) and the Iron Age (the pottery from Olbia, Nora, and Tharros). These indicate the existence of low-level, secondary relations of exchange over the course of the first millennium BC, relations which were probably subsumed in the commercial routes and relations of greater importance, such as those of the Phoenicians and the Romans. To infer the migration of people from Iberia to Sardinia from this constitutes a qualitative and quantitative leap that is difficult to justify with the fragmentary and scarce evidence in our possession.

Bibliography

Bartoloni, P., and C. Tronchetti
   1981   *La Necropoli di Nora.* Rome: Consiglio Nazionale delle Ricerche.

Bermejo, J.C.
   1978   La Función Real en la Mitología Tartésica: Gargoris, Habis y Aristeo. *Habis* 9: 215–32.

Bruni, S., and M.J. Conde
   in press Presencia Ibérica en Etruria y el Mundo Itálico a Través de los Hallazgos Cerámicos de los Siglos III–I a.C. *Rivista di Studi Liguri.*

D'Oriano, R.
   1984   Ceramica Ispanica d'età Ellenistica in Sardegna. *Nuovo Bolletino Archeologico Sardo* 1: 247–52.

Fernández-Miranda, M.
   1987   Relaciones Entre la Península Ibérica, Islas Baleares y Cerdeña Durante el Bronce Medio y Final. In *La Sardegna nel Mediterraneo tra il Secondo e el Primo Millennio a.C.: Atti del 2° Convegno di Studi 'Un Millennio di Relazioni fra la Sardegna e i Paesi del Mediterraneo', Selargius-Cagliari, 27–30 Novembre 1986,* 479–92. Cagliari: Amministrazione Provinciale di Cagliari.

García y Bellido, A.
   1935   Los Íberos en Cerdeña, Según los Textos Clásicos y la Arqueología. *Emerita* 3: 225–56.
   1954   Expansión de la Cerámica Ibérica por la Cuenca Occidental del Mediterráneo. *Archivo Español de Arqueología* 27: 246–54.

García Iglesias, L.

1979   La Península Ibérica y las Tradiciones Griegas de Tipo Mítico. *Archivo Español de Arqueología* 52: 131–40.

Hübner, E.

1899   Addimenta Nova ad Corporis, vol. II. In: *Ephemeris Epigraphica: Corporis Inscriptionum Latinarum Supplementum*, 8: 517. Berlin: Georg Reimer.

Lamboglia, N.

1954   La Ceramica Iberica Negli Strati di Albintimilium n'ell territorio ligure e tirrenico. *Rivista di Studi Liguri* 20: 250–73.

Martín de la Cruz, J.C.

1986–87   Problemas en Torno a la Definición del Bronce Tardío en la Baja Andalucía. *Cuadernos de Prehistoria y Arqueología de la Universidad Autónoma de Madrid* 13–14: 205–16.

Pallotino, M.

1952   El Problema de las Relaciones entre Cerdeña e Iberia en la Antigüedad Prerromana. *Ampurias* 14: 137–55.

Ridgway, D.

1989   Nota di Rettifica sul Fragmento Ceramico THT/81/6/6 da Tharros. *Rivista de Studi Fenici* 17: 141–44.

Ruiz-Gálvez, M.L.

1986   Navegación y Comercio entre el Atlántico y el Mediterráneo a Fines de la Edad del Bronce. *Trabajos de Prehistoria* 43: 9–42.

Ruíz Mata, D.

1987   La Colonización Fenicia en la Península Ibérica. In: *Historia General de España y América*, 1: 31–91. Madrid: Rialp.

Santos Velasco, J.A.

1982–83   La Difusión de la Cerámica Ibérica Pintada en el Mediterráneo Occidental. *Cuadernos de Prehistoria y Arqueología Castellonense* 9: 135–48.

Siles, J.

1985   *Léxico de Inscripciones Ibéricas*. Madrid: Ministerio de Cultura.

Index of Place Names[1]

Adra 142
Africa 121, 130
Agroal 26
Albacete 33, 34, 37, 38, 40, 42, 43, 53
Alcudia de Elche 81, 102, 155
Alemany (Calvia) 60, 63
Alentejo 19
Algarrobo 96
Algeciras 95
Algeria 95
Aliseda 137, 138, 139
Almanzora 96, 122, 143
Almería 96, 122, 141
Almuñécar 124, 137, 142
Alorda Park (Calafell, Barcelona) 155, 157
Amathus 109, 110
Amendola 18
America 99
Andalusia 3, 4, 15, 18, 19, 34, 123, 131, 143, 147,
    154, 155, 156
Apulia 18, 20
Arene Candide 2
Athens 147
Austis 164
Australia 28

Baelo 129, 131
Baiões 102, 103, 104, 105, 109, 110
Balearic Islands 51, 55, 57, 59, 69, 70, 71, 82, 84
Baria 122
Barranco de los Grajos 4,
Barranco del Tollo 38
Baza 142, 143
Biniac L'Argentina 65
Bolinches 41
Bóquer (Polença) 60
British Isles (Britain) 77, 105

Ca Na Costa 71
Cabelluela 41
Cabezo de los Vientos
Cabezo N 147
Cabezo Redondo 102, 105
Cádiz 95, 96, 121, 125, 129-31, 135, 137-39, 142,
    162,
Cagliari 128, 136, 164
Calasparra 153
Cales Coves 65, 67
Calzada de Vergara 38
Can Ballester 4
Canaries 95

Cancho Roano 157
Cantabria 95
Capocorp Vell 64, 67
Carmona 131
Carthage 123, 124, 126, 128-30, 135-39, 145, 147
Cascais 29
Castellar de Santisteban/ Casteuar 153, 157
Castellet de Bernabé 155
Castellón 3, 154
Castile 114
Castillico del Jardin 41
Castillo de Doña Blanca 121
Castillo de Guardamar del Segura 154
Cástulo 142, 143, 153
Catalonia 155
Cehegín 151, 153
Cendres 2, 4,
Cerro de la Virgen 55
Cerro de los Vientos (Santa Barbara de la Casa) 16,
    17, 20, 22, 23
Cerro de San Cristóbal 137
Cerro Villagordo 142
Chaves (Aragon) 4
Chinflón 111
Ciudad Real 34, 43, 38, 53
Ciutadella 65, 67
Clariana 60, 63
Coimbra del Barranco Ancho (Jumilla) 151
Cola Caballo 43
Collado de los Jardines 153, 156, 157
Coppa Nevigata 18
Córdoba 153, 154
Corsica 51, 59, 69, 70, 80-82, 84
Cortijo de Ebora 139
Coto da Pena 105, 110
Cova de l'Or 2, 3, 4, 7, 10
Cova de la Sarsa 2
Cova Fosca (Castellón) 3, 4, 5
Crete 69, 70, 192
Cuenca 3, 12, 34, 38, 44, 102
Cueta 95
Cueva Chico de Santiago 4
Cueva de la Cariqüela (Granada) 2, 4
Cueva de los Murcielagos (Córdoba) 4, 13
Cueva de Nerja 3, 4, 5,
Cueva Dehesilla 4, 5
Cueva del Calor 153
Cyprus 70, 92, 98, 102, 104, 109, 126, 135

Danebury 77
Dehesa de Las Carnes 41